Praise for *Alfie & Me*

"This is a book about a foundling owl, and infinitely more. As it turns out, the universe and all its mysteries, our relationship with our wild kin, and a better future for ourselves and the planet—all are reflected through the prism of an eight-inch ball of feathers named Alfie. Carl Safina has never been more eloquent, or more urgent. *Alfie & Me* is masterful."

—Scott Weidensaul, *New York Times* best-selling author of
A World on the Wing: The Global Odyssey of Migratory Birds

"Alfie's story is wonderfully told, drawing back night's curtain on these feisty and intelligent birds."

—Julie Zickefoose, *Wall Street Journal*

"Like Blake, Safina sees the world in a grain of sand, holds infinity in the palm of his hand. In addition to Blake's poetic insight, Safina brings a great deal of scientific knowledge to his work. . . . Safina's interrogation of each interaction results in provocative, insightful asides, a pulling-together of the many tributaries of attention to a particular animal, employing his career in the life sciences and the vast reading of world literatures and philosophies."

—Michael Sims, *Washington Post*

"In his new book, *Alfie & Me*, Carl Safina, one of the United States' best science and nature authors, adopts an injured owl and writes: 'Our deeply shared history as living things is why we had the mutual capacity to recognize each other, and be brought into relationship by that strange binding called *trust*.' The healing, Safina discovered, goes both ways."

—Kim Heacox, *Guardian*

"Just like humans' lives, the lives of owls follow a narrative arc, and it is a pure joy to discover, chapter by chapter, Alfie's own arc as she matures, mates, and raises a family."

—Barbara J. King, *Science*

"A must-read. This wonderful story offers a life-changing and moving account. . . . [A] landmark and deeply personal book."

—Marc Bekoff, *Psychology Today*

"The book is brilliant. It made me laugh, weep, marvel . . . at Alfie, at humanity, at you, Carl, and your remarkable insights and sensibility. Bravo! May Alfie and her book soar!"

—Jennifer Ackerman, *New York Times* best-selling author of *What an Owl Knows*

"The rescue of a little screech owl brings Carl Safina the unexpected joy of companionship and propagation of the species, leading him to philosophize about humanity and how much we're part of nature. A delightful read!"

—Frans de Waal, author of *Different: Gender Through the Eyes of a Primatologist*

"How right to choose an owl, symbol of learning, to help us see anew the twinned truths of compassion and connection—gifts our kind desperately needs to keep our world alive."

—Sy Montgomery, author of *The Soul of an Octopus: A Surprising Exploration into the Wonder of Consciousness*

"Little Alfie unleashed a meditation about life itself and how our culture has shaped our way of seeing the world and our place in it. A unique book that is scientific and spiritual at the same time."

—Isabella Rossellini

Alfie & Me

ALSO BY CARL SAFINA

Becoming Wild

Beyond Words

The View from Lazy Point

A Sea in Flames

Voyage of the Turtle

Eye of the Albatross

Song for the Blue Ocean

FOR YOUNG READERS

Learning to Be Wild

Beyond Words: What Elephants and Whales Think and Feel

Beyond Words: What Wolves and Dogs Think and Feel

FOR CHILDREN

Nina Delmar: The Great Whale Rescue

Alfie
& Me

What Owls Know,
What Humans Believe

CARL
SAFINA

W. W. NORTON & COMPANY
Independent Publishers Since 1923

For information about permission to reproduce selections from this book, write to
Permissions, W. W. Norton & Company, Inc., 500 Fifth Avenue, New York, NY 10110

For information about special discounts for bulk purchases, please contact
W. W. Norton Special Sales at specialsales@wwnorton.com or 800-233-4830

Manufacturing by Lakebook Manufacturing
Book design by Beth Steidle
Production manager: Lauren Abbate

Library of Congress Control Number: 2023290649

ISBN 978-1-324-08648-2 pbk.

W. W. Norton & Company, Inc., 500 Fifth Avenue, New York, N.Y. 10110
www.wwnorton.com

W. W. Norton & Company Ltd., 15 Carlisle Street, London W1D 3BS

1 2 3 4 5 6 7 8 9 0

For Paula, Jack, and, of course, Cady

There are more things in heaven and earth, Horatio,
Than are dreamt of in your philosophy.

—SHAKESPEARE, *HAMLET*

Contents

✦

Prologue

THE LITTLE OWL HAD FOR MORE THAN A YEAR BEEN LIV-
ing a comfortable, healthy life. A developmental setback stemming
from her almost fatal infancy in 2018 had delayed her departure. Now
she was perfectly fit, her new feathers soft and sleek and luminous
with youth. She was a strong and excellent flier who could execute
tight turns and precision pounces. And she was perfectly at home in
her roomy enclosure. But I knew—as she did not—the relative mean-
inglessness of a life without risks. An owl who is not out doing owly
things is just a bird in a cage. But after this soft and secure salvation,
could I really subject her to those meaningful risks? How "meaningful" would be injury, or starvation, or getting eaten? All this was on
my mind that morning as she flew from the coop to me while I was
offering her food. But it was she who made the decision. She merely
touched my arm and flew across the yard, and suddenly was taking in
the world from a new vantage point atop a tree. She hadn't vanished.
Not instantly. Not yet. She had been braided into our life. But now
she was tugging back, pulling us into hers.

THE COVID-19 PANDEMIC THAT FORCED us to spend our year
at home coincided with the unprecedented free-living presence of that
little owl—rescued from near death and raised among humans and
dogs and chickens—who decided to stay around our backyard, got
herself a wild mate, and became a mother who successfully raised
three youngsters. Despite the pandemic and partly because of it, the

year generated some good memories to ameliorate the not so good. The owl, the songbirds, and our pets gave us a daily off-ramp from the jammed-up highway of worries and dread. This is a story of profound beauties and magical timing harbored within a year upended.

The little owl in this story is a living being in all the ordinary, extraordinary ways. She is not here to "represent" anything. She is not an omen—as many people believe owls are—nor was she sent as a messenger. At least, I don't *think* so. But she is in no sense "just an owl." Our deeply shared history as living things is why we had the mutual capacity to recognize each other, and be brought into relationship by that strange binding called *trust*. Trust was the bridge across which she and I, and my wife, Patricia, shuttled. Pulling the balloon string of the universe to the door of our existence and then through the keyhole of our life, Alfie became a portal to the parallel reality adjacent to our human experience. She was my passport to that older, saner realm, usually denied to foreign visitors. She was my little friend.

HAD THE YEAR PROCEEDED AS planned, my scheduled travels would have caused me to miss all the fine details of her life, courtship, mating, and their raising of youngsters. Had the year proceeded as it did—but without her—it would have been all the more grueling. She was literally a bright thing in our nights. And she was a metaphor for sanity, at a time when sanity seemed increasingly at risk.

Even in a "normal" year, the perspective she offered would have felt like something new, a deeper perception of being. She brought us into intimate proximity with a more original world, allowing us to see softer borders between light and darkness, deeper perception beyond the normal view. If that sounds a bit mystical, there's that, too.

ONE CAN TRAVEL THE WORLD and go nowhere. One can be stuck keeping the faith at home and discover a new world. In this story most of the action takes place within a hundred-foot radius around our house. But that circle contains histories. This was a year in which we stayed closer but saw farther. We came to see the many ways in which our daily existence is strange and romantic, unpredictable and quirky, buoyed and burdened with exotic customs as any place is. Home is always too close and yet too distant for us to fully know it. It can take a kind of magic spell to let us see the miracles in our everyday routines. Our enabling wizard was the little owl.

Something like a trillion and a half times, daylight has rolled across our planet of changes. About how we came to be, we are privileged to understand a few things. Devoted workers have lifted some sketches from layers of clay, from cells of the living, and from the lights of distant galaxies. No two days are the same, regardless of how small and petty and blurry we make them, how much we blunt our edge on imaginary surfaces that would be better avoided. Written in every rock and leaf and the lyrics of every bird's song are invitations. If we accept, and attend, we see that billion-year histories are the thrust that sends each blade of grass, that dreamscapes whir within each traveling shadow.

My easy intimacy with an owl helped me understand what is possible when we soften our sense of contrast at the species boundary. My growing relationship with her made me want to better understand how people have viewed humanity's relationship with nature throughout history. Why do we happen to have a strained relationship with the natural world? How have other cultures throughout time and around the globe seen humanity's place in the order of things? Turns out, it's complicated. Since earliest times, various peoples have developed differing realms of thought about the human role in the world. Beliefs and values that developed in antiquity among Indigenous, Asian, African, and Western cultures retain astounding power to clarify the sources of illumination and darkness that cast their light and shadows across our lives today. Values that held sway deep in humanity's cultural past are not past; they're very much with us.

SO NOW, about that little owl . . .

PART ONE

First Summers

1

Down from Heaven

THE PHOTO IN THE TEXT MESSAGE LOOKED LIKE A WET washcloth. The text, from a wildlife rehabilitator, explained that it was found on the ground. No nest in sight. I could make out that this was a baby bird. But if this bird was still alive, I'd be surprised. It was the next-to-last day of June, one of those long days that anticipate all the suns of summer. But even in the season of fullness, not all are lucky. The winnowing begins.

This barely living baby's dirt-matted down was full of fly eggs. In a matter of hours those eggs would hatch; maggots would tunnel into the bird. The poor chick was about to be eaten alive. But fate had disrupted the imminent trajectory of events, and humans—this time—would intervene between bad luck and certain death.

Washed, dabbed dry, warmed, and stabilized, the chick remained so bedraggled that it wasn't obvious what kind of bird this was. Based on size—the little being fit into one's palm—I figured that this tiny baby whose luck had just turned a corner must be an Eastern Screech Owl. They nest in dark, secure tree cavities. Somehow, out of a hidden nest, this owlet had been dragged and dropped. Had some predator raided the nest? A crow? Perhaps a raccoon or opossum? Was this disheveled nestling the only survivor?

Presently this baby joined our other-than-human family members. The roster of the latter: dogs Chula and Jude; our four hens, Paulette, Zorro, Stripey, and Smokey; Patricia's king snake Frankie; and our adopted parrots Kane the Quaker parrot (Psittacine Kane), and our cheeky little green-cheeked conure, Rosebud.

And now an owl. Odd word, owl. Three letters, one vowel. It's said to originate from the sound of them calling. While a wolf's *"Awooo"* became its "howl," from a bird heard as *"Ooo,"* voila: an "owl."

This wasn't the first orphaned owl to come my way. In my twenties I had helped found a wildlife-rehabilitation group, I was currently a university ecologist, and I'd had permits for wildlife rehab, falconry, and bird banding.

WITH THE HEALTH OF OUR new foundling stabilized, we needed a name. A baby bird's gender clues are usually internal. How about a gender-neutral name for this downy little rascal? One of the other Little Rascals—of the old Our Gang film and TV series—was named Alfalfa. Shortened to Alfie, it sounded like "Owlfie."

Just to be contrary to the usual default bias of referring to a creature of unknown gender as "he," we began referring to Alfie as "she." The chances of being correct were fifty-fifty. Anyway, pronouns reinforce distinctions. English most commonly offers the options of "he" or "she" for humans but generally forces us to refer to other living beings as "it." Contrastingly, many Native American languages distinguish the living; animate nouns, such as "dog," take different grammatical forms than do inanimate nouns, like "shoe." But English conventions strongly favor phrasing such as "The dog that is barking," not "The dog who is barking." Language reflects its culture's values. Our language makes our tongues turn life-forms into mere objects, more easily abused. In English we don't call a human "it." So to keep a more level pronoun playing field, I try to avoid calling other animals "it." I prefer "male" and "female" to terms like "bull," "cow," "boar," "sow," "bitch," and so on. "Father and mother" rather than "sire and dam." Those labels perpetuate bias and baggage, and I find that dropping them lets me see things that the labels work to deny.

Birds and humans have not had a common ancestor for three hundred million years. That seems a long time on our human scale. But the vertebrate skeleton, organs, and nervous system were by then already blueprinted. Everything since, including us, represents rather recent variations on a theme that all our bodies hum, even when we don't know the words.

And so it came to be that this babe began a new phase of life—a growing, thriving phase—with us.

LIKE ALL BABIES, THIS NEW owl didn't arrive with instructions. But we had a parenting philosophy. We frequently let "her" join us, whether in the backyard or the kitchen. We wanted plenty of stimulation and freedom of movement to develop an active mind and a strong body. Meanwhile, we'd back her up; we'd keep her safe and well.

Our doggies, Chula and Jude, were preadapted to being friendly with small birds who could only flutter. They had grown up around our two small rescued parrots and our little flock of free-roving chickens. The training I devised stemmed from a simple premise. I presumed the dogs would chase because of curiosity and impulse, rather than hunger. If I did the catching for them and let them investigate at the closest range, it should quench their curiosity. Repetition should take the novelty out of it. My training routine consists of holding a parrot or a chicken on my lap while letting the dog sniff or lick; meanwhile, I feed the dog super-tasty treats. This both splits their attention, taking their fixation off the bird, and rewards them for not harming. When, inevitably, they open their mouth or try to nip, they get a firm "No," followed immediately by a treat for drawing their head back. This phase takes two to three weeks. During that time we closely watch them when the birds are loose. The idea is not to "restrain" their prey drive but to extinguish it by letting the newness wear off, to make the birds matter-of-fact, ever present, and thus rather boring. I've tried this with half a dozen dogs. It still surprises me that *none* ever bit or hurt a bird. Our chickens are loose every day, and so are the dogs. The dogs are not just trustworthy. They are proprietary and protective; they bark away any hawk that dallies for a look.

The dogs had also been gentle around an orphan squirrel we'd raised—even though one of their favorite hobbies was chasing wild squirrels up trees around our bird feeders. The difference between how they treated our baby squirrel and the wild squirrels was in itself a fascinating study into the dogs' ability to mentally sort individuals into differential categories. When the baby squirrel grew to full size and took up life outdoors full-time, our dogs could no longer tell the difference between her and the wild squirrels by sight. At that point, when she came daily to visit and we'd see her making her way along leafy tree branches toward our porch, the dogs assumed she was one of the wild squirrels and readied for a chase. But all we had to do was say the squirrel's name—"That's *Squirrlie!*"—and the dogs' recognition was total. Often we'd sit in chairs with the squirrel on our shoulders or playing in our laps and with the dogs at our side—or with *their* heads in our laps—and we'd be giving all of them the same treats: peanuts, say, or grapes. Squirrlie moved by degrees to different nest sites in the woods behind our backyard, increasingly distant from our house. She returned daily for most of fourteen months. In her second summer we could see that she'd been nursing babies of her own. Her visits became irregular, then ceased.

By the time Alfie arrived, Chula and Jude had been through a couple of generations of fuzzy new chicken chicks. They'd presided over the chicks' upbringing with a gentle protectiveness that we had modeled and they had absorbed. What they seemed to bring to the situation was an innate sense that new chicks were like a new litter of helpless babies in our family pack. Whether that's right, I'm not sure. But it seemed that way. For at least some Native Americans, dogs occupy a unique position between other animals and humans: the people know other animals but they *understand* dogs because dogs and humans are engaged in a working partnership and share a way of life.

All this is to say that Chula and Jude instantly understood that

Alfie the owl was just one more helpless baby within our sphere of care. They knew what to do.

But it soon became apparent that our developing relationship with Alfie was not just about us caring for her. She had a wing in our world, and that meant, too, that we had a foot in hers. Something mutual was going on. The intimacy allowed us glimpses from Alfie's point of view and made me wonder about questions that Alfie had not exactly asked but had nonetheless planted in my mind, questions about the relationships that various peoples, through time, made with the natural world, how they viewed humankind's place in the cosmos.

I wondered how to approach such questions. Can we detect answers among the remaining evidence of Indigenous hunter-gatherers who flourished for deep millennia in dappled forests and open plains and along the world's watercourses and coastlines? How is it that people who etched spirit animals into rocky hillsides or journeyed deep into lightless caves rendered their beasts and torch-lit dreams with such humanity that, tens of thousands of years later, their strokes speak with the power to make us gasp? Should we consult the ancient Greek classics for their perspectives on humans and nature or seek the views of pyramid-building Egyptians or the horse peoples of Asian steppes? Or perhaps the early spiritual probings of India, of China? Or the ancient Hebrews and founding Christians? Bodily, all the ancients lie in dust. I began realizing, however, that their thinking lives on, in our minds. In many ways and often without knowing why, we are merely playing out roles written for us thousands of years ago.

For most of human history, Native peoples, more intimate with their existence than we with ours, perceived that Life and the cosmos are mainly *relational*. People of many Indigenous cultures on every continent and humanly inhabited island wondered, What webwork of matter and spirit binds together the world and time? Later, Asian traditions such as Buddhism, Hinduism, Taoism, Confucianism, and others also focused on the human being's participation in material and spiritual harmonies, in dynamic balances and forces.

Then, in ancient Greece, something happened. Plato posited an ideal realm outside of space and time and disparaged our existence in the flawed material world. Rather than attend to the unity of all things, this view segregated the spiritual from the material. If I may oversimplify: in most ancient and traditional beliefs, the world comprised the most holy and important things; in the European, or "Western," perspective that developed after Plato, the world was the least holy, least important thing. The Western view has globalized, and the global economy reflects this Western devaluation of the world. And here we are.

As our relationship with Alfie continued to blur boundaries, I wanted to better understand how various peoples have sought and seen answers about how to be human in the living world.

❖

OUR HOUSE SITS ON THREE-QUARTERS of an acre. It's in an old and historic Long Island neighborhood (several houses from the early 1700s yet stand) that has accumulated a recent suburban look while retaining a semirural feel. On two sides our backyard abuts about thirty acres of young woodland that was mainly farmland when our house was built, around 1910. Across the street a small wetland flows into two ponds down the block; the old millpond spills into tidewater connected to Long Island Sound.

When Europeans arrived in the region Alfie, my wife, and I now deem home, the place had been long inhabited, hunted, and farmed by Algonquian people whose lifeways did not noticeably harm land, soil, water, or air. Algonquian views typify Native American views of nature. And Native American views themselves share much with many other Indigenous worldviews.

Indigenous people were, of course, the first to think about the human place in nature. The Native American writer Paula Gunn Allen tells us that the fundamental Native idea is that "We are the land . . . the Earth is the mind of the people as we are the mind of the earth." The most basic teaching is that the world is sacred and that a web of relationships is fundamental. A good relationship with the world is foundational to good spiritual life and health.

WITH ALFIE AT OUR HOME, a new routine emerged. Alfie was free to hop around the house during the day. (We did a lot of cleaning up.) She spent most nights in our mudroom, where she got her big meal. Wild screech owls eat a broad diet of mostly small rodents and large insects, but they also eat everything else they might catch, from worms to lizards to birds. Alfie accepted any offered animal food, from crickets on up. Sometimes she shared our meal when we were eating fish or eggs. She grew to be one very healthy, vigorous, plump little owl. Caring for Alfie meant that I needed to find a reliable main source of food. I decided on a supplier whose website promised that their frozen mice had been raised with high standards of cleanliness in a low-stress environment, cared for with respect, and killed humanely. I hoped they were telling the truth, and clicked "Add to cart."

The predicament of Life on Earth is that plants make, animals take. All owls are hunters. Unlike Alfie, we have wider choices. And our decisions have greater consequences. Algonquian storyteller Ken Little Hawk tells a story of a boy who asked his grandfather to teach him. The grandfather took the child to a lake. Giving the boy a stick, he said, "Stir up the water." The child happily stirred the water and mud and sand and leaves, having fun making a cloudy swirl. Grandfather then instructed, "Now put everything back as before." The human power to change things exceeds our power to simply put things back as they were. So proceed thoughtfully; reversing course may not be an option.

2

⁘

Flight Delayed

OUR MUDROOM HAD BEEN THE DOORWAY TO GRADUAL explorations and eventual freedom for our orphaned squirrel. And before that, for a little raccoon who'd fallen from forty feet up in a maple at the edge of our yard, emaciated and near death after her mother had been hit by a car. For a while she came and went from the mudroom, sleeping in a comfortable wooden den-box I built for her until she was ready to find herself an outdoor den. One time, Patricia and I watched as she approached a deer. Instead of leaping away as we expected, the deer lowered her head and they touched nose to nose. I would never have guessed that such different wild creatures would be so mutually curious. It took a tame raccoon to show us. She came running back to us in excited bounds, quite as if saying, "Did you see what I did? Did you see me?" She visited us regularly for a year, during which she learned to interact with fully wild raccoons. As a behavioral ecologist, I learned a lot, but—. Raising a raccoon is hazardous. Not recommended. When they disagree with you, they bite; often they don't growl first. They can acquire rabies (ours was vaccinated); and they usually carry certain roundworms that in very rare instances have killed humans. Right around her first birthday she, like her mother, had a fatal encounter with something even more dangerous: an automobile.

Allowing a young creature to come and go, and backing them up while they are trying to figure out what things are good and what to avoid—without natural parents to model how to survive—is called a "soft release."

The plan for Alfie was a similar soft release based out of our mudroom. She'd be with us for a couple of weeks, and then at her own pace would develop her independence. Parent owls care for and feed their young for several weeks after they leave the nest. With parental backup giving them the needed time, young fledgers sharpen new skills while learning how to become wild.

BUT SOON A PROBLEM EMERGED. Actually, the problem was in what *failed* to emerge: feathers crucial for flight. Like our upper arm, forearm, and hand, birds also have a humerus bone, in their case as the upper wing; the radius and the ulna are next, and the end of their wing, corresponding to our hand, has fused "carpometacarpal" bones. From their "hands" grow their main flight-powering feathers. These are called their "primary" feathers. From their "forearms" grow their "secondary" feathers, the feathers that give the wing its main lift. Along a bird's humerus grow the "tertial" feathers; these also help create lift. In a baby bird, all the primary, secondary, and tertial feathers grow at the same time. Alfie's problem was: while the primaries of both wings had grown out beautifully, none of the other flight feathers were coming. Alfie looked normal except that two-thirds of each wing was essentially bare.

That problem was physical. The second was psychological. Together, they'd doom Alfie if we carried out our planned soft release. Development of a baby bird's feathers and their behavioral urges must be synchronized. Alfie acted like a bird ready to take on the sky. She knew that her *time* had come. Her mind was ready. But with her missing flight feathers, Alfie could only do a lot of flapping and hopping. A normal fledger would have spent all their time up in trees. Alfie could only flop around. Alfie did not sense her disadvantage. And what I knew—that she didn't know—was that one night of hopping around on the ground would likely be all she'd get. Our neighborhood was home to raccoons and great horned owls and the occasional fox—not to mention several free-ranging cats, who posed perhaps the greatest threat. The cats kill chipmunks and mice and birds, all of which are food for owls. A cat could kill a baby owl, too.

So we kept her and cared for her. I provided some instruction about life by pulling fake mice on a string with food attached. I gave her toys to play with. She began pouncing on small fake animals and pillows and even things like smartphone videos of mice. When I saw her attack and eat a spider in our living room, I began collecting crickets; Alfie was keen on catching them on the floor. We were doing our best to nurture a housebound hunter's body and mind. But I worried that Alfie's abnormal flight-feather growth was a result of her having nearly starved to death. I worried that the problem might be permanent; I'd seen that before.

My fears were largely relieved when all of Alfie's secondaries and tertials began a belated emergence. Growing evenly. Shaped correctly. Looking good. Because her primaries were already fully grown, when the rest of her wing feathers hit a half-grown point, Alfie could—quite suddenly—fly.

Now we had a very different dilemma. What makes a soft release soft is that it is gradual. It requires time. But all at once what neither Alfie nor we had—was time. Many years ago I'd known an owl who was also a nearly starved foundling and who grew a beautiful set of first feathers but then *lost* the ability to fly because he was unable to molt and replace feathers normally. He was never released. So I wanted to be sure Alfie would be able to normally molt and acquire a proper set of new feathers. That would mean waiting.

Patricia and I were scheduled to go away for two weeks, a long-planned trip among eagles and salmon and bears in the wild splendors of Alaska. An excellent pet sitter would be coming to the house to keep Alfie and our other wards well cared for. But a soft release is more than care. It's the management of a fraught transition. It requires quite a bit of attention, time to watch and follow, and the ability to make adjustments depending on how things are going.

As a suddenly flying Alfie collided with our imminent departure, the choice we confronted was: open the door and wish her well or keep her longer. With no parents to bring food while she experienced many failed attempts to catch a first wild meal if we simply let her go, Alfie would be—at best—faced with low odds of surviving. We thought that just letting her out and then leaving town was tantamount to abandonment.

And so began a prolonged, unplanned captivity.

◆

WE ENJOYED ALASKA THOROUGHLY, NOT least because Native people and their stories remain prominent there. Cultural anthropologist Richard Nelson, who lived among Koyukon Athapaskan people of Alaska's interior forests, helped prepare us to understand their perspective, writing that in the Natives' view, "Humans and animals share a communality of being, a mutual sphere of influence, a spiritually bound moral unity where the ethics of fish and humans are not separated."

Everyone on Earth has Indigenous ancestors who left no scars, no straight lines, no crumbling ruins more obtrusive than stones around charcoal. Where they were purged, scarcely a memory holds their place. Where we now live, their place-names, such as Amagansett ("Place of Good Water") and Setauket ("At the River Mouth") now bear postal zip codes. The names can help us remember. But memories fade.

"An Indigenous person," writes Native Australian Tyson Yunkaporta, "is a member of a community retaining memories of life lived sustainably on a land base." Where Indigenous peoples persist, their values often reflect their deep identity. Indigenous peoples still constitute perhaps 5 percent of the world population, in about five thousand distinct societies in Australia, Africa, throughout Eurasia, throughout the Pacific, and in the Americas. The human mind originated in place-based cultures. From such moorings, almost all of us have long been severed.

WHEN CHRISTOPHER COLUMBUS FIRST ENCOUNTERED Caribbean people, his European background had not prepared him for such nonaggressive human beings. He wrote, "They are so guileless and so generous with all that they possess, that no one would believe it who has not seen it." (The Natives were guileless, but Columbus's scheming was reflexive. He wrote to Spain's King Ferdinand, "I found very many islands, filled with innumerable people, and I have taken possession of them all for their Highnesses." After explaining to the king that the Caribbean people "do not know what weapons are," Columbus promised Spain's royal highnesses "as much gold as they may need," as much spice, aloe, and cotton, "and slaves, as many as they shall order.")

When James Cook first touched the continent now called Australia in 1770, he wrote of the Natives, "They are far more happier than we Europeans. . . . They live in a Tranquility which is not disturb'd by the Inequality of Condition. The Earth and sea of their own accord furnishes them with all things necessary for life. . . . In short they seem'd to set no Value upon any thing we gave them, nor would they ever part with any thing of their own for any one Article we could offer them. . . . They think themselves provided with all the necessarys of Life."

Edward S. Curtis, who published twenty volumes of photographs of Native Americans in the early twentieth century, wrote, "They were marvelous in the beauty of their free, poetic thoughts full of imagery such as white men have never known. Their souls were those of poets."

I risk oversimplification when generalizing about "Native" or "Indigenous" beliefs. And while I aim not to oversimplify or idealize, there appears one key generalization worth hazarding. In general, Indigenous peoples have understood themselves as living in a network of relationships within the oneness of existence. Many Indigenous cultures see in nature's diversity *a unity*, in which all things past, present, and future exist embedded in a relational webwork. Indigenous people also wield what Richard Nelson called an enormous wealth of empirical knowledge about natural relationships, "an ecological perspective essentially identical to that recently evolved in Western scientific thought." Physics, chemistry, astronomy, geology, biology, and ecology all explore the world and the universe. Their findings affirm in great detail that existence is *relational* at all scales of space, life, and time. My bond with Alfie and her reliance on us was primal, elemental, and mutual. In other words, our affiliation affirmed, in its crucial innocence, that life is indeed relational.

Indigenous people widely perceive all of existence as neither material nor spiritual but always both simultaneously. Their spirit-infused natural world tends to be conscious, feeling, and forceful. Spirits occupy the relational fabric and all things, having no clear boundaries. Powers act not from remote distance but with present, highly tangible agency. Any event can be a manifestation of such forces. Winds, lands, waters, plants, animals—all are sacred, and all aspects of existence are bound by spiritual threads into a tight weave of power. Nature is a "watchful and possessive" second society of physical and spirit forces in which people live. No wilderness is desolate, because nowhere are you ever alone. Indigenous people move in landscapes whose creatures, plants, and weather continually decide what to do. Beliefs and rituals are tailored to a world wherein the powers between humans and wider nature are two-way, with human and other-than-human entities constantly engaged in a spiritual intercourse. Intangible forces deliver direct consequences. Humans are compelled to move with, yield to, and perhaps coax favors from such forces. Nature can nurture, can withhold, or can punish the wasteful and impertinent. And attempting to alter physical and spiritual forces without their permission can compel catastrophe.

I can't say I saw the world that way, exactly. But there was something resonant here that I felt, and that I knew. As an ecologist I understood that the currency of Life is the shuttling of energy, which is always flowing. Two rocks are in many ways isolated. But among living things, individuals are not isolates. In a real sense there are no individuals; there are only living nodes in flowing networks. Whenever I saw or even thought of Alfie, I felt something between us that united us. We did, after all, interact. We had a certain mutual understanding. To create a metaphor from physics, we had developed a covalent bond. And that was real enough to hold us.

3

Tilting Toward September

RETURNING HOME AFTER TWO WEEKS AWAY, WE FOUND the lush air of summer tilting toward September. And we were confronted by a very different, much more physically capable Alfie. Her feathers were perfect. She'd developed excellent flight skills, easily and swiftly maneuvering through doorways and turning tight curves within rooms. Owls' advantageous ability to hunt at night is completed by flight that is *silent*. Tiny comblike serrations on the leading edges of their main wing feathers, as well as minute trailing fringes (and generally softer feathers overall), let them ghost—rather than swoosh—through the air. Alfie could be in the same room with us— on a chair, say—and we'd glance away and she'd be gone. We'd wonder, "Where—? Oh, there she is on the bookshelf." Alfie could fly right past our faces without us hearing anything.

With a good, vitamin-enriched diet, we could keep her physically healthy. And with interaction, the sight of bird feeders, and the comings and goings of us and the dogs, she had continual visual stimulation. Sometimes she'd leave a bookcase she was dozing in and come looking for us, often ending up in Patricia's office, where, perhaps feeling safer because she was not alone, she'd take a prolonged snooze. We loved having her around. And she didn't mind the only life she'd known.

But it was a human's kind of life, not an owl's life. For a young owl it was a safe, healthy, pleasant dead end.

What was the solution? If we simply let her out now, she'd likely vanish in the exuberance of new wings and strong flight and the sudden feeling of life in a world without walls. An exhilarating world. A hungry world. One might think that any young owl "knows what to do." That may be, but they need to learn *how* to do it. Hunting requires skills. Learning skillfulness requires a parental cushion for making errors; that takes time. And survival requires luck, because time is limited. Young screech owls depend on their parents for food for about two months after leaving the nest. After those couple of months the young disperse, usually moving out a mile or more, to establish independent lives. This transition to independence is dangerous. Few survive their first year. In one study, two-thirds of young screech owls died soon after leaving their parents.

Knowing this, my mind was bookended by worrying that if she simply bolted she'd likely starve—*and* knowing that captivity led nowhere. Neither choice was good. Captivity was all she'd known; meanwhile, I could improve it. I gave her the outdoor part of the chicken coop. She was out in the fresh air and exposed to the changing seasons. I included a variety of perches and landing shelves to facilitate activity. I made these landing spots different sizes and textures, because constant pressure on the same spots can cause foot sores. She got a big water dish for bathing. And I placed a little shelter box for a daytime snooze room. She might perhaps even pounce on the occasional mouse who'd sniffed out some birdseed I'd sprinkle in there, so she would not forget what her talons and her fascination with motion were for or how to use them at speed.

She took to the place very well. I was concerned that she might cling to the chicken wire, fluttering, trying to get out. Birds who do that can easily demolish their tail feathers, break wing feathers, and abrade their face. But she seemed quite comfortable and at home, instantly settling in.

In the evenings of September's shortening days, nighthawks and swifts migrated right through our neighborhood in the hours before sunset, sometimes by the hundreds. Meanwhile, Alfie was living in her outdoor chalet. So now we had this situation: Alfie was healthy. Alfie could fly skillfully. Alfie had at least some idea about hunting. And Alfie was molting normally, shedding her first flight feathers in proper sequence and pace, with new ones coming in nicely. That showed me that all her developmental delays were behind her. She was in top shape. She was comfortable. She was well cared for. She was safe.

I could not duck the nagging question. Potentially she had quite a few years ahead of her. Potentially Alfie could breed. Should I open the door? What *always* stopped me was the thought of her bolting and quickly starving or getting killed. As a flightless chick, Alfie had been an early casualty. Luck had intervened. But Alfie was not living the life she was born for. She seemed comfortable with the status quo, and I was kind of stuck there, too.

ALFIE MOLTED FULLY—wings, body, tail—and by mid-autumn she was simply stunning. Her fluffy fledgling flannel pajamas changed into a sleek new set of adult feathers. And if she really was female, she was a knockout debutante. All of her feathers were lustrous. I could hardly take my eyes off her.

Eastern screech owls come in two colors, brick reddish or gray. These forms are genetic, like whether a human has naturally red or black hair. With the owls, parents of either color can mate and chicks of either color can come mixed in the same brood. Alfie was a "ginger," the more common tint in our region (the majority in parts of their range are gray). A highly successful species, eastern screech owls cover a realm stretching from southern Maine to the Gulf of Mexico and west to the Great Plains. They range through almost all of Texas, north to much of Montana, and a bit into Canada. They're nonmigratory, so some endure harsh winters and others face high heat and humidity or aridity. They're tough and adaptable little buggers, surprising and admirable. (In Brazil once, our searchlight illuminated a closely related species called a tropical screech owl, flying. When the bird landed on a fence post and turned to look our way, I was stunned to see that the entire left eye was occluded by scar tissue. The owl was hunting and surviving with only one functioning eye.)

Of our locally breeding owls, screech owls are the smallest. From where Alfie's feet rested on a perch, she stood only about five inches tall. Adding perhaps three inches for her tail, she was roughly the length and color of a large sweet potato, but in shape so oval as to be almost cylindrical, a bit like a beverage can. We see other owls here on Long Island. Great horned owls have nested in sight of our house (the "horns," you probably know, are just feathers). The marshes and grasslands host short-eared owls (again, the short "ears" are just feather tufts) and barn owls (who somehow managed to exist without us millions of years before barns). Barred owls, common on the mainland, are rare visitors here. Saw-whet owls, our smallest, breed farther north but visit our region in winter. Snowy owls, too, regularly visit in winter; some years they are not difficult to find amid tundra-like dunes along our ocean shores. Very rarely—not every year, not even every decade—a great gray owl shows up; they have the largest body length of all the world's owls and look surreal.

A birder could glance at Alfie and instantly recognize a "screech owl." But labels often make us feel as if we know and understand things we don't know, don't understand. Labels sometimes cause us to stop observing. Alfie's voice, behavior, and her species' role in the web of life far surpassed anything communicated by "screech owl."

WHEN SHE WAS AT REST, Alfie's soft, dense body feathers made her look full-figured. When relaxing, her contours were those of a big-headed Russian matryoshka doll. Black eyeliner made her large, prominently lidded eyes utterly striking. Those eyes and her small hooked bill were a similar light yellow-green straw color. In many owl species, the ears have different-sized openings (one large and one huge), with one lower than the other and one a bit farther forward than the other, all of which allows such pinpoint hearing that some owls can catch moving prey in total darkness, even by locating the sound of a rodent moving beneath a covering of snow. The "facial disks" that give most owls their characteristic flat-faced look are specialized feathers that help funnel sound into their unique ear openings. Alfie's were outlined the color of dark chocolate, giving cheek-like definition to her face. Astride her bill were bristly feathers of a light cream, whose color continued upward to create eyebrows like little clouds. As if extending those eyebrows, feathered tufts shaped like cats' ears broke the round outline of her head. Her throat was white. Below her throat, dark-chocolate markings on her upper breast gave a brown-sweater-open-at-the-neck look. Just below, a loose and indistinct whitish line traveled down to her toes like a drip of vanilla ice cream. And to the left and right of that, vertical streaks of dark chocolate, softly barred as though swished gently with finger paint, wrapped her body outward to her underwings. Those streaks were her main camouflage, breaking the outline of her body into something like tree bark. If ever feeling threatened, she'd be able to complete a vanishing act by stretching up like an elongated branch, squinting her eyes into invisibility, and erecting those head-feather tufts into little sticks. Her brick-red color dominated most of her head, back, wings, and tail. Many of those feathers also bore lighter or darker markings, and in particular her long flight feathers had waves of alternating light and dark banding, visible when she stretched a wing.

On a perch, two talons of each foot projected from beneath her skirting feathers. Most birds have three toes forward and one back. Woodpeckers are an exception, grasping vertical trunks with two toes up and two down. Parrots, who often use their feet for climbing and for bringing food to their mouths, are another exception. Owls yet another. With two toes front and two back, an owl's opened foot hits prey with four evenly spaced curved needles. At their base, Alfie's talons matched the color of her eyes and bill, darkening as they attenuated to piercing points. Alfie could swivel her head in famous owlish fashion, about 270 degrees. Depending on the species, owls have about fourteen neck vertebrae (mammals—even giraffes—have seven), and they differ a bit in structure from one another to allow a wide range of motions. The spinal cord and arteries run through roomy canals that are bigger than the nerves and blood vessels themselves, so they don't get pinched when the head swivels.

Night habits and silence make owls seldom seen. More often we hear their haunting, sometimes bloodcurdling calls. When one shows up, their appearance can be startling, even disturbing. My grandmother shared a common European belief that owls are ill omens. Hieronymus Bosch frequently painted owls into his scenes as his solemn warning that the devil is ever present. Yet an owl symbolized the ancient Greek goddess of wisdom, Athena. Messengers of both good and ill is how various Native peoples see owls. Native Hawaiians hold Owl, called Pueo, in great esteem as a powerful and positive messenger. The Koyukon of central Alaska believe that owls can both foretell and influence events to come. The Kiowa see owls as omens of impending death in one's household. In what is now Primorsky Krai, in Russia's Far East, the Udege people hunted eagle-sized Blakiston's fish owls for food, while across the Sea of Japan, the Ainu people of Hokkaido consider them divine protectors. Silent in flight, vocal by disposition, predatory by vocation, with the power to command impenetrable darknesses that humans seldom dare venture into, owls are a formidable presence.

Beyond Alfie's resting exterior, much else about her remained to be discovered. Much would lie always beyond words. Looking at her I'd think, "She has her own life, impulses, urges, her times of comforts and fears." She is flesh and feathers and organs, wants and needs; her heart pumps blood as red as ours. These are everyday things. But this day rests on our planet's foundational quirks and Life's 3.5-billion-year history; there is nothing simple here. Alfie is a very real little being, yet she harbors many mysteries beyond my understanding. She knows things I do not and perhaps cannot know. She is material and seems magical. Looking at her looking at me, I feel myself within a more miraculous existence. I suppose one could say that yes, she is, after all, a messenger.

AS THE FOREGOING SUGGESTS, MANY Indigenous cultures view owls, other birds, mammals, fishes, and plants as thinking and emotional beings who have minds, communicate among themselves, act with agency on their own behalf, and exert spirit power. Western believers might see a guiding hand of the biblical God, whose "eye is on each sparrow." But in the Native apprehension, the sparrow herself decides how to respond. If you make a prayer to a raven or disrespect the carcass of a deer, Raven spirit or Deer spirit will determine what happens next. An owl or raven, aware of what people say and do, might, by calls or flight patterns, aid a hunter or forecast something good—or bad—to come.

"Each animal knows way more than you do," one Athapaskan elder advised. "We always heard that from the old people when they told us never to bother anything unless we really needed it."

By understanding and responding to signs and warnings that the world sends, Indigenous people enhance luck—or spoil it. Spirits can either guide humans to sustenance or act in retribution when offended. Human practices strive to maintain harmonic balances among living and spirit beings within the integral fabric of the world. Consequently, humans and the world dance an elaborate code of respect and morality. This binds human existence into a moral drama of duty and conduct. Nearly all daily acts include gestures of reverence. Rituals precede, for example, felling a great cedar. Or, for instance, a shaman in the Maasai lands of Kenya might stop at the edge of a forest and ceremonially ask permission to extract medicinal plants. Good luck is not random but *granted*. When Indigenous people hunt, they often prepare with ceremonial cleansing and prayers to the hunted, seeking their agreement to offer themselves for human need. If all is in balance, the hunted allows the hunter to succeed.

"The interaction here is very intense," notes Richard Nelson. A successful hunter offers thanks *not* to a third-party god but directly to the killed, who has given this life for the hunter. Afterward, their remains must be treated with the deference owed to something sacred. Sensitive to insult, the spirit of an animal who has not been treated correctly may take offense. All members of the offended species may avoid the offending hunter for months. By disrespect, humans create bad luck. One foolish man, angry at jays for taking bait from his marten traps, plucked a trapped jay and left it alive. For causing the jay to suffer in the cold, the man froze to death in his tent.

Richard Nelson experienced deep unease, realizing that his Native companions experienced "in the fullest measure a different world than I did, or than people of my culture could perceive." He "never found access" to their perceptions. His companions saw what he had not learned to see—or what he'd been taught does not exist. Intellectually this did not surprise him, but, he writes, "I was entirely unprepared for it emotionally, unready for the impact of living it. My clear and certain comprehension of the natural world was ended."

Though spirituality infuses everything, Indigenous beliefs are not "religion" in the Western sense. Indigenous people generally don't worship gods; rather, they converse with spirits and ancestors as with elders. There are generally no houses specified for worship, no holidays, no scripture, no dogma. No pressure to conform. What it amounts to, writes Native scholar Evan T. Pritchard, is not religion but "a way of life that nurtures deeply religious experiences, which is a different thing."

It is quite possible to be religious, to feel spiritual, without religion. The Latin root of the word "religion" means to be bound in relationship, to feel an obligation and a bond that one holds in reverence. The feelings come from sensing connections. And, oddly enough, most of those words—"obligation," "bond," "connection," perhaps even "reverence"—applied with respect to my relationship with Alfie.

4

Shortening Days

WHEN PATRICIA AND I LEFT FOR A THREE-WEEK SPEAKING trip in early October, our close friend Linda stepped in as pet and house sitter. Linda's experience made her perfect for caring for Alfie, our doggies and chickens and parrots, and the wild birds at our feeders; she enjoyed it all.

We live with gratitude for the privilege of our travels. But we love our real life, too. I don't feel a need to "escape" from my normal day-to-day, and the love and beauty that we've braided into being at home. The sacred lies in the mosaic of the everyday. Attend, in great detail, as you again fill the bird feeders for the morning. As you wash, again, the dishes in the sink. You and the dishes are here together now in this moment of your life. Enjoy the process. The little things are the big things. The moments pass.

Indigenous people tend to sense a world continually in communication with things deeper, bigger, more eternal. Physicists have indeed found deeper, bigger, more eternal realities working beyond our senses. Unseen things create the material world we see. Light travels as both waves and particles. Subatomic particles behave with probabilities, not according to certainties. Solidity is illusion. Matter is a form of energy. Gravitational forces suggest that "space" is connected by time and a suspected thing called dark matter. Time has strange properties and prompts stranger questions. Energy, matter, time, and space may all be aspects of the same thing. And why is there anything, rather than nothing?

Earth-based peoples apprehend all things as expressions of greater mystery, of the power working everywhere in nature, throughout the cosmos. "The creative eternal" is my phrase for how I understand the concept.

BY LATE OCTOBER, THE FIELD crickets' calls were slowing. Releasing Alfie into a world with temperatures getting too cool for crickets, moths, and other insect prey seemed, to me, a worsening prospect. As the nights chilled, the so-called cave crickets started moving indoors. I whisked them off our basement walls with a butterfly net. When I tossed them one by one onto the kitchen floor, Alfie could get herself whipped into a minor feeding frenzy, zooming down and catching a snack and flying to a rafter to anticipate the next one.

Autumnal impulses were stirring the lives of many beings. Monarch and admiral butterflies and "darner" dragonflies began migrating in droves. Along our coast, whales and turtles turned tail and left us. Ducks, geese, cormorants, and loons streaked the sky. Shorebirds flickered along foaming ocean surf. Hummingbirds were buzzing southward, following new flowerings along the coastal corridor. Weather fronts propelled south-bounding swallows and warblers, sparrows and finches, hawks and woodpeckers. They spent all the urgent day feeding, and in the restless night, sometimes over long stretches of turbulent sea, they moved. White-throated sparrows and juncos arrived and would be with us through our months of cold.

Before people knew that the world was round, the seasonal appearance and disappearance of birds and other animals appeared wholly mysterious. For most of human history, people knew only the world they saw, perhaps a large valley, or a few ridges, or a ribbon of coastline. No one could have imagined the physical diversity of the world, because no one imagined the world as it exists. No human mind conjured images of regions with wholly different habitats and climates, the range from tundra to rainforests, deserts to coral seas, polar ice and so on. Birds saw and knew more of those things than did human beings. The magnitude and distance of even the most visible migrations—those flocks of birds—were impossible to imagine because no one understood the size and shape of the continents, oceans, or planet.

Here in our yard, juncos appear only in winter, the only time of year when cowbirds disappear. Ancients such as Aristotle, knowing so little of the world's wider horizons, believed that the birds of summer *changed into* the birds of winter. Perhaps seeing some birds molting from breeding to winter plumage abetted this reasonable leap of logic. On Aristotle's authority, the view held for millennia. In the 1600s, the English minister Charles Morton wrote a persuasive (for the time) claim that birds annually migrate to: the moon. Many birds migrate at night, and in those days of vastly higher bird abundance, people frequently saw migrants silhouetted by the moon. "Now, whither should these creatures go," Morton asked us, "unless it were to the moon?"

No one had a telescope of any kind until the early 1600s, and the first ones were far weaker than today's birding scopes. (English mathematician Thomas Harriot appears to have looked at the moon through a telescope four months before Galileo did, in 1609, but he saw only "strange spottednesse.") At that time, the moon and planets were assumed by many to be Earth-like, replete with air, water, and life. So, sure, wherefore not a lunar solution to the seasonal vanishings and reappearances of Europe's birds? We can call this kind of argument "must be the moon" thinking. You can't imagine another answer, so you conclude that the answer "must be" the one you've imagined. People have long used "must be the moon" thinking to believe mistaken things. Science has shown a methodical way to consider evidence, to accept or reject conjecture, but many people prefer "must be the moon" thinking.

In centuries past, some people believed that various birds disappeared in autumn to spend winter underwater. A woodblock print from 1555 depicts fishermen raising a net full of hibernating swallows from a lake. Such stories, passed along as fact for centuries in writing and art, acquired an air of authenticity. In the late 1800s the American ornithologist Elliott Coues, who knew a thing or three about swallows and wrote extensively about them, seemed perplexed by nearly two hundred written accounts claiming that swallows hibernate. Coues had never seen such a thing, nor spoken to anyone who had. But because he knew that, for instance, some bats hibernate, Coues felt that he could not simply dismiss the many claims of hibernating swallows. Today, the only bird known to hibernate is the poorwill, *Phalaenoptilus nuttallii* (though most definitely *not* underwater.) We now know that swallows don't hibernate; they migrate. Here where Patricia and I—and company—live, we can see them moving down the autumn coast in long, low flocks, still sometimes by the thousands.

Migration is a regular movement between one place and another. Commuter rush hour is a kind of daily human migration, though we don't usually call it that. Some birds migrate thousands of miles over the surface of the world every year. Some insects—certain butterflies and dragonflies, for instance—make continental, birdlike migrations. Some bats, too. Sometimes, as with sea turtles and the biggest whales, migration is mainly about breeding in one place and eating in another, at different times of year. Squid, lanternfish, and many tiny sea animals collectively called zooplankton migrate thousands of feet up and down in the ocean every day. Most people have never heard of this daily vertical migration, but it's the biggest migration on Earth.

The world's longest-distance migrators are Arctic terns; they spend summer in the Arctic and then fly to the Antarctic for the austral summer, experiencing more daylight than any other creature. Some hummingbirds cross the Gulf of Mexico nonstop. Some shorebirds travel thousands of miles across oceans without a rest. They may double their weight before embarkation and shrink their internal organs for efficiency. One satellite-tagged bar-tailed godwit left Alaska and flew more than seventy-five hundred miles nonstop over the open Pacific Ocean for eleven days before landing on the shore of a bay near Auckland, New Zealand.

SCREECH OWLS DON'T MIGRATE. Alfie would be content to stay put. For us, approaching winter means accommodations to the shortening, chilly days. Around Thanksgiving—late November— my kayak and Patricia's paddleboard get stored. Outdoor furniture migrates indoors. I button up the boat. When cold can bring inactivity, splitting and hauling firewood from trees downed by storms constitutes fit exercise. The wood-burning stove augments our home heat, reducing our use of oil. We continue taking the doggies for walks on the beach or in the woods—they *always* want to go, and chilly days energize them. These are some of our routines, our ways of living in the world.

Native Americans universally developed their own sense of how best to live in the world—a "way." It is the Mi'kmaq "way of truth," *agulamz*; the Cherokee "way of good," *dohi*; the Navajo "beauty way" of harmony and balance, *hózhó*. "Our ways, not our things, sustained us," writes Tyson Yunkaporta. The most fundamental way: "move in the world with respect and care." These views survive. "I am always in awe, and always in relationship," says the contemporary Potawatomi writer and scholar Robin Wall Kimmerer.

Native ways of being and knowing are often the same. Knowledge is not just absorbed; it is done, an active thing. The Navajo word *bee*, "by means of," refers to knowing by doing. By means of gardening, I know of flowers. Knowledge comes through living the act. By means of Alfie, I know of owls.

Indigenous peoples draw from their landscapes the psychological shapes and material contents of their lifescape. "This is how spirit works," writes Tyson Yunkaporta. "In these contoured dimensions of existence," he explains, "time and space are one concept." (Modern physicists say there is a "space-time continuum.") Space-time continuity creates space-time community when stories layer up hundreds of generations deep. This generation experiences the results of prayers made and plans laid generations ago. And what is decided now will cause what will be.

In the long-ago of many Native Americans there were no "animals," only different people known as Raven, Deer, Wren, Wolf, Eagle, Bear, Loon, and so on. All those people eventually transformed into the plants and animals we see today. In the United States, business corporations are legally considered "persons," but many Indigenous peoples have for millennia viewed other-than-human beings as "people." In many Native origin stories, human existence originates through the cooperation of preexisting animals. A raven releases the first people from a clamshell, for instance. Or a swan's wing cushions the first woman's fall out of the sky and into this world. Distinctions between humans and other animals are soft. Native Americans widely refer to Life in its entirety as "all my relations." In this intuited evolution, today's diversity originated in a primordial world of equals. The insights of Charles Darwin and Alfred Russel Wallace that struck Europe in the late 1800s as a disruptive shock wave—that all Life is related, diversified from a common origin—were in essence long presupposed by Indigenous minds. DNA confirms our kinship with other creatures and maps that genealogy. Perceiving existence as a fine mesh of relationships is a new path called "ecology." But it is also the human mind's oldest path.

The great blindness of the West is to grope the world as inventory. The great wisdom of the Indigenous mind is to understand the world as relationships. Life is connection in the present and across time. Each owl and crow, every living being is today's working expression of the memory of Life. Each negotiates their lifescape by maintaining relationships. These major aspects of life are not fundamentally competitive; they are fundamentally networked. Life is *symphonic*. Alfie was magical for me because she added to my flow.

Shall we see Raven, or shall we see a raven? Perhaps the truth lives somewhere between the sense that Raven possesses powers that can affect your luck and the sense that a raven is just a bird. I don't *think* a raven will affect my luck, but I *know* a raven is not just a bird. Nothing is "just" anything. Everything is the present manifestation of deepest histories, most ancient yet always unfolding. Could Alfie affect my luck? The revealed answer was becoming increasingly plain. She'd been lucky. And so was I.

THANKSGIVING'S APPROACH AND A CHILL in the mornings got me thinking of a steamy pot of chowder. So I went to the harbor to collect a basket of clams. The local Natives who'd lived alongside these waters as their own would have understood. Our Natives so admired the blue blaze that inexplicably lines the inner shell of our hardest clam that they strung this part of the shell as a medium of record keeping and of exchange called *wampum*. This species' Latinized name, *Mercenaria mercenaria*, refers to that mercantile function. While clamming I always imagine the Natives who took shellfish from these very places.

Full moon meant low-low tides. And so with waders and rake I went to worship at the corner of mudflat and first light. As dawn turned the sky to stained glass, I stepped into the faint current and bowed deep, putting my rake into the sandy sediment and tightening my back and arms against the long handle.

While I watched scarves of ducks crossing the autumn skies, I could feel my rake's tines undermining the security of the shellfish I sought. Quiet as a clam? Oh, a clam has plenty to say. You can read, on each and every one, many verses of sung praise. Each clam is a poem slowly written, its humble ambitions inscribed in its shells. One. Line. Per. Year. Each line's quest and re-quest: live simply, simply live. Within their homespun calcium carbonate fortresses, they gap open just enough to get on with the art of living, the soft pumps of their bodies filtering fodder from incoming water. Prized from the safety of their sediment, they tighten their limestone bodies like hands clamped in some lost-cause prayer. How wondrous they seem: rocks that grow, filled with meat. Finding them feels like homage. Taking them feels like theft. Into my basket with each clam I drop a small apology for the inescapable sin of my animal existence. Lacking a centralized nervous system, clams *probably* feel little. So clamming carries less of the dilemma that accompanies fishing: the concern over causing pain. This makes clams among the less guilt-inducing of edible animals. The other plus: I can bypass farm and supermarket and get a meal. Gathering *requires* the wild and the untended, and so is compatible with the rest of life on Earth in a way that farming, as practiced, is not.

At home I hosed the salt off the clamming gear and put the clams away for later. Alfie watched, her head turning to follow my movements. I yearned to know what Alfie knew and to sense what she sensed. What, I wondered, were her impressions? She looked at me, and blinked.

CLAMMING CONNECTS ME TO MY home place, to my food, in ways that seem simple—though nothing really is. Indigenous belief systems are anything but simple. For instance, African belief traditions at first seemed "so superficial" to one Christian writer, but he later came to appreciate "the extreme profundity of native thought. . . . It is infinitely more involved than the white man's logic."

In traditional African beliefs generally, writes African religious scholar Jaco Beyers, "There is one reality, with no distinction between physical and spiritual." The fundamental African understanding is of connectedness. Spiritual practices and rituals express the unity of existence; morals and ethics maintain it. There is nothing from which humans need saving. Creation has no hierarchy, but humans do have a special role in caring for the world. Maintaining harmony is humanity's greatest obligation. "Every generation and every individual is merely a part of a never-ending chain that stretches backward into the past and forward into the future," says Beyers. Ensuring continuity of that chain is the present generation's responsibility. In many Indigenous value systems, community supersedes the individual. For the Nuu-chah-nulth (formerly Nootka) people of the Pacific Northwest, a person who needs help and does not ask for it is not admired for self-sufficiency but instead is considered unkind, because honoring mutual dependence is seen as fundamental. Among southern Africa's San people, a person returning from the bush says, "I am here." The reply comes: "I see you!" We all want to be seen. But for that to work, we must also see. "I am here." "I see you!" Everyone wants the opportunity to have that conversation. "I see you" is what Alfie was softly whistling when I appeared at the edge of night.

◆

ALFIE REMAINED THE PICTURE OF health. But one of our birds' health was failing. On November 27 our little adopted green-cheeked conure, Rosebud, had a series of terrible seizures. We took her to the vet, who ruled out some things but found nothing definitive. She had no deficiency of vitamins or of calcium, which can cause seizures in captive parrots. After seeming okay for most of the day, she suffered another series of seizures, much worse, at times screaming for prolonged periods as though in great pain or fear, and at times looking as though she might be seeing threatening things, as if hallucinating. It was terrible to watch our little friend suffer while we remained so helpless to assist her. At the end of that torturous series, she lay exhausted, on her back as if dead, on the floor of her always-open cage.

Patricia rose in the dim predawn. Rosebud was "crying softly," so Patricia picked her up and soothed her a bit. A few minutes later, Patricia came upstairs and woke me in tears to say, "Rosebud just died."

I've seen many pets pass. It actually gets a little harder each time. Pets become family because in some ways they are a bit better than us. More peaceful, less manipulative, more forgiving, more eager to reconcile and smooth things over and move on. They show us how to be better than we are.

The next day, Patricia and I laid Rosebud on a bed of roses in a hole I dug. Chula had known Rosebud since she was a little puppy; Rosebud and Kane were already with us when Chula arrived in our lives. Chula came over to the open grave, sniffed, lay down, and pawed the edge a bit. We covered the grave. I placed a stone over it specifically so the dogs—or raccoons—wouldn't dig it up. But after we walked away, Chula went back sniffing and scratching the ground around the stone. I think she was concerned that Rosebud was stuck in there.

We were so sad. I am not sure whether Chula understood that Rosebud was dead. Various animals have varied understandings about death. Predatory creatures such as owls need to have at least a working understanding of the difference between alive and dead, because after they catch something that they need to kill, they must know when they can relax and begin eating.

That afternoon the veterinarian called to say that Rosebud's blood analysis indicated a virus that can cause seizures. Rosebud had such a cheerful and cheeky personality, often landing on our shoulders and sharing our meals, nibbling bits from our plates and sipping our drinks. This was doubly sad because she and Kane had been inseparable, and now he, with his permanently injured foot and wing, would live quietly without his friend, his preening companion, his interspecies mate. Alfie could never be a companion to him, not least because screech owls are bird-hunting birds.

LIFE GOES, LIFE COMES. LATER that day we were on the train to Manhattan to accept a seven-month-old puppy from our friends Paula and Jack. A mini Aussie shepherd with the energy of a nuclear reactor, Cady had proved too much for a city apartment. Fearful, loud, and not well socialized, this pup, we knew, might not fit into our peaceable kingdom. At our home a dog had to be chill around chickens, at peace with a parrot, and A-OK with Alfie.

When we introduced Cady to our doggies, things were tentative at first. Then Patricia got them all playing and chasing—and the throw rugs went flying. Much fun. But by the evening our dogs had had enough of the visitor. They looked at us as if saying, "When are you taking this puppy back to her home?" Chula growled at her.

In our yard the next day, a leashed Cady wanted nothing more than to chase our chickens. For their part, our chickens, though raised with Chula and Jude, were terrified of unfamiliar dogs.

Alfie had also grown up with Chula and Jude. In her young flopping and flapping phase before her flight feathers grew in, she would sometimes even hop right onto them. But the sight of Cady freaked her out. When Alfie first laid eyes on Cady, her immediate reaction was panic. For the first time in her life, Alfie banged around her enclosure, then went into full-stretched alarm-camouflage mode. We'd never seen her *do* that. I started thinking that Cady might not work out here.

On Cady's second full day we all went to the dog beach. Unleashed, Cady did some mingling and mixing, but she already knew her pack and continued following us. At the end of our walk, however, Cady decided to run after someone jogging with a dog far down the beach, back where we'd just come from. To my surprise, Chula and Jude stopped, turned to look at the receding Cady, then at me. Jude then lay down in the sand facing Cady. Cady soon came running back to us at top speed. When she reached Jude, he leapt up and followed Cady back to us. The dogs understood that now we belonged together. It would require weeks before Cady could be trusted around the chickens and Alfie would be fully accustomed to her. But I was sure I wanted to make it succeed, so I put in the time.

Artificial units of time such as our hours, minutes, and seconds are generally unknown in Indigenous traditions. No "week." No word for "work." The more we inhabit such artificialities—glancing at the clock, hurrying our bites while rushing toward our next online meeting—the more we hand the bucket of our time to someone else. We get it back with less room for experiences and relationships that would keep us situated within our own lifetime. When my time comes, I would rather kick a bucket that I myself have filled. Alfie was in my bucket because luck and I—with an assist from Patricia—had put her there. And she was light as a feather.

IN THE WARM PADDING OF her thick, brick-red plumage, Alfie was well prepared for her first winter. She avidly came down for her meals when we stepped into the coop. She napped in her shelter box. She could change her view by moving around on her perches, watching songbirds and the hens, and the deer, cats, raccoons, and possums ghosting through night's whispering shadows. She remained relaxed and healthy in a captivity that felt like home in the only life she'd ever known. She was comfortable.

I was not.

The fact that she'd been rescued from certain death went only so far toward justifying things now. She never sought a way out of the coop and her situation. I did.

But no better plan occurred to me. I remained afraid that if I opened the door she'd simply fly away and starve. Refusing to face pain can create a numbness that pushes joy beyond reach, according to Nuu-chah-nulth tradition. Wise words but—they must be paired with a bit of courage.

MEANWHILE, I TOO RETRACTED INTO a limited routine as January edged into February, which melted into March. I settled into winter rhythms of writing and teaching, my science-oriented ways of knowing and sharing. Ecological scientists and Indigenous people might recognize in each other a similar resonating awe. But Native and scientific ways of knowing travel different paths. For discerning objective reality—what exists regardless of what we believe, perceive, or prefer—science has the stronger claim. But science only maps reality; and the map it produces does not decide destinations, or routes of travel. Indigenous ways chart paths that work for humans and other beings, based less on objective facts than on subjective truths. As Albert Einstein noted, "Science can only ascertain what is, but not what should be, and outside of its domain value judgments of all kinds remain necessary."

The cold weather also prompted the meditative yard work of cutting and splitting and stacking the stored sunlight we call wood. How strange that in the stove it bursts its pent-up light, which radiates as heat throughout our home. The wood, the dogs, the clamming—it all helped get me outdoors, get me moving, get me cold and warm me up, made our kitchen smell good and our home feel cozy. Different components creating one shared life, unity from diversity, diversity within unity.

ONENESS FROM CONNECTED DIVERSITY, A world enspirited, responsive, and alive, was perceived by many cultures. For thousands of years, human beings worldwide puzzled the world's perimeter from their accustomed views of natural contours and the stars. Perspectives changed as some peoples began living settled agricultural lives that created new concerns: crops could be raided, animals could be stolen, drought or insect swarms threatened desperate famine, and despots arose who both defended and oppressed. Various peoples' whirlpools of worries created different perceptions about ancestors, spirits, gods, and human responsibilities for maintaining the cosmos in working order. Egyptians focused on preparing for an afterlife. Some Iron Age Hindu sects elevated one god over other coexisting gods. So did certain ancient Chinese belief systems, as early as four thousand years ago. Much later, China's Taoist and Confucian thinkers prescribed behaviors in keeping with cosmic balances, practices sometimes seen more as philosophical systems than religions. Alfie needed no instruction on connection; she needed no philosophy. She came naturally to herself, and the world came naturally enough to her.

◈

COLD-WEATHER BIRDS SUCH AS JUNCOS and white-throated sparrows continued to empty our feeders. But spring was well underway, with the tiny frogs called spring peepers strongly chorusing from well-watered vernal pools, forsythias preparing to pop their yellow blossoms, scarlet-billed oystercatchers again stalking the shores, and returning ospreys wheeling over warming waters. Bald eagles were new in the neighborhood. We watched spectacular sky chases between ospreys—who seem to abhor eagles for stealing their food—and the majestic white-collared thieves that are our national symbol. Songbirds began returning from Central America and other southern points in early May. Yellow, black-and-white, blue-winged, and other warblers; orioles; scarlet tanagers; great crested flycatchers; various vireos; savannah and chipping sparrows; all returned. A pair of peregrine falcons took up residence overlooking the shores of one nearby harbor. They'd wait for a migrating grackle, say, or a jay to cross the water. And when the bird was far from shore, they'd launch spectacular tag-team attacks. More breathtaking was how often their targets skillfully evaded the two living missiles.

The wild birds were going places. Alfie kept close counsel. The more adjusted she seemed to her comfortable confines, the more I fretted.

Whip-poor-wills and toads filled the night air of June. In July, whales shot their steamy breath skyward within sight of our beaches.

Alfie ate, rested, and watched her little bubble of the world.

———

LIKE ANY GOOD PARENT, I had accepted some responsibility for a little bit of the future. So I'd been tempting fate a bit. In early summer I'd started feeding Alfie on my hand most of the time. Then I opened the door so she would fly to me; I'd walk her back into the coop while she was eating. At first her focus was on me and the food. But she soon began finding the new views pretty interesting, looking around, acting distracted. In the practice of falconry, the trainer keeps the bird's focus through controlled hunger. Leather ankle straps allow the falconer to restrain the bird. I wanted none of that for Alfie. She was plump, and she was free to leave my hand.

And there she suddenly was, up in a tree. I got her down using something familiar that we'd practiced with during her first summer: a fake mouse on a string.

Crucially, she didn't just fly wildly off. This tempered my paralyzing fear that she would bolt and vanish. And she did not abruptly become skittish at my approach. These were pleasant surprises. They let me consider a next step.

During the first week of August, I finally let her out with the intention of allowing her to go up into a tree. She did. And again she was not inclined to wander off.

But she was immediately beset by angry blue jays. Alfie's "ear" tufts went straight up, and she uttered a softly screeched threat. Indignant about the presence of a predatory owl in their territory and emboldened by her vulnerable exposure during daylight, the jays— about Alfie's body mass—pressed their numbers and their advantage.

Several struck her. The same world that has nurtured all of Life into existence can nonetheless be a harsh place.

Alfie shifted her position into a protective lattice of English ivy about fifteen feet up the trunk of a maple. There she weathered the jays' insults and replied with open-mouthed threats.

I might have left her there in the sheltering ivy all day. And I might have had no choice; it was up to her. But after the scolders left, I heard the soft whinnies she often made to me. So I went with food and the fake mouse on a string.

"I don't think she'll want to come down," Patricia predicted.

"I'll make an offer," I said. "She'll decide."

I tossed the lure, and it landed on the ground. Alfie immediately oriented toward me. But she had a hard time figuring out how to free herself from that protective ivy cage she'd wiggled into. And—it looked like she wasn't sure she wanted to come.

Alfie and Patricia watched, unimpressed, as I waved food and dragged the lure. Alfie worked her way to a lower branch and seemed inclined to stay there, mulling her options. This could last for hours. The only thing about the situation that I knew and she didn't was that I didn't have hours.

I was able to climb onto a stump, reach up, and offer food where she could lean down and bite it. Rather than nicely stepping onto my hand, she tried energetically to yank the food from me. So, considering the situation—and my need to depart—I grasped her legs between my fingers, put her back into the coop, and let her eat there.

I was relieved. But had I thought this through? Shouldn't I have fed her *and* left her out? She didn't bolt; she seemed inclined to hang around. Ideally she would have dozed in the ivy all afternoon and come down for food in the evening. That would have counted for a successful first day of freedom at the start of a soft release. But I was again preparing to leave for several days. I wanted to be around if she was loose, especially the first day or two (assuming there might be two). So, again, I opted to play it safe. And again I wondered whether keeping her safe was the right thing—or even a good thing.

PART TWO

Openings

5

◈

Departures and Arrivals

THE FIRST DAYS OF SEPTEMBER SAW THE HIGH SUNS OF
summer shift to more angled light. Dawn and sundown crossed the
horizon much farther south than in June. The cycle of the year was
sliding toward another autumn. Flocks of blackbirds were gathering;
chimney swifts and nighthawks and bats started migrating through
our neighborhood; swallows and falcons and warblers and many others appeared along our ocean beaches as the continent began to drain
southward.

And Alfie was facing the possibility of a second fall and winter in
the safety and comfort of her roomy coop. Apparently that did not
bother her; of course it bothered me. What was the right balance here
right now in my little dot of the world? I wished I knew.

FINDING AND ASSISTING BALANCE HAS been on the minds of
many for thousands of years. Ancient South and East Asian cultures
sought a life harmonized with the universe's order. This they pursued
with a concept called *rita* in Vedic Hinduism (which gives us "right"
in English) and *dharma* in Buddhism and certain other South Asian

religions. It resonates with the Chinese philosophical and spiritual tradition called Taoism (or Daoism).

The Tao is pure reality, everything that makes up existence. The fourth-century B.C.E. text *Tao Te Ching* teaches that the universe coheres in harmony due to the Tao's patterns, rhythms, and substance. The *Tao Te Ching* intuited:

> There was something nebulous existing
> before Heaven and Earth.
> Soundless and formless it depends on nothing and does not
>   change.
> Moving cyclically without becoming exhausted,
> It operates everywhere and is free from danger.
> It may be considered the mother of the universe.
> I do not know its name;
> I give its alias: Tao.

It is said that "the Tao that can be spoken of is not the eternal Tao." Such mystical-sounding sayings, these little linguistic contortions, stop us long enough to do a double take and ask, "What? Why?" They seem intended to quiet us so that we may stop projecting and begin receiving. "One who knows does not speak," declares the *Tao Te Ching*. "One who speaks does not know." So, the Tao that is spoken of is not the Tao that is. I think of it as analogous to music. Music spoken of is not music itself. Words are always just code for something. One can nonetheless seek to live harmoniously with the rhythms of life and the cosmos—in a word, with the Tao. Even without understanding *how* the universe operates, knowing that the world exists according to the Tao suggests a way of living in accord with natural order. "The Way is to humans as rivers and lakes are to fish: the natural condition of life," said Chinese philosopher Zhuang Zhou (also known as Zhuangzi) in the fourth century B.C.E. Physical, mental, emotional, and spiritual health are thoroughly interwoven. Strive for simplicity, spontaneity, humility, frugality, and compassion. Taoists see no divine lawgiver. What impresses them is the *spontaneity* of the world, its inherent motion, its seasons, how plants come forth—all without central directives and without self-conscious thinking.

So, one's ways must not block the Tao. The *Tao Te Ching* advises:

The world is a spiritual vessel, and . . .
one who acts upon it destroys it.

Modern physicists sometimes propose an unknown force or particle whose existence—if confirmed—would solve a perplexing observation. Quarks and dark matter are examples. Analogously, Ancient Chinese thinkers posited a universal shared essence called *qi* or *ch'i* (pronounced "chee"). When dispersed, *ch'i* is invisible and without substance. Condensed, it becomes matter. Material things, from rocks to humans, are composed of condensed *ch'i*. What looks like creation and destruction is actually continuously changing densities of *ch'i*. Said Mengzi (sometimes Latinized as Mencius, who lived from 372 to 289 B.C.E.), "When it accumulates there is life. When it dissipates there is death." Out of the chaos of energy, Chinese philosophers saw the universe ordering and disordering itself. *Ch'i* has no outside cause; no god moves *ch'i*. Flowing and ebbing, *ch'i* connects and pervades everything. There is nothing that is not *ch'i*. Similarly, modern physics holds that the total amount of energy and matter in the universe is constant, merely changing from one form to another. Albert Einstein's famous $E = mc^2$ describes matter and energy as different forms of the same thing. Mengzi might tell us that the thing is *ch'i*.

Self-concentrating, self-dissipating *ch'i* creates complementary opposites. Hot and cold, sunlit and shaded, male and female, alive and dead—. Chinese thinkers generalized such complementary opposites, calling them *yin* and *yang*. Condensation of *ch'i* is the yin force, and dispersion is the yang force. We cannot have up without down, front without back, over without under, because yin-yang balance yields the wholeness of existence, creating harmony on Earth and throughout the cosmos. Rather than create a dualistic *split*, as did Western philosophers, the Chinese saw a unity of necessary opposites, fruitful paradoxes by which the whole is more than a sum of parts.

PATRICIA STAYED HOME WHILE I spent a night about sixty miles to the east at our cottage on the bay. In the morning I bought coffee and an empanada and went to the ocean. Through binoculars I watched the translucent yellow tail tips of many thousands of fish wagging through the water's surface, glittering in the early golden sunlight. Herring-like fish called menhaden (their name derived from their Algonquian term), recovering from a century of overfishing thanks to recent catch limits, had been massing just outside the surf in schools tens of miles long. I'd known this species of fish almost all my life but had never imagined such numbers were possible. The new schools spoke eloquently of the abundance of which this coast was capable, abundance that had supported the Natives and countless larger fishes, whales, and seabirds. Most of that wild plentitude has been forgotten. But with the industrial boats restrained, that time was remembering itself. Every few minutes a humpback whale—finally recovering nicely from near annihilation in the 1900s—exploded from beneath the schools like a bus suddenly airborne. Fish tumbled away from spectacular gaping jaws that engulfed hundreds in each lunge. Pods of overfed dolphins lazily worried the edges of the vast schools, while an osprey took in the scene from above, their "hunting" now as easy as picking grapes. Alfie wasn't with me of course, except that of course she always was, on my mind as if sitting on my shoulder like a little muse. Alfie was like a new lens that admitted more light, that gave me sharper images, more vivid views. The renewals of these rhythms and relationships—fish, whales, dolphins—felt wonderful.

Rhythms and relationships were on the mind of Kong Fuzi, or Master Kong (whose name was Latinized as Confucius, 551–479 B.C.E.), in ancient China. He emphasized family and kindness and gave humanity the Golden Rule: "Do not do to others what you would not wish for yourself."

In the eleventh century, the Neo-Confucian Zhang Zai (Chang Tsai) observed, "What fills the universe I regard as my body; what directs the universe I regard as my nature. All people are my brothers and sisters; all things are my companions." I wondered whether all this philosophical work labored toward the place where Alfie was effortlessly taking me, a sense of soft borders and openness. Did Alfie also see herself as one within everything? Or did she see herself more as an autonomous actor on the stage of her terrain? I could not yet know. Zhang Zai further observed, "Wealth, honor, blessing and benefits are meant for the enrichment of my life; while poverty, humble status, worries and sorrows are meant to help me find fulfillment."

For China's later strategists, entering the globalizing Western capitalist economy meant pursuing enrichment rather than fulfillment. (The China of the twentieth century had already suppressed Confucianism. Balance and harmony—and the way the monarchy had manipulated Confucianism to support itself—conflicted with China's newer political ambitions and Mao's form of communism. Nowadays teaching and discussing Confucianism has been resumed to some extent.)

Original thinkers of South, Central, and East Asia developed many ideas about human participation in the mysteries of existence. Jainism, Sikhism, Tengrism, and Shintoism are among the many Asian religions and wisdom traditions. Jainism is noteworthy for its core principle of *ahimsa*, a devotion to nonviolence so thorough that adherents sometimes mask their mouths and sweep their path as they walk to minimize the possibility of accidentally inhaling or crushing the smallest creatures. Shintoism, developed from ancient roots, holds all nature sacred. In Shintoism, reality is divinity and all things living and non-living have a spiritual power called *kami*. Some Asian belief systems speak of many cycles of death and rebirth prior to enlightenment and ultimate release from the karmic wheel. Meanwhile, though, they generally advance the idea that the best life is lived in harmony with what exists within and without us.

ALFIE HAD FOR MORE THAN a year been living her comfortable, healthy life in home and coop. She was a strong and excellent flier who could execute tight maneuvers and precise strikes. Such an owl who is not out doing owly things, with no chance at the gene pool—such an owl is not truly an owl. But maybe in a sense she *did* know. Each night Alfie had been moving her toys around. Was she getting antsy? Was she feeling bored?

A grim arithmetic backs the fact that most creatures raise many young, yet adult numbers don't fluctuate much from generation to generation. A breeding pair of screech owls might manage to raise three young every year. But the territory can support only one pair of adults. Outside their territory, all the good habitat is usually occupied. The young must look for holes left by recent fatalities. Some may drift and lurk. Until an opportunity opens up, they might remain unable to secure their own territory, their own mate, a stake in the future. Most of the rest cannot survive.

Could I really subject Alfie to those harsh odds? On the other hand—could I really deprive her of the opportunity to have a real shot at life?

Patricia shared my misgivings. "Let's just proceed with caution," she counseled. "We agree that softening Alfie's boundaries is the best course."

Alfie's outings suggested that she might be inclined to hang around rather than fly straight and fast and never be seen again. For a year I had paced back and forth over the sparse options. It came down to either leaving the door closed or opening it—and seeing what Alfie decided to do. "Yes," I answered, convincing myself. "It's time to rip the Band-Aid off."

THE NEXT MORNING—IT WAS THE sixth of September—Alfie flew from the coop toward me while I was holding food. But she merely touched my arm and continued across the yard. This time she was out all day, watching the world from a new vantage point in one of our dogwoods. She hadn't vanished. Not instantly. Not yet.

Near the usual evening feeding time, I began trying to lure her down. She seemed to be ignoring me. But my displays of food must have gotten her thinking about eating. She suddenly streaked across the yard, directly into her coop.

I was doubly ecstatic. Again she was safe. And she showed, by voting with her wings, that she had in fact felt comfortable there. If she could be free and continue regarding her coop as a home base, we could support her widening explorations by backing her up with food. We might—even after these months—have begun a soft release after all.

I fed her as usual. The forecast called for hard rain all night. I didn't want her first free-living night to be spent wandering in a downpour, perhaps getting too drenched to fly. Bad weather gave me an excuse to wait. I shut the door.

WAKE UP, WAKE UP. ONE never steps into the same sunrise a second time. The clearing morning promised fine late-summer weather. Patricia and I walked to the coop. Patricia is an excellent photographer, and we were hoping to get some frames of Alfie flying out of the coop to me for food. We didn't know whether this would be our last photo op with Alfie.

I'd considered the possibility of electronic tags that could track her. I've leg-banded thousands of birds. But something in my mind had shifted with the intimacy of knowing Alfie so well. I didn't want to impose anything physical on her.

I opened the door, walked out about ten paces, turned, and raised my arm, offering her a morning meal. She fluttered out and landed on my arm. But she did not take the food.

Instead, those big eyes of hers scanned the wider world, scanned the trees, scanned the sky. Taking it all in.

I was pulling off a little piece to hand-feed her and refocus her attention when she flew into a maple on the side of the yard. But not high, and then she came down low enough for me to give her some food and pick her up and put her in the coop. This time I left the door open. Now the Band-Aid was off. Would it hurt?

ALTHOUGH ALFIE AND I HAD not shared a common ancestor for about 300 million years, we very much shared present moments. Alfie responded to me, and always enjoyed a little head scratch. Our nervous systems can still entangle each other. Although 300 million years sounds long, it is less than the last one-tenth of Life's history. (Dinosaurs existed for about 180 million years—three times as long as the 60 million years they've been extinct.) By the time of that last common ancestor, our basic skeleton, our organs, and the brain chemicals involved in mood and motivation were all in place. Both Alfie and I inherited them. The broad imperatives of our lives remain shared: find food, dodge dangers, acquire some space and shelter and mates with whom to possibly raise young. We share overlapping perceptions and pleasures. We can, these hundreds of millions of years notwithstanding, relate to one another in the moment.

Alfie sat in her comfortable accustomed corner all day. In the evening I actually had trouble luring her out. I tossed a piece of food just outside the doorway. She took it, then flew back *into* the coop.

Would she continue to hang around the yard, coming into the coop for food until and unless she was feeding herself sufficiently to become independent? That would be perfect.

I tossed a second piece of food in the same spot, right outside the doorway. She flew to the doorway and gripped the wood frame briefly, hanging a bit sideways. Then, without taking the food, she flew out. She headed toward my writing studio at the corner of our yard, veered around it, and disappeared into the foliage near the great maple from which our little orphaned raccoon had fallen nine years earlier.

Around nine p.m. Patricia and I came out to look at the orb-weaving barn spider we'd been watching. Each night she spent hours remaking her whole web from scratch, over our back deck.

We abruptly heard Alfie calling very loud and close. She was in a dogwood over the yard gate. I hurried inside to fetch food to offer.

But she wasn't calling for me. She was calling back and forth with *a wild owl*, whom she then flew toward, into the woods. Was this a potential friend or a determined foe who'd already claimed this yard? Either way—but especially if the wild owl was inclined to be hostile—could Alfie cope? Did she even realize that she was *an owl*?

The calls stopped. We waited awhile, then readied for bed.

————

IN THE MORNING, THE EIGHTH day of September, I checked the coop. The food I'd left remained untouched. I called. And called. No answer, no owl.

I feared that the wild owl had promptly driven her away. Soon I noticed something even more worrying. Just outside the back steps were several screech owl body feathers. They appeared to have been forcibly pulled out. There seemed little question that something had attacked a screech owl. Possibilities included: the wild owl we'd heard or, worse and more decisively, a Cooper's hawk. The latter seemed more likely. This would mean that she'd come back this morning and gotten killed.

I'd let a perfectly tame, rather comfortable little owl face the harsh world. Whose best interests was I really concerned about? Hers? Or my imagined ideal outcome? I'd opened the door. She'd chosen to come out. It had been a gamble.

My worries about her over the last year had not gotten me as far as the possibility that a day-flying predator would snatch our little night-flying friend one fine morning. Yet that's what the evidence most suggested after her first night out.

Patricia looked on in silence.

I cursed myself out loud.

A FEW DAYS AFTER ALFIE'S possibly fatal disappearance, I had to temporarily disappear again. I'd been asked to participate in a conference titled "The Future of the Planet" in Lisbon, Portugal. So I flew away from my present, across the Atlantic toward an uncertain future.

Alfie's future—and whether there was such a thing—was much on my mind. A possible reason for the feathers on the ground had not previously occurred to me: blue jays might have attacked Alfie and pulled several feathers without otherwise injuring her.

But as I'd always feared might happen, the week passed with no sign of Alfie. Food that Patricia was leaving out remained untouched.

IN LISBON THE NIGHT BEFORE I was scheduled to head home, a ding from my cell phone woke me in my hotel. A text from Patricia read, "Guess who's back!"

Patricia was sitting outside with a friend at around eleven p.m. New York time when Alfie showed up. Alfie followed Patricia to the screened coop. Alfie went in. Patricia gave her food and closed the door.

Later Patricia emailed me:

> There is a wild screech owl sitting on a branch just over Alfie's coop. I heard vigorous calling earlier. I just went to see how Alfie was doing. She was just sitting up near her box. I decided to look around with the flashlight and found the other owl sitting there on the branch, also quiet. I had the dogs out with me but the wild bird did not seem to be disturbed. I went to get my camera, and left the dogs inside. The wild bird was still there. They continue to be quiet and the wild bird does not seem to be too concerned about me. We will decide when you are back whether we want to let Alfie roam again.

Alfie's week-long disappearance was one part of what I'd most feared. But she *hadn't* starved. So when I got home, we opened the door and left it open. In late dusk the wild owl again appeared. This time the wild owl hit the wire of the coop, hard. That seemed hostile. The wild owl flew back and forth and disappeared into the woods past the studio, as if burrowing into the dimming light. Alfie didn't come out. That Alfie might try to stay around only to be *driven* from her home by a wild owl was something I hadn't fully considered.

Alfie was still inside when I went to bed early. Through open windows we heard several bouts of calling. At Patricia's last check at ten-thirty p.m., Alfie had come out and was inspecting a cavity in the huge old mid-yard maple. She seemed to be browsing real estate possibilities. This did not seem like an owl in fear. If anything, she was making herself quite at home.

The owls traded calls off and on during the night. Screech owls don't hoot. An eastern screech owl's main call is a whinny, as if the owls are tiny winged horses. Sometimes they loudly broadcast; at close range they whisper. Often they alternate those high descending whinnies and lower-pitched trills. When frightened or annoyed, circumstances when a growl might seem appropriate, screech owls utter a soft, high screech.

At dawn an owl was whinnying close by. Wrens were scolding. We got right up. Outside, we did not see her. Yet when I held up my glove with a defrosted mouse, she arrived instantly. She took the mouse to a low tree. Patricia thought she'd be safer from blue jay mayhem inside the coop. I got on a stepladder and—after almost falling—brought her into the coop. There she ate, then dozed in her accustomed spot. I left the door open. Alfie would henceforth be free to choose whether and when to come and go. She would start a new phase on her own terms. I jotted a note to myself. "Best case: Alfie comes and goes and eventually becomes independent—and breeds."

I didn't yet realize something more profound. That open door was an invitation for us, too. Alfie had been braided into our life. But now she was tugging us into hers.

I WENT TO CHECK ON Alfie at seven p.m. There was plenty of light left. She flew to a branch next to me. I handed her a piece of fish. She took it to a maple tree. Fish might seem strange food for an owl, but eastern screech owls have been known to catch small fish while wading. Four owl species actually specialize in fishing, including the eagle-sized Blakiston's fish owl of far-eastern Russia and Hokkaido. In Nepal one evening I observed as two owls—likely tawny fish owls—landed on rocks in a stream riffle and waited watchfully there for movement. In Connecticut after dark one night a great horned owl grabbed my bass lure from the surface of a pond (luckily the bird did not get hooked, and let go of the lure). Alfie herself was always pleased with a morsel of fish.

Cady appeared at my feet. When I looked back to Alfie, she'd ghosted. We are all, always, in pursuit of something that is sometimes tangible and sometimes not. As babies we all seem to discover that the world consists of self and not-self. Modern Western culture nurses our infant impression into adulthood, raising us to split existence into self versus others, body versus mind, human versus nature, creation versus Creator, rich versus poor, us versus them—. We come to see ourselves as if operating in a world we are not quite part of. But as the Nobel-winning physicist and mathematician Frank Wilczek observes, "Detailed study of matter reveals that our body and our brain—the physical platform of our 'self'—is, against all intuition, built from the same stuff as 'not-self,' and appears to be continuous with it." He added, "There's a lot to unlearn."

Many cultures have in fact *not* taught that existence is composed of opposing dualities. In the fifth century B.C.E., Siddhartha Gautama (who, after his enlightenment, was referred to as Shakyamuni and called the Buddha) taught a method that is known as *dhyana* in India, *Ch'an* in Chinese, and *Zen* in Japanese. To oversimplify, one attains enlightenment when fully apprehending that all existence is one. Buddhism holds the understanding that no separate self is possible.

"The most important thing," wrote Zen master Shunryu Suzuki, "is not to be dualistic." He elaborated: "Our usual understanding of life is dualistic: you and I, this and that, good and bad. But actually . . . you and I are just swinging doors."

Individuality is real. When I leave my desk, my desk remains. When I am no longer myself in the world, loved ones will note my absence. We are selves in a real sense—but not in a closed sense. As a river depends on new water, one's body is an interchange. To test this, stop breathing. Our flow of food originates as sunlight's energy. We drink water molecules whose atoms have been recycling for eons and will do so when they are no longer part of us. Observing relationships that we have, that we *are*, we approach the realization that no isolated separate self is possible. We are participant members in one existence of life, of the cosmos, of time. Buddhism has always appreciated the living world. In East Asia especially,

Zen Buddhism absorbed the Taoist habit of immersion in nature's sensory richness: sights, sounds, scents, rhythms, and textures. A thousand-year-old poem, "At Home in the Mountains," says, "This patch of earth delights the mind."

The ancient Buddhist concept of "dependent origination" (*pratitya-samutpada*) is the profound observation that there is no entirely "new" life. Europeans believed that life continually arose anew from non-living things such as soil and rotting meat. This belief in living things arising from the non-living—"spontaneous generation"— persisted until 1859, when Louis Pasteur experimentally disproved it. Pasteur's proof was hardly news to Buddhists. True, life must have originated at least once from non-life. But for more than three billion years since then, each of the unimaginable multitudes of living cells burning their brief candles, through all the living past and flickering present, has emerged directly as *a preexisting living cell that divided.* No known exceptions exist. No spontaneous generation. After the very first, each cell that ever has been alive, and that is alive now, was part of a living cell that split. Only life makes life. Much is always changing as life diversifies, but humans retain copies of DNA from Earth's earliest cells, the common ancestors of all living things. *That* is connection, is relation.

A relevant Hindu scripture, the *Chandogya Upanishad,* tells of a humble father and his precocious son. The son is chosen for an auspicious education with holy Brahmans. Now the son looks down on his simple father. One day the father says, "Come with me." He leads his impatient, reluctant son to a tree. He picks a fruit and asks, "What do you see?" His son curtly answers, "Nothing. I see nothing." The father asks him to break open the fruit and look at the seeds. "What do you see?" Again, the son says, "Nothing!" The father holds a seed close to his son's face and says, "You are this, my son; you are this 'nothing.'" All is one thing, and we are all things, existing in a single interpenetrating unity, the family of Life, the oneness of the cosmos.

When Buddhists from India arrived in China, they brought the

Hindu concept of *dharma*, the cosmic principles harmoniously relating all things. Our human task is to live in resonance with these natural harmonies. The Chinese welcomed dharma as an independently derived view of Tao. Teachers exchanged ideas, and sometimes debates got vigorous. But there remains no pressure to conform, no concept of blasphemy or heresy, no dogma. Oxford professor and writer David P. Barash says that when introducing audiences to unfamiliar ideas, "I have consistently found Eastern audiences to be more comfortable and even welcoming than those in the West." He continues, "A Buddhist perspective—often creatively combined with that of Hinduism, Taoism, and/or Shintoism—generates openness to the interconnectedness of all life."

A Zen proverb advises, "Before enlightenment, chop wood, carry water. After enlightenment, chop wood, carry water." I first encountered that idea in my twenties in Nepal while reading Peter Matthiessen's monumental *The Snow Leopard* not far from where he'd begun the trek upon which he based the book. I'd been reading while sitting alongside a mirror-calm blue lake that reflected the shining peak of Annapurna towering within a snowy panorama of Earth's highest mountains. I was sipping tea. Matthiessen had just informed me, "The universe itself is the scripture of Zen." The practice is simply the endeavor to grasp the infinite within each moment. Peter rendered the wood-and-water proverb as an aphorism: "How wondrous, how mysterious! I carry fuel, I draw water." The line so arrested me that I took a moment to absorb it. Reaching for the tea, I felt the profound mystery that enabled my eye and mind and arm to grasp and direct the teacup. In order for me to reach that warming sip, every precedent of Life's history had to be present in the thing I call me. Before enlightenment, reach for a cup. After enlightenment, reach for a cup. Had I just been gently awakened? As if confronted with a newly unveiled work in a wholly new idiom, I felt a life shift that ushered me into a world of miracles. Aided by the soaring, psychoactive view, I felt the power of everything.

The word created by joining "a" with "we" is "awe." Each of us is joined to all things and all of time. Of course, we can't always fully inhabit that elevated awareness. We have emails to answer and on and on. So perhaps we can aspire to something slightly more achievable. Before emails, chop wood, carry water. After emails, chop wood, carry water. That's what my woodstove and the chickens and dogs and our other daily vital signs do for me. They help start the days real and help keep things authentic. The little things—are the big things. The routine helps guardrail the journey toward being present in our own lives and loves. It can inspire a life's work. It can be as simple as a little owl at the back door.

Alfie knows something about presence in relationships. After all, she herself has managed to convene us here on this page, you and me, in this moment. "Everything is here now" is a tenet of Zen Buddhism. Arriving here required the full trek, and that whole journey is present in each second. The deep ancestors' essence is everywhere. In our mother's womb, our temporary gills, fins, and tail manifested the genetic memory of Life's family portrait. As adults we retain and pass along our fish-originated spinal column, ribs, and organs, and the gill-originated jaw with which we voice human thoughts. We are one point in the unfolding of all. We are not just a speck in time and the universe; we are the universe and all of time in a speck.

One cannot step into the same river twice, said Heraclitus; change is constant. But we often succumb to distraction while our days flow untended. Worse than obsessing on the future or past is eddying in what I'll call "the parallel present," the now that is not now: the nags, the to-dos, the static our minds can't tune out, the tedium we insist upon, the hurts we nurse. That is how we deflate our sexiness, douse our talents, imprison our passions, neglect our loved ones, darken the sun, overlook the moon, and forget to taste our food while we're chattering. Life is flowing by whether we are in beauty full immersion or drying out on the wrack line of desiccating distractions. The present passes instantaneously. There is nothing to attain except attention. When dancing, you are not trying to get anywhere. Easily said, but it is hard to be fully here. The moment you start thinking, you place yourself outside all that is. I've observed that much of what passes as thought isn't worth that price.

Alfie is the perfect little Zen master. And she is Heraclitus, too, flexing with the constant flow of change. Alfie lives a freedom untainted by critique or doubt, a liberty buoyant and volitant and as reliably accessible to her as the air beneath her wings. Resisting nothing, she is pure presence, here now.

AT TWO A.M. I HEARD calling and went out into the drench of moonlight. Alfie was in the dogwood by the back door. "There you are," I said. "Here I am," she softly answered. There we were, united.

6

◆

On the Loose

CLOUDS SCUDDING ACROSS A SETTING MOON. COOL AIR.
In the east, the swelling bud of dawn. Alfie was again in the dogwood by the back door, as if we had an appointment. I walked to the
screened coop and was entering its open doorway when Alfie flew
past, brushing my head, and landed on one of her little perches. I gave
her a meal.

Patricia came out briefly with the dogs. They were riled with
morning energies and hungry and she didn't need to say anything to
get them to follow her back inside for their breakfast.

This was everything I'd hoped for at this stage. More than I'd
dared expect. Leaving most of her meal on the perch, Alfie went to
rest in her favored day spot alongside her shelter box. Clearly, she
wasn't very hungry. Perhaps she'd been hunting successfully. For her
to remain motivated to hunt, I thought, maybe I should dial my feeding back a bit. But what she'd been catching in these last few nights—
if anything—I really didn't know.

I'd gone out so early because I had a new fear: that if she remained
outside waiting for me much past dawn, a Cooper's hawk might notice
her. The back-door dogwood Alfie had started to frequent was close

to the bird feeders. Those bird feeders were often under surveillance. To make that point, one afternoon while Patricia and I were standing under the dogwood, the sudden sound of a dry splash in the branches just a few feet above our heads was followed by a rain of dove feathers. No one saw the hawk coming. That is the hawk's way.

Alfie's winter safety would depend on her being situated in her snooze roost by dawn, either inside the coop or in another sheltered place of her choosing, perhaps in a secure tree hole, concealing herself like the wild owl I hoped she could become. Easiest for us would be to feed her early in the evenings. But I wanted her to be hungry enough for most of the night to want to hunt. So it looked like I'd be getting up in the dark.

Alfie was now a longer-term commitment. One day I saw Patricia browsing house listings. Maybe a quieter neighborhood, she said, perhaps something nearer the water.

"We can never move," I advised.

Patricia looked at me with her eyebrows high.

"Screech owls have lived more than a decade in the wild; captive ones, twice that," I reminded her. "If Alfie survives and stays close but remains dependent on us—"

"We could take Alfie with us."

"Not that simple. She might try to return here. And a new place could have an established pair of wild screech owls." If so, they would not tolerate a newcomer. We'd have to find a place listed as available not just by the human owners but also by the local owls. That was not happening.

◆

WE ATTENDED A RELIGIOUS WEDDING in a splendid sylvan setting that inspired the officiating priest to acknowledge, with appreciation, "this beautiful world in which God made all things for us."

He meant no harm. But it would never occur to me to think that Alfie was made for me. What if, instead, the story we told ourselves was that God made us *for* all things? "What people do with their ecol-

ogy is deeply conditioned by beliefs about our nature and destiny—
that is, by religion," wrote the Christian and historian Lynn White Jr.

Akhenaten, who ruled Egypt from 1353 to 1336 B.C.E., may have
been the first to invent a sole god. In a clear first, he brutally imposed
forced worship of his sun god, Aten, abolishing all other gods, destroy-
ing their statues. Egyptologist Jan Assmann calls it "the most radical
and violent eruption" of a religion in history. People had always felt
spirits pervading the world. Akhenaten moved spirit off to the heavens.
The world no longer participated in creation; it became a mere result.
Other cultures sensed no segregation between material and spiritual;
they did not see existence at odds with itself. Splitting the universe into
a *duality* consisting of nature and a god outside of nature was the most
counterintuitive idea yet about how and why we exist.

Akhenaten's new monotheism was, to state it mildly, unpopu-
lar. Three regimes later, Egypt's boy-pharaoh, Tutankhaten—possibly
Akhenaten's son—quickly changed his name, becoming the now-
famous Tutankhamen. Later rulers purged Akhenaten's name from
Egypt's roster of leaders. After Akhenaten's death, monotheism was
quickly buried. Egyptians reinstituted divine diversity and returned
sacredness to Earth. But monotheism would be back, with a vengeance.

Meanwhile, during the second millennium B.C.E., pastoralist
people began spreading out from a thousand-mile-wide region north
of the Caucasus Mountains and the Black and Caspian Seas. We call
them Caucasians. Archaeologists call them "Proto-Indo-Europeans."
They tended cattle and rode horses descended from those their ancestors had domesticated centuries earlier. Their fifteen-hundred-year
spread brought them as far as India in the east and Greece in the west.
They are the reason that "brother" is *bhrater* in Sanskrit and *brathir*
in Old Irish, the reason that Sanskrit, Persian, Greek, Latin, German,
and Celtic are related languages.

Perhaps seven centuries B.C.E. (scholars debate the timing) in
what is now Iraq, Zoroaster (a.k.a. Zarathustra) saw a self-antagonizing
universe wherein "good" and "evil" were constantly at war. He personified the good with the god Ahura Mazda, creator of a perfectly
ordered universe; disorder and chaos he personified by the devilish god

Angra Mainyu. Zoroastrianism injected several monumental concepts into the world: that we exist in a dualistic universe of opposing good and evil forces; that a law-giving Creator of the spiritual and material world exists in a kingdom of justice; that this good Creator is opposed by an evil force; that people have free will to choose good or evil; that after death their acts will be subjected to a divine judgment; that a virgin will give birth to the savior of the world; and that this world will pass and a renewed existence will be inhabited only by goodness. Zoroaster's views reverberated. From Zoroaster's Persia to Egypt to the eastern Mediterranean, voyagers, traders, and travelers exchanged everything from goods to alphabets to ideas about existence, influencing Greek philosophers and eventually—most importantly—Judaism, Christianity, and Islam. Zoroaster gave us ideas in whose wash and waves our Westernized minds are still bobbing.

SOME THINK THAT THE DISSOCIATION from nature began with agriculture. It's true that agrarian civilizations developed straight lines and hierarchies. But the Americas and many Pacific islands homed Indigenous peoples who depended substantially on agriculture yet never lost their reverence for nature. And, of course, the Asian peoples whose dharmic religions were respectful of nature were mainly agriculturists. As Richard Nelson has mentioned, Indigenous peoples' ethics of reverence often remained unperturbed by the introduction of outboard motors, chain saws, and guns. Present-day American Natives in the Midwest, Plains, and Pacific Northwest continually oppose government policies about things ranging from pipelines to wolf killing to bear hunting to mining, because their traditional ethics remain unvanquished by their avail of pickup trucks and internet accounts.

Something happened in Western culture. Something different.

◆

IN THE WARM MONTHS, WE leave the doors open for the dogs to come and go all day. Our windows stay open day and night for the breezes while birds and frogs and bugs are chanting praises.

But in the third week of September an evening approaches—and this was it—when a breath of autumn first prompts us to close the doors and lower the windows. "Indian summer" will come and go for weeks, but the earliest of turning leaves means that the season has inflected into fall.

AT SIX-THIRTY P.M. I HAPPENED to be filling the pets' outside water bowl when Alfie flew into her favorite dogwood. With plenty of remaining light, wrens, cardinals, and sparrows were soon mobbing her. But their protestations were mild and to no effect.

When the light lowered and the songbirds departed, I watched as Alfie showed that in these few days of freedom she'd acquired considerable knowledge of her territory. She went first to the big, ivy-clad fifteen-foot-high maple stump outside our kitchen window. She appeared to be hunting, scrutinizing the dense ivy. This is a place where sparrows spend the night. Another place is in the front bushes, and that is the next place she went. Alfie was acutely tuned, scanning the bushes from shifting locations in a low tree as though she'd indeed been hunting roosting sparrows all her life. She kept this up for about forty-five minutes, then flew across the street. I lost sight of her.

Fifteen minutes later, I was inside with the doors and windows closed when I heard her calling loudly. She was right there in her favorite dogwood by the back door. I called her up to the coop. She followed me in. I gave her some food. A little while later she was gone.

◆

BEFORE DAWN, I WAS ELSEWHERE. I was out in my boat, looking for dinner. I enjoy most aspects of fishing, except, ironically, harming fish. But from the heat of that friction we can try to create some light. The fish bring to our table a story from the authentic world. For that connection, we are always grateful. Who thanks a can of beets, a box of crackers, the hill that grew the coffee, the hands who picked the beans? The anonymous lives contained in purchased foods go thanklessly through us. Fishing causes pain, but agriculture—even organic farming—obliterates wild animals and plants. No free lunch. Only balances to be sought. Fishing helps me keep my distance from the industrial food system. That's my main justification. But my main *reason* is the beauty of venturing upon the ocean in angled light, among wandering seabirds, among mindful tribes of dolphins, into the world's most humbling realm.

I view the fish as gifts. I see gifts not as free, however, but as expensive. A monetary transaction merely transfers ownership; both parties walk away. A gift exchange is an acknowledgment that we are with each other in the world, a little gesture of understanding that, simply, we may help each other, that we will live in reciprocity. And that's no small task. Accepting a gift entails offering a little bundle of ourselves. When a fish comes into my boat, I say thank you and I apologize as an admonishment to myself to live up to the life I am taking. Fishing alerted me to the ocean's depletion, a realization that has powered a lifetime of work, the enactment of my gratitude.

So as I said, before dawn I was out in the boat, looking for dinner. Not long after the planet had spun the sun up to dazzle the sea, Patricia texted: "Good morning Sweetie. I hope you are enjoying your time on the water. Alfie was in the dogwood this morning. She wasn't following me to the coop. I picked her up and brought her there and put her food on the platform and gave her some head scratching. She loves that. I guess she's decided to stay in there for the day."

WARM TEMPERATURES RETURNED; IT TOPPED 80 degrees Fahrenheit during the day. In the evening, Patricia still had the doors open for the doggies. She was sitting in the living room when she suddenly noticed Alfie on the dining room lamp. Alfie flew silently out again and landed on the deck railing, then flew to the edge of the woods and landed in the raccoon tree. Patricia went to the coop; Alfie followed. Patricia gave her a head scratch, fed her.

I returned late from my time on the ocean.

At first light, Alfie was calling from the back-door dogwood. The temperatures remained so warm that even with windows open, we'd slept with just a sheet. That was unprecedented here during the third week of September. Even at dawn it was T-shirt warm outside.

In the emerging light Alfie flew to the huge old maple in the central part of our yard, a tree in the declining part of a long life. We'd had to trim back some massive dead branches that threatened to fall on our house. But I'd resisted advice to cut the tree down. A dead trunk can be home to many. This tree's five huge trunks offered many cavities, several of which interested Alfie. I watched as she landed on the rim of two, still house hunting.

I fed the dogs. When I reappeared, Alfie had vanished. She was now making all the choices. Her flight, soundless as a snowflake, was literally something to behold. So many things about her had a savor of sweetness. It felt magical that a little owl who was not hungry enough to take food would arrive and softly call, seeking contact before retiring into some nook of quiet safety for the day, making a last little connection.

CONNECTIONS WERE, FROM ANTIQUITY, ON the minds of most cultures.

In the Homeric Hymn to the goddess Gaia, she is the mother of all. Gaia and the worldly earth were continuous, not separate. The seventh-century B.C.E. was perhaps the last time that the leading edge of Western thinking viewed the world as sacred.

Around that time a Greek named Hesiod told stories of how gods who had sprung from primordial Chaos engaged in violent struggles and lustful intrigues, like superheroes in a cosmic soap opera.

But by about the sixth century B.C.E., several Greek men from Ionia had asserted that the classical gods and goddesses were all silly. Historian Colin Wells says that these Ionian thinkers recognized that the world is "governed by orderly operations of its own," that gods or spirits are not necessary for understanding how those operations work. Rather than see the sun as a god, for example, they speculated about what the sun is and how it functions. Seeing a world of worldly processes, they advanced speculations that others could critique. This was the world-rocking invention of free rational inquiry.

An Ionian named Anaximander thought that an original undifferentiated cosmos had separated out into the different things we see. Thousands of years ahead of his time, Anaximander realized that fossil seashells on hilltops indicated that the world had been different, that it changes. He believed that life had originated in moist mud or slime and that land animals—including humans—*evolved* from fishlike animals. Modern science did not catch up with Anaximander until Lyell, Darwin, and Wallace in the 1800s.

In the face of natural forces, the old, all-too-human classical gods were not standing up well. Xenophanes (born around 570 B.C.E.) mocked the classical gods as merely imagined beings reflecting the foibles and physiques of the people who projected them. He prodded those who believed in this pantheon with the idea that if horses, oxen, and lions could invent gods, they'd invent horselike, bovine, and feline gods. Xenophanes viewed *thought* as having enormous power, complete purity, and existing independent of the material body. He believed that human thought could approximate divine understanding. Further, Xenophanes was among the first who considered the natural and the divine as separate. This view has never stopped reverberating.

Pythagoras (born around 570 B.C.E.) believed that we possess an immortal soul, which reincarnates through many creatures. He also believed that the universe functions by fixed, reliable laws that could be measured. Contrastingly, Heraclitus speculated (around 500 B.C.E.) that nothing can ever really be known because everything changes. Heraclitus, who told us, "One cannot step into the same river twice," also said, "Change is the only constant" and, "All things must pass." Anaxagoras (born around 500 B.C.E.) stunningly intuited a cosmic Big Bang, writing, "All things were together, unlimited both in amount and in smallness, for the small, too, was unlimited." All things had been together *with one exception*: mind or intelligence—called *nous*. Wrote Anaxagoras, "*Nous* has power over all things." Then, the momentous event: "*Nous* set in order all things that were to be." This was the suggestion that the universe was created by something *outside* of it.

Parmenides (around 460 B.C.E.) concluded that appearances

are pure illusion. His contemporary Democritus (born around 460 B.C.E.) said that the growth and coming apart of things implies invisible building blocks. From this he developed a complex theory of invisible particles: atoms. Democritus said that because the universe is built of things unseen, our senses deceive. "Of knowledge there are two forms, one legitimate, one bastard. To the bastard belong all this group: sight, hearing, smell, taste, touch." He also said, "Actually we know nothing; for truth lies deep." His message: Distrust what seems real. Believe what you *think*.

A problem was brewing. Rationality had suggested that nothing can be known, reality is invisible, and all is illusion, but rational people disagreed among themselves. Worse, philosophers lacked hard evidence; experimentation lay in the distant future (Democritus's atomic theory sat untested for nearly two thousand years). If this was all just debatable conjecture among thinkers who did not agree, was rationality of any value to real people? Was there *anything* here upon which we mortals could base right and wrong and how to live? Anaxagoras's student Archelaus said in essence, "Well—of course not."

Civil laws had been considered divinely ordained. Rationality made people feel like society was losing its grounding, drifting on a rising tide of conflicting perceptions. One can almost hear the average person say, "Enough already with this useless 'reasoning.'"

Rationalists' explanations prompted the faithful to close ranks. Further, religion and patriotism were thoroughly entwined. In the face of reason's destabilizing effects, many people wanted to make Athens great again. So around 432 B.C.E., in perhaps the Western world's first religious backlash, the Decree of Diopeithes authorized legal action against "those who fail to respect things divine or who teach theories about the heavens." Anaxagoras was charged with "impiety" for saying that the sun was not a god. Socrates arrived and said with emphatic humility that knowledge *was* possible. Together, he urged, we should search for what is knowable. His search brought him eternal fame, a death sentence for impiety, and a very famous pupil: Plato.

◆

WHEN I'D CALL ALFIE, I'D imitate a screech owl. But now—no response.

For Patricia, a simple "Where are you?" often worked. Alfie knew her voice, of course.

Alfie suddenly appeared, calling strongly from the front of the house. "I am here!" She flew over our vegetable garden and into the edge of the woods. Patricia, watching her, continued calling, "Where are you?," and like this they dialogued back and forth.

Meanwhile, I went in and got Alfie a mouse from the fridge, took the chill off—six seconds in the microwave—and exited via the back door. Alfie flew like a silent shadow against the sky, crossing the yard from the woods, into the back-door dogwood.

I went up to the coop and called.

"She's coming to you," Patricia said.

Alfie swooped straight through the doorway and landed on her preferred eating platform. I served her dinner. Patricia came up and indulged her in a little head scratching. Then we let her eat in solitude.

A LASHING GALE DROPPED ALL-NIGHT driving rain and delivered a treetop-swaying dawn. I went out the back door and called. Alfie popped into the dogwood and whinnied. I walked toward the coop; she flew. I fed her, I fed the wild birds, I fed the chickens, I fed the dogs; I made coffee for myself and Patricia. When I went to inquire of Alfie whether she wanted some head scratching, she was already gone.

She was no longer regarding the coop as a base. Now it was only a feeding place.

IN THE EVENING I WAS at a book-signing event when Patricia texted me: "No sound, no call, I just looked up and . . ."

Accompanying the message was a photo of Alfie on top of Kane's living room cage. Alfie had grown up with him all the previous summer. Fortunately, Kane's door was closed. Surprisingly, he did not seem frightened. When Alfie had first started flying, she would streak around the house, attacking pillows and small items. That was all practice for the real thing: hunting. During those days of fun and frolic in the house, Alfie once snatched Kane off his kitchen perch, took him to the rug next to the dining room table, and immediately began ripping feathers from his head. Kane's previously injured foot and wing disadvantaged him further, and he was well on his way to getting killed. Luckily, I was right there.

I was astonished that Alfie would attack someone about as large as herself, but I chalked that up to juvenile misjudgment. I guessed—but would not trust—that a more experienced Alfie would no longer attack Kane.

Alfie, standing on Kane's cage, wasn't hungry. Patricia offered some hard-boiled egg; Alfie passed. She spent some time flying around the house—her childhood home. Then, as if she could materialize and dematerialize at will, she flew out into the night.

At two a.m. she began calling loudly enough to wake us, with a kind of screech I'd never before heard. Lying in bed listening, I wondered whether these calls were her claim of territory, her advertisement for a mate, or her attempt to locate the wild owl we'd seen. We had not heard or seen the other owl for about two weeks.

AT FIRST LIGHT, SHE WAS waiting on a low branch. After eating in the screened coop, she hopped into her water dish and shook herself a brief bath. Then she flew out. It was light enough for a cardinal, wren, and blue jay to all come scolding. Alfie might pose a lethal threat to these birds when the world went dark, but in daylight they had the tactical advantage and the numbers. Alfie replied with a soft, threatening screech.

When the dogs came bounding out, with Patricia following, the sudden commotion prompted Alfie to fly into a maple and spend about fifteen minutes observing the world from on high. Eventually, and with a bit of difficulty, she got situated in a cozy nook in the lush, branching sprays of English ivy festooning the trunk. Camouflaged among the leafy shadows, she was so hard to see that I moved a small fallen branch to mark exactly where I was standing so I could relocate her. After breakfast, Patricia came to see. Standing on that bit of wood, I could not spot Alfie. Had she left? All at once I realized she was perched exactly where I was looking, exquisitely blending in.

I LEFT TO DO A bit of teaching in California for a few days. Patricia emailed:

> Last night Alfie came in the house again and flew around a bit but soon went right back out. Just came to say hi I guess. A great horned owl called in the distance so I worried for her. I went back to bed. She continued to call for a bit but not as loudly.
>
> This morning I heard a few birds mobbing. I went out and saw that she was up in the ivy growing on the big maple trunk next to the bird feeders.
>
> That is the update from Happy House.

I was packing to head homeward when a text lit my phone: "We have an owl in the house. She is currently in the bathroom. Just hanging out."

WHEN I GOT HOME, AFTER midnight, Alfie was on a beam above the kitchen table. She wasn't hungry. I climbed onto a chair, plucked her from her perch, and carried her, protesting, to the open door. I opened my hands and she flew into the night.

◆

THINK OF A BASEBALL, A football, a golf ball. We recognize them all as balls, because we have an abstract concept of "ball." Some twenty-five hundred years ago Plato, born around 429 B.C.E., imagined that for each thing in the world, an ideal, perfect, eternal "Form" actually existed on an abstract plane in a non-material dimension.

There is, he said, a perfect ball, the quintessential horse, ultimate blackness, exemplary courage, a model table, an absolute circle, flawless love—. All things we see and have (and are), he reasoned, exist in the world as defective reflections of those eternal perfect Forms that exist beyond space and time. Things get from ideal to real via Plato's divine craftsman, known as the Demiurge, who uses the perfect Forms as templates for crafting our imperfect world. Until this, most people viewed matter as animated by divinities that commingled with worldly realities or as simply both matter and divinity: a river, say, might also have been seen as a god. A personified god working from *outside the universe* was something very new.

Plato reasoned that our ability to imagine a perfect circle, say, means we must actually have come in contact with those perfections beyond space and time. How? Borrowing from Socrates's and earlier philosophers' spiritual views, Plato believed that spirit guides drew lots to determine which unborn human they would inhabit. Arriving in our material body, this immortal guide remembers its contact with perfection. In us these eternal guides remain trapped until death frees them. Plato viewed the soul and the mind as the same thing, so these guiding souls generated human reason and goodness, steering our decisions in matters of right and wrong. They accounted for our ability to think about thinking—something so pure that Plato saw the soul as essentially a route to contact with the divine.

The body, however, was subject to baser emotions, desires, and decay. Consequently, Plato disparaged desire. Controlling desire by applying reason yields virtue. The problem, though: desire exerts continual pressure upon reason. The soul, in continual friction with the body, is not a happy tenant. Plato writes in the *Phaedo*, "We must get rid of the body." Then what? "Contemplate things by themselves with the soul by itself." In the dialogues of Plato, "the soul is most like the divine." It is "deathless, intelligible, uniform, indissoluble, always the same." The body is contrastingly mortal, inconsistent. Any ideal, such as *the good* or *the beautiful*, that finds its way into material existence gets "tainted with human flesh and a mass of perishable rubbish." We cannot know truth "as long as we have a body and our soul is contaminated by such an evil." Therefore, humans should work toward freeing their souls, and the perfect way is: death.

In sum, Plato gave us a creator-god to craft perfections into earthly facsimiles; an eternal soul imprisoned in decadent flesh, yearning for release upon death; and—most consequentially—denigration of material existence. Plato moved the sacred away from the body, from Earth, from Life. Viewing intellect as divine and disembodiment as ideal, Plato moved goodness off the planet. It was a long, strange surgery, performed not to remove something bad from the body but to remove the body from everything perceived as good. Plato and his followers were perhaps the first people to feel revulsion toward the world. By forever separating our material world from the realm of perfection, Plato propounded a stark *dualist* doctrine. This might be the most consequential idea in the history of human thought, its implications almost literally Earth-shattering. Most fundamentally, we are left with: an existence at odds with itself.

THE DOGS HAD PENT-UP ENERGIES. Cady had hurt a leg playing with Chula, and we'd given them all a week's rest. This penultimate day of September was unusually warm, and the harbor tide was very low on the new moon. I was hesitant to let the dogs loose; I wasn't sure about Cady's leg. But she was. They went running along the shore and splattering through the shallows. Soon enough, Cady was on three legs again, holding one leg up but having a ball. It's sometimes a balancing act, sometimes a guess, but I always try to "let our dogs be dogs." Home we went with several wet pooches. At home, Cady was back on all fours and followed me to my writing studio, where she curled happily into a deep snooze, dreaming perhaps of flying sand and salty mud.

I haven't mentioned that our dogs are color-coordinated. Cady has very pretty markings of black and tan, with a white throat and belly. The dogs are unrelated, but she looks like a perfect cross of Jude, who is black with a white underside, and Chula, who is a lovely kind of brown that I call mahogany; she's also been called auburn.

For Plato, a brown dog was a reflection of perfect brownness and pure dogness. But for Plato's star student, Aristotle, a brown dog was a dog who was brown. Aristotle believed that philosophy should explain the world, not deny it. For Plato, justice and virtue were conditions of the soul. For Aristotle, they were practices put into action. To Plato's credit, he did not claim certainty, and he invited further consideration. And, indeed, Plato's fantasies drew thoughtful dissenters. Epicurus (d. 270 B.C.E.) and Lucretius (d. 55 B.C.E.) had more incisive insights. Epicureans eschewed superstitions; they sought happiness in a modest life free of pain and fear. Lucretius took a swipe at Plato's belief that our world was the center of the universe, positing instead an infinite cosmos. (Lucretius wrote this a millennium and a half before the Catholic Church charged Copernicus with heresy for concluding likewise.) And Lucretius thought it absurd to believe that the world was made for humans, noting the obvious hostility of deserts, dangerous animals, and many toxic plants.

These cooler heads assailed but did not prevail. They failed to dislodge Plato.

◆

I SQUINTED UP INTO THE umbrella of ivy festooning the huge old fifteen-foot-high maple stump outside the kitchen window. Alfie was again spending the day tucked up there, in deep shade.

A few hours after dark she flew into the house again, taking positions around the living room, from chairs to window shutters, before flying back out the side door. I went out. She soon landed hard on a branch in front of me. She brought her foot to her mouth a couple of times. She seemed to have caught a bug.

Her responsiveness amazed me. When I worked with hawks, food was the prime motivator; a bird that was not hungry would ignore you. Alfie was coming to be near me without my calling, without my showing food, and often without being hungry.

Having Alfie physically free yet perpetually dependent would not reflect good parenting. So we generally did not feed her until shortly before we went to bed, so that in the night's earlier hours she'd have an appetite, motivating her to hunt. Tonight she showed up early, but instead of focusing on me she was scrutinizing the ground shadows near some bushes. Perhaps she'd seen a cricket or spider, maybe a shrew. Suddenly she launched and *hovered* like a kingfisher over the shadowy spot before zooming back to her dogwood. For an owl, that hovering and hairpin boomeranging was a most impressive display of flying skill. She launched a second sortie, again hovering and hairpinning back to the dogwood branch. On her third sortie she pounced, but seemed to have missed whatever she was targeting.

Later she started calling back and forth—with the wild owl. But who was this wild one; were their conversations friendly?

AS USUAL, AT FIRST LIGHT I let the dogs out and filled the bird feeders. Summoned by the activity, Alfie showed up on her favored branch in the back-door dogwood. She soon hopped down to the back steps' banister. I gave her some head scratches—she was very sweet—then handed her three small pieces of fish and some fried egg from our hens. She took each morsel, remaining eager for more. Lastly I offered a larger piece of fish. She flew it into a tree, ate it, loafed for twenty minutes, then went to roost under her ivy umbrella, her Ivy Tower.

LEAVES WERE FALLING. WILD ONES were migrating full-swing. Birds, fishes, whales, dolphins, sea turtles—. The whole quickened world, whether in the air or in the sea, sought its southing. In this seasonal tectonic shift in the distribution of life, migrating seabirds and whales drew their travel fuel out of the living swarms flowing below. Big fish followed trillions of smaller fishes, thinning their ranks and growing fat enough to reach their own destinations far offshore and down the coast. It was as if the ocean itself were a living, traveling stew, creating its own food for its own travelers. The waters were cooling, but weeks of migratory movements remained. My friend Johnny D called and generously offered me half of a hefty bass he'd caught. He described the gulls and gannets that had shadowed the moving schools. Autumn outings used to entail knit caps and gloves, flannel-lined pants and heavy socks, and thermoses of something hot and indulgent. If we were going boating at dawn, the first task would be to splash a bucket of salt water on the deck to melt off any slippery frost. But October isn't what it used to be. Now it was warm enough to sit outdoors as we dined on fresh fish sandwiches, our coastal autumnal comfort food.

AT EIGHT P.M. OUR FRIEND Mayra arrived so I could show her how to feed Alfie now that she was on the loose. Mayra frequently cares for all our furred and feathered when we are gone; Patricia and I would be away the next day and night. It was the first time we were leaving a free-flying Alfie, but things were so mellow that I simply showed Mayra where to leave food on the back-steps banister.

Did I say "mellow"? Mayra texted me that Alfie had taken the food but had *also* hit her in the head, followed to her car, and hit her again. Mayra had known Alfie since the little orphan owl's first days among humans, and had taken care of her numerous times during her months in the coop. I hadn't expected hostilities. Good thing screech owls are too small to do damage. But the next time, a wide-brimmed hat would be needed. I wondered if an owl who was really female would be so aggressive. On the other hand, a female might indeed, and in no uncertain terms, take it upon herself to usher a female coming from outside the territory—even a human one—off the premises. No help there in determining Alfie's gender.

◆

ALFIE HAD DEVELOPED FOR HERSELF a regular routine: she centered her activity in our yard, usually came when called, and had found a very convenient day roost in her Ivy Tower, outside our kitchen window. But every day was different, and she continued to unveil little surprises. Like a flame, like the sea, like love, she was both steady and constantly changing. One evening well before sunset— the hens hadn't yet gone into their coop—she spent a lot of time in bushy branches just a couple of feet above the ground. From there, she simply hopped onto the ground and looked around. That was new. I couldn't discern quite what she might be searching for.

Two hours after sundown, I went looking for Alfie in the moonlight flooding the woods and our yard. In recent days she'd been coming instantly. But tonight when I called, Alfie did not come. Neither did she come the following morning. Maybe she'd caught something good and filling. Maybe something was going on with that other owl.

THE MOON SWELLED TO FULLNESS in mid-October. I worried when a big nor'easter slammed us with several days of severe wind. But I watched Alfie perched on the back-door dogwood while gusts rocked her cradle. It didn't seem to affect her. A body built for flying, after all, could handle the flow of air.

That weather reminded me to keep my eye on the calendar. In a month, my boat would be hauled out for winter. Time to think about our winter food supply. When seas calmed into a window of settled weather, Patricia and I ventured forth. At three of my favorite fishing spots, we found little. Twelve miles from the harbor, we decided to try a place I did not know well, a rubbly glacial hill under sixty feet of ocean. Patricia's lure hit bottom, and immediately her rod bowed. Migrating fish were foraging while sheltering from the tidal current among the food-harboring boulders. Drifting repeatedly over that long-drowned hill, Patricia and I handily assembled our day's limit of black seabass and bluefish. Each fish, I quickly killed and chilled. By the time I turned the wheel homeward, we had enough for more than thirty meals that would mean something to us. All winter we would eat with connection, a humbling twinge of mindful remorse, and gratitude for the gifts we've accepted, which require, in turn, something from us.

❖

LIKE FISH WHO DON'T REALIZE that they are in water, we're not aware of the ideas we inhabit. We don't know we're swimming in Platonist-Abrahamic dualism. Yet ideas steer us and limit where we go.

Plato based his cosmic valuation on figments of his imagination. That's all they are. We may say he's a dreamer, but Plato has been called "by any reckoning, one of the most dazzling writers in the Western literary tradition and one of the most penetrating, wide-ranging, and influential authors in the history of philosophy."

There is a reason for that influence. Plato's ideas framed a structure that could house a monotheistic faith separating a putrescent world from a "transcendent"—outside of the universe and time—God. Further, Plato taught that there should be classes of rulers, soldiers, and producers. Europe's kings claimed they ruled by "divine right," a mandate from God that set them above human law. And notably, Plato was averse to democracy. So for many centuries Plato's ideas would befriend Europe's monarchs and theologians, who perpetuated them. Most consequentially, Platonist dualism—preference for mind as opposed to matter, and devaluation of the material world—has been the bedrock of Western thought ever since.

This could very well be history's biggest intellectual mistake.

I HAPPEN TO FIND THE material world rather wondrous. So I again ventured out into the first light of a new morning. I called. I went to the coop. No sign of Alfie. I turned and came back to the porch. I called again. I heard a soft whinny coming from—my feet. I looked down. Alfie was sitting in the chickens' water bowl. Well, that was a first. I'd walked right past her, twice.

She hopped onto the deck railing. With a finger, I preened around her head. I offered a piece of fish. She took the morsel into her beak, then grasped it with her foot and flew off to the cedars.

After Alfie chugged a few quick bites, the other owl began calling from the woods just behind my writing studio.

Alfie held her peace.

She ascended into her Ivy Tower. And from that relatively secure citadel she now began calling loudly and long, alternating whinnying and trills.

Who *was* that other owl; what *was* their relationship? I had the impression that Alfie was asserting ownership while retreating to her protective green tangle to delay a physical confrontation. If the other owl *was* hostile and also claimed this territory—and things eventually came to blows—who would remain when the feathers settled; who would be driven away?

The calling trailed off with the fullness of daylight.

I let the chickens out, filled the bird feeders, made coffee, and lowered a rack of bluefish fillets into the smoker. Then I went to work. Such was my modicum of success in balancing work and life. Not bad, if I do say so.

Around eleven-thirty that evening, Patricia and I came home from a concert. Alfie did not appear. I left a piece of fish on the back banister. In the morning it remained.

I went to her Ivy Tower and peered up into the leafy shadows and braided branches. Alfie was visible up there. Seeing me, she immediately shook her feathers into place and gazed down attentively. I got the piece of fish that she had not touched. She descended, ate it, and accepted a bit of head rubbing. When I turned my cheek she leaned out, returning a little preening. I readied my cell phone for a selfie, turned to face her, and pursed my lips—and got an owly kiss. Then Alfie ascended hop by hop into her bedroom in the dense cascading ivy like a fairy princess who'd been turned into an owl. Fortunately, she was a real owl—otherwise that kiss could have caused trouble.

While I'd been smooching with Alfie, blue jays had been going to and from the bird feeder just a few steps away. Normally they would not have tolerated me at that proximity. But seeing me with a live bird may have let them judge me as safe. Or at least may have let them judge their nighttime nemesis as preoccupied. I guess we were all preoccupied; they didn't bother to mob Alfie while I was there with her, and they were busy stuffing their throats with sunflower seeds to cargo away.

Alfie was gone that evening and absent at dawn. The feeders swarmed with grackles and cowbirds, fall migrants still shifting southward in waves, by droves. I heard the coming winter in the song of a first-arriving white-throated sparrow.

7

Chilling

MY FAVORITE UNCLE, TONY, HAD AN UNTRAINED EYE FOR
the beautiful and a willingness to share a little time near water with
his adolescent nephew. That was long ago.

Now he's in a two-person room on the far side of the curtain.
Our visit is a surprise. As we file past the partition, Tony takes in his
visitors. It's my mother, me—.

"Here's a person I haven't met," he says as we fully materialize.

"My wife," I say, and before I can add, "Patricia," he points to the
wall; there's a photo I'd sent him of Patricia on a boat.

Tony had always been drawn to the sea, to boats, and to fish. That
drew me to him. But today is only the third time I've seen my uncle
in ten years. He's not much of a talker, so I seldom call. At age eighty-
seven, he's got diabetes and recently fought a bout with pneumonia;
everything hurts. He refuses to complain, but his energy is limited. So
those phone calls, which he always ends with "I love you," are short.

We all know he will not go home. Shameful of me that this is
only our second visit here, and that he's not previously met my wife of
five years, considering how much a few brief experiences I'd had with
him when I was in my teens have meant to me.

In recent weeks he'd suffered several days of episodic hallucinations. His devoted stepdaughter, Emily, advised that we come soon. Thus this hastily arranged trek to Staten Island. I've been bracing for how we'd find him. But though physically diminished, he is mentally very much himself.

His roommate has his TV tuned to a game show that he's not watching. Same, it seems, with everyone on this floor. Except my uncle, whose TV is never on. He's got the window, a view of distant Raritan Bay, and his wall of photos.

A crowd is gathered in front of a Brooklyn tenement on the day the government declared the end of World War II. "That's me, that kid on the right, half-hidden by the flag." The next photos of him are in military clothes in Korea. There's Josephine on the boat, fishing rod in hand, the late-arriving love of his life beaming her eternal smile. In fact, the majority of the photos that keep him company are of people in boats, their faces sunlit.

It had momentarily slipped Patricia's mind that it was Tony who had painted the masterful reproduction of Winslow Homer's *The Herring Net* that dominates our living room.

"When I brought that painting home and you saw it," Tony recalls with a chuckle as he adjusts his oxygen tube, "you said right then, you wanted it."

I was seven years old. I had to wait fifty years.

My uncle's extraordinary talent for painting came to him effortlessly. Unfortunately, nothing else did. He was almost five when my immigrant grandfather hanged himself in their Brooklyn apartment, plunging a seamstress with four kids aged three to fourteen into dire poverty, setting the family on a stagger from which no one ever quite recovered. Despite enormous ability, painting was never more than a temporary avocation for my uncle, and after a few years he put his brushes down. He'd been a starving child; he couldn't afford to become a starving artist. He bounced around a bit. Eventually he got a steady job in a boating supplies store in Sheepshead Bay, a paycheck he stuck with for as long as he worked.

I never saw him much, but his interest in the sea interested me, greatly. When I was fourteen, I decided to take a vacation: four days in my grandmother's Brooklyn apartment just so I could hang out with Uncle Tony. In his Mustang we drove to the New York Aquarium, where we marveled at the improbable sizes of old and obese specimens of fish that we loved to catch. I snapped photos of doormat-sized flounder, pillow-sized black seabass, and striped bass like logs. At his home I pored through his stacks of *Sea Frontiers*, an early magazine of scientific discovery for non-scientists. Best of all, I was invited aboard *Happy Days*, the boat owned by Tony, my uncle Sal, and their friend Sonny.

"You remember that huge turtle?" he says, knowing where this conversation will go.

"Huge turtle?" Patricia asks attentively. "What was it, a big snapper?"

"Leatherback," he says.

"You saw a leatherback? Where?"

"We were off the Rockaways that day."

I was fourteen. We were fishing for bluefin tuna a few miles offshore, within easy sight of Brooklyn. Tuna fishing is often hours of waiting that, sometimes, instantly turns to out-of-control pandemonium. I was wound with suspense. Studying the surface for any swirl or fin, I noticed the mild waves breaking over something just below. Suddenly a surreal, mechanical-looking head the size of my torso lifted from the sea foam and gasped a deep breath—a thousand-pound leatherback, by far the world's largest sea turtle. The indelible sight never left my mind.

Tony turns to me and says, "I never really got a great look at it when it was right under the boat. I backed up when we cut the line."

Soon after coming up for air, the gigantic turtle tangled in our heavy fishing line close to the boat. I bent over the gunwale and got a clear look at its massive soft shell and angelic flippers. An unstoppable force, quickly cut loose.

"You gave me a lot of work to do by getting me to see that leatherback," I say. Thirty-seven years later, my book *Voyage of the Turtle* was published. "I went to see leatherback turtles nesting and migrating on three continents and in three oceans. Then we did the PBS show. You know how much time and money that all cost?"

"Sorry," he says with mock sarcasm. "Excellent book, by the way," he adds, surprising me a bit.

"And that was after the tuna fishing itself made me decide to write my first book." I add. "Hey, do you remember the article I wrote for *Sea Frontiers*?" About twenty years after I'd pored through his magazines, I had beamed with pride when I showed him my name below a feature in that publication's pages.

He doesn't remember. He's getting tired. We get up to say bedside good-byes.

Patricia tells him she is so glad she's finally met him and how much we enjoy having his painting of *The Herring Net*. It's so masterfully done, you might think it was the original.

"I gave them a few extra herring," he confides.

For a man who never had the means for much generosity, he did what he could for the fishermen on the canvas, and the result has lasted decades. About what he did for me, the same applies.

I want to kiss him. But the cluttered reach to him in bed is awkward; I'm afraid of yanking on a tube. I take his hands and say good-bye and walk into the hall.

I'm putting on my coat when we overhear Uncle Tony say to his ninety-three-year-old sister, "I guess this is the last time I'll see ya."

"You didn't kiss him," Patricia points out.

I march back in and, without mishap, give him a kiss on his stubbled cheek. It crosses my mind that this might be the first time I've ever kissed him.

"Thanks for that," he says.

"Thank *you*."

◆

ALFIE DID NOT REPORT UNTIL the following morning. Then as the sky was just flushing with new light, she streaked in to snatch her food off my hand in a nonstop blur, arcing away with breakfast "to go." That was a new move. A few hours later, the white-throated sparrow caught my eye. I looked where the sparrow was looking. Alfie was in the birdbath by the feeders in broad daylight. Another first for our little bird of routines with her knack for exceptions. Perhaps it kept her life interesting; it certainly did mine. And then the fairy princess was back in her Ivy Tower, singing for a few minutes of alternating whinnies and trills.

◆

IN THE 1600S, BARUCH SPINOZA offered that God was not separate from nature. For belief deemed incompatible with Christianity, Europe ostracized him. Three centuries later, Albert Einstein dissented: "Spinoza is the greatest of modern philosophers, because he is the first philosopher who deals with the soul and the body as one, not as two separate things." But Einstein's assessment of Spinoza's primacy and rejection of dualism was true only in the West.

And the twentieth-century poet Robinson Jeffers concluded,

the race of man was made . . .
to butcher beasts and to slaughter men,
And hate the world.

But he, too, was summing up the West. Indigenous peoples worldwide and many philosophers throughout Asia had long assumed cosmic integration, focusing their spiritual explorations on how worldly diversity creates unity, how the many form one.

In Hinduism's Upanishads for example,

Those who realize that all life is one
Are at home everywhere and see themselves
In all beings

A key Indian text, the *Katha Upanishad* (likely composed a few centuries B.C.E.), posits a wise eternal self-essence—a soul, termed

"Atman"—that differs fundamentally from Plato's: "Atman, smaller than the small, greater than the great, is hidden in the hearts of all living creatures." The fundamental difference: the Indian religions teach that *all* life is ensouled. In the sacred Bhagavad Gita, the divine Krishna says, "I look upon all living beings equally; none are less dear to me and none more dear" (9:29).

The Greeks elevated reasoning above all. In stark contrast, Hindu Vedas advise one not to overthink. The *Katha Upanishad* instructs that a person can behold the majesty of their true essence "through tranquility of the senses." The Vedas themselves advise, "Atman cannot be attained by the study of the Vedas, or by intelligence, or by much hearing of sacred books." The body must be calmed, and the mind, too, must also be quelled, so that the soul may enjoy the world through the senses and connection with the divine, and ultimate reality can be found within. "The wise call the Atman—united with the body, the senses, and the mind—the enjoyer."

Such sensual ideas would have horrified Plato.

Indian thinking flourished into Hinduism, Jainism, Buddhism, and other religions. The objects of conquest: not land or people but, rather, fears and sufferings. By self-improvement—less con, more quest—humans could find betterment in balance. Souls are not just trying to escape bodies; they have a worldly mission. Jains, for instance, live by the motto *Parasparopagraho Jivanam*, translated as "souls render service to one another" or "the function of souls is to help one another." Various sects in India's complex religions see a soul distinct from the body. Yet the major flavor in South Asia is not a duality of body versus soul bickering over their nasty divorce but a strong marriage, a correspondence, a weave of the eternal throughout the material, a view of sacredness in Life, in everything.

Hindu scripture contains a metaphor called Indra's Net. The net stretches forever in three dimensions. Close your eyes, imagine it. At each knot in the net there hangs a jewel, and in this jewel are reflected all the other jewels in the net's infinity. This is the relational universe. All lives and all existences are encompassed. This infinite, interdependent universe, first mentioned in the *Atharva Veda*, was adopted into Indian and then Chinese Buddhism. In Book 30 of the Buddhist *Avatamsaka Sutra*, all things everywhere arise interdependently. And "the cosmos is unutterably infinite." (In Europe around 1600, Italian Dominican Friar Giordano Bruno also came to believe that the universe was infinite. The Catholic Church convicted Bruno of heresies.)

Generalities about Hinduism and other so-called dharmic religions and lifeways are fraught. Ancient texts offer guidance, but no central authority exists. Various sects lean into beliefs ranging from many gods and their avatars to one, even to spiritualized atheism. And not all is ideal; woven throughout Hindu tradition is its hideous caste system. But if we were to hazard a generalization, it's that for most dharmic followers, divinity unifies, connects all beings, all things. And Hinduism includes powerful female divinities. (Female divinities also preside in numerous African traditional beliefs.) The Hindu caravan of reincarnation affirms all living things as relatives in the shimmering net of existence. Dharmic souls are genderless, and as each soul dips in and out of material existence, matter and spirit entwine throughout many forms of living beings. For this reason, protecting all animals becomes fundamental.

Westerner colonizers such as the British mistook such reverence for lack of ambition, cluelessly mocking the sacred cows who roamed under their own agency, making them a metaphor for unexploited opportunities, casting pejoratives that revealed their own blindness to that deep, accommodating respect for life and coexistence.

I LEFT A COUPLE OF mice for Alfie on the back-steps banister and we departed for a weekend of friends and doggies running the beaches of ocean and bay. We watched gannets raise geysers of white spray as they bombed the autumn ocean, seizing mackerel, menhaden, and herring.

After two nights away, we returned home a couple of hours after dark. Alfie started calling from a tree alongside the driveway while we were still getting out of the car. I didn't remember her doing that before. Was she merely hungry? Or had our absence Friday night into

Sunday bothered her? She flew toward a different tree, and from a branch she snatched and ate a moth.

After Monday's sunrise she began loudly whinnying and trilling from her ivy fortress. I went out to have a look at her up there, and to make a recording of her song. But immediately upon seeing me, she softened her calls. Her singing appeared to be a kind of checking in, to ascertain where everyone was before settling in for the day. Presumably another owl—a mate or a competing neighbor—would engage in a back-and-forth. So I tried that the next morning. When she began to sing, I called back. Her song immediately softened and quelled. Sight unseen, she appeared satisfied about my presence. A touch is momentary; a bird's notes swiftly fade. What we want to know is: today we are not alone.

A FEW YEARS AGO, I traveled to Rome and to India. Italy's magnificent sacred art varies mainly upon themes of people either writhing in agony as they are cast into eternal fire or blissfully ascending to heaven. Little celebrates life itself. India's ancient temples shocked me. The thousands of stone carvings on the sacred structures include abundant depictions of humans, sometimes with other animals, in various acts that would get you cast into eternal hellfire in Rome. Why, I wondered aloud, were holy temples covered with what the West would call pornography or, to put it nicely, free-form eroticism?

"Not erotic," my docent explained. "Sacred. Sex brings life. The West thought sex is dirty because they believe life is impure; your religious art worships only what is in heaven. To our religions and the artists of our temples, life is sacred. So what *brings* life is sacred."

That brief, stunning exchange instantly cast Western sacred art in a lighter shade of pale.

Hindus perceived the creation, continuity, and decomposition of life and assigned a corresponding divine trinity: Brahma, Vishnu, and Shiva, who preside, respectively, over each of those major aspects of lived existence. Their Bhagavad Gita enshrines principles for human relationships with nature, the divine, and society. Meanwhile, Christianity's trinity, the "father, son, and holy ghost"—Christians say they're three "persons" in one god—corresponds to little about earthly life. The focus is resolutely on "Our Father, who art in heaven," not here with us. The French Revolution's "Liberty, equality, fraternity" constitute a distinctly more pro-social trinity than America's me-first "Life, liberty, and the pursuit of happiness." The U.S. Constitution proclaims, "All men are created equal," but in practice, "life, liberty, and the pursuit of happiness" is the starting gun of a rat race that confers dominance to some and alienation to many.

Why not something more uplifting? I see another trinity. Beyond me, beyond us, beyond now. Imagine a nation predicated on pursuit of: community, compassion, understanding, commitment, environment, equality, creativity, beauty, service, health, nurturance, nature, and what's next. Trinities are catchy, so pick any three. Imagine this: having the enshrined right not to compete but to matter. Come together. Right now.

◆

DURING THE FIRST WEEK OF November, Alfie several times silently strafed me fast and close in the dark backyard, her talons raking through my hair. Startling. Aggression? Fun? I never knew. She stopped doing that as suddenly as she'd started. With her, there was always something different.

THREE NIGHTS OF FROST USHERED us into mid-November. Alfie's insect larder essentially vanished overnight. Hungrier now, she followed me around the yard in the dark when I went to and from my writing studio after dinner, often landing next to me or on my shoulder. She even landed on my hand as I reached for the back door. I let her into the mudroom. She hopped onto the little shelf where we used to feed her. Her *memory* certainly seemed good. When I opened the kitchen door, she flew inside. I got her some food from the refrigerator and put it on that mudroom shelf. She took it out into the night.

Before I went to bed she was back, perched on the propped-open screen door. I gave her more food, and more at dawn. Before we released her, I'd been worried that she'd starve if we opened the coop. Now I worried that I was overindulging her. She knew how to catch bugs. But did she have the skill to hunt mice? Indeed, were there mice to hunt? I'd always had the impression that we did not live in high-quality screech owl habitat. Wild screech owls seemed to arrive, but then go. And the trees surrounding us—mainly Norway maples—don't produce nuts and acorns as would native hickories and oaks, or stashable fruits as do wild cherries. Where those native trees are abundant, they supply well-stocked winter larders for high populations of our lovely native woodland white-footed mice.

So I didn't know what her winter prey base was like, but I suspected that mice and voles, anyway, were not abundant. Sparrows were, but I found no evidence that she'd become an able bird stalker— no piles of feathers under the cedars, for instance.

Parent owls continue to feed their young for weeks after they fledge from the nest. During those weeks, the owlets may observe their parents foraging. Various birds pick up their parents' skills and specialties. The terns I studied during grad school follow their parents to sea, watching them expertly dive for fish, making their own first awkward attempts and gaining skill while their parents continue feeding them for weeks on the open ocean. Those shorebirds called oystercatchers specialize in opening mussels by either stabbing or hammering them. Chicks whose parents stab mussels develop the stabbing technique; those whose parents hammer mussels join a hammering culture. Juvenile New Caledonian crows stay with their parents for up to two years, learning tool-making by closely watching. Young scrub jays learn from their parents how to choose the best acorn-storing sites. Young macaws learn foraging routes from their parents; human-raised macaws who've learned to raid food from tourist lodges raise their wild offspring to a similar life of larceny. The importance of copying parents' behaviors has been documented in everything from falcons to finches to kittens to fishes.

Alfie grew up bereft of wild parents, deprived of critical weeks of parental care after fledging. How might I guesstimate the right balance between backstopping her so she'd stay healthy while avoiding making her an eternal juvenile, a panhandler content to wait until we provided another handout?

I didn't know. I knew it would seem like failure to have her just waiting all night to hear the back door open. To top my unease, Alfie was now acting "clingy." Anytime from sunset to dawn, she was usually waiting just outside the door. She habitually landed on me or flew into the mudroom. Alfie wasn't really hungry; she was plump to the touch. Her begging seemed more like that of a juvenile who simply always wants food from a parent. With the cold weather, she seemed increasingly fixated on her human caregivers rather than developing independence. Ironically, her intensified begging might have indicated that I was feeding her too much, enough for her to get complacent, lose any motivation.

So one night I fed her less than usual. In the morning at first light, she was not waiting for me. It was the first time in days that I had to call her, wait, listen—. I heard her answering, but she took her time before flying in and carrying my offering over to the cedars. So perhaps she'd caught something earlier and was full.

Complete recovery from her long-ago fall as a tiny nestling would mean being free-flying, being able to provide for herself, being able to interact normally with wild owls, and eventually raising young. But so far on that list we could confidently check off only the first item.

And now Patricia and I were scheduled to leave for a month on an overseas speaking tour. Alfie's fine-tuning would go on hold. Linda was returning to house- and pet-sit for us. I advised her to wear the sombrero. She looked skeptical. Regardless, she assured us she was looking forward to a relaxing interlude at our place with all our furred and feathered companions. Linda bade us a warm farewell, and Patricia and I headed to the airport.

I KEPT THINKING ABOUT ALFIE, of course, about our relationship with her and with the natural world generally. To the extent that anything in the world makes sense, our relationship with Alfie made sense. Traveling and experiencing various places got me thinking again about how other peoples related to the natural world, and about the ancient Greek thinkers' present-day influence on our minds and values. My wonderment was not about why Plato thought as he did, but why his views continue to be wholesaled so cheaply, generation to generation, millennia on end. After all, we now have such better questions and more relevant answers, such different and crucial current needs.

I think the answer is that Plato's devalued world became foundational to the globe's major faith tradition. The original religion of ancient Israel, Yahwism, worshipped a hierarchy of gods and goddesses. But Jewish views continued evolving. Most scholars believe that the first five books of the Hebrew Bible were compiled (incorporating some much older material) in the fourth or fifth century B.C.E.—around the times of the major Greek thinkers. Likely through such Jewish Platonist philosophers as Philo of Alexandria, Plato's divine crafter profoundly influenced Judaism and, later, Christianity. Plato had positioned his divine crafter as outside of space and time, creating the world we're in. In the Bible's Genesis, a similar God, existing before everything, outside of everything, creates Heaven, creates Earth, and then:

> God created mankind in his own image, in the image of God
> he created them;
>   male and female he created them. . . .
> God blessed them and said to them, "Be fruitful and increase
> in number; fill the earth and subdue it. Rule over the fish in the
> sea and the birds in the sky and over every living creature that
> moves on the ground."

And so at the Creation, the Abrahamic tradition pounds a cosmos-splitting dualist wedge, inaugurating a world created to be subjugated by its newest tenant. All is "put here for us," making the Abrahamic tradition perhaps the most self-centered of all the world's belief systems.

By contrast, Indigenous stories tell of other animals cooperating to bring humans into the world, giving us a soft landing and a well-supported start. In a widespread Native American story, as Sky Woman falls toward a world of water, Swan cushions her plummeting descent, while the aquatic animals of this world risk their lives to create the dry land and plants she'll need to thrive and establish her kind on Earth.

Plato and his followers saw material existence and our bodily impulses as polluting the mind; the West's religious thinkers came to see them as polluting the soul. In the Abrahamic story, we soon encounter Adam and Eve. The account delivers the theology's original distortion: a woman comes out of a man. All implications for her consequent status flow from that falsehood. God almost immediately weaponizes the intellectual endowments he gave them, tempting them in their innocence. When they fall for his setup, he banishes them from the Garden of Eden and condemns them to a life of toil. Quite a start. Our own legal system would call this entrapment and likely throw out the conviction on appeal.

When God breathes a soul into Adam and the rest of Creation doesn't get one, this is essentially Plato's thinking infused into what became the world's dominant theology. Plato's ideas, so foundational to Western thought, became Western belief, which concretized into Western faith, which created Western values, which eventually went global. Consequently, Plato casts perhaps the longest shadow across our lives—and thus the life of every living thing on Earth.

The newer religions of Christianity and, later, Islam would build their mansions right in the gap between Heaven and Earth, defining "faith" as a victory of things unseen over the world we see. A Christian definition of faith attributed to Paul the Apostle is "the conviction of things not seen." Jesus tells a doubting Thomas, "Blessed are those who believe without seeing," and Islam's Qur'an says its text is "a guide for those mindful of Allah who believe in the unseen" (2:2–3). Plato's cancellation of attention and reverence for the seen world became a matter of *faith*.

A FEW DAYS INTO OUR speaking trip I emailed Linda, asking whether Alfie had shown any of the attitude that I'd advised her to be on guard for. She replied, "One night she got me on the lip and chin. Next night on the top of my head. Not badly though. I'm using my hood now. Tonight she came and got the mouse without flying at me at all."

Confident about Linda's capability—and grit—and reassured about her prospects for survival during the duration of our absence, Patricia and I enjoyed the remainder of our trip and the terrific people and places we encountered.

We landed in New York at nine-thirty p.m. on December 21, the year's longest night, and walked in our front doorway at midnight. Chula, Jude, and Cady clearly loved the fact that we were home. There were hearty rubs and waggy tails and bright eyes and smiley faces all around. We appreciate the sheer luck of seeing so much of the world and—more so—we live in constant gratitude for having so much love and life to come home to.

Moments after we walked out the back door, Alfie appeared. We went inside. Around three a.m. I stepped outside again briefly; she was there instantly.

We spent the next day in a jet-lag fog, unpacking and unwinding. At dusk, Alfie flew directly at me—not very fast—and though she hit me on the forehead with all eight talons, the impact was not hard enough to scratch. Was this a reprimand for having been gone—or what?

I resisted feeling guilty. I had other guilt to deal with—about the indulgent air miles of the fabulous trip we'd just been treated to and the entire journey's attendant luxuries. I didn't know it then, but the guilt of such privilege would soon meet a partial counterbalance. A disruption was hurtling our way, as unseen as the asteroid that extinguished the dinosaurs. The trip we'd just completed would be the last travel for years.

By the next day Alfie was back to normal. She landed next to me on the railing, and I indulged her with some head scratching.

On December 23 Patricia and I went downstairs around five a.m. I fed the dogs; Patricia made coffee. As always upon return from travels, it was wonderful to reinhabit those small sacred gestures that make up real life. We had no inkling that Alfie was just about the only thing that was going to remain normal for Patricia, the doggies, and me. But for Alfie, too, a new normal was in store. Coffee wasn't the only thing brewing.

———

ADAM AND EVE'S EDENIC TROUBLE seems an allegory for our war with ourselves. God's temptation creates friction between our mind's emotional ability to enjoy life's garden and our mind's intellectual desire to understand the world. Eve and Adam choose the analytical. What they *want* is: knowledge. God does not offer them a balance such as the Hindu Atman, understanding truth through the senses. With their story abruptly curtailed by its unfortunate turn, Adam and Eve never get the chance to show us what they would have done with knowledge. Would they have loved and tended the Garden with deeper wisdom and compassionate coexistence or subdued and cleared it to serve self-aggrandizing desires? Their immediate banishment from Eden by a punishing Creator, their sentencing to a life of labor, initializes one culture's view of life as a struggle against nature. The foundational dislocations are neatly wrapped and served: we've warned ourselves against our own curiosity, deprived ourselves of our welcome into Creation, made ourselves wary of our mates and their motives. Seeing ourselves through the lens of so ugly a story became the West's self-fulfilling prophesy of drudgery and alienation. But must we, as the poet Robinson Jeffers observed, learn to "hate the world"? Other cultures do not. Basic human nature does not. We learn to hate the world only if we are taught to hate it.

WE STEPPED OUT THE BACK door into the predawn darkness. Alfie showed up right away. Patricia had just started a conversation with her when the wild screech owl streaked in. Alfie leapt off the branch and they both disappeared into the woods. In the low light I was not sure whether she was the one being chased or was chasing the intruder. Was this a territorial attack? Intended courtship? Would this other owl become an ally—or an implacable foe? We still didn't know.

Alfie silently returned to the back-door dogwood. The other owl continued calling, loudly, from the tree shadows at the north edge of the yard, just inside the dark woods wherein dwell, in equal measure, delights and dangers.

8

✦

Suspended Winterlude

THE HOLLY-DAZE AND NEW YEAR'S CAME AND WENT. WE saw friends, worked, read books, made our morning coffee, and took good care of our furred and feathered. The blessed usual.

We had not thought much about it when the *New York Times*, on New Year's Eve, published an article informing us that "Chinese authorities treated dozens of cases of pneumonia of unknown cause."

Like that wild owl streaking in, this would be a year that no one saw coming. But I was still thinking of the whole quirky ancient entwinement of Plato into the development of Western belief: no one could quite have seen that coming.

When the Christian Gospel of Thomas was discovered in a buried jar, a partial copy of Plato's *Republic* was among the thirteen accompanying papyrus codices. Scholar Ivan Miroshnikov remarks that Thomas's writing "makes great sense in light of the Platonist body-soul dualism." Thomas and other early theologians of Christianity widened Plato's dualistic split until the spirit world and the material world were not just different but diametrically opposed. Thomas (29:3) has Jesus commenting on the soul and body, saying, "I marvel at how this great wealth has taken up residence in this poverty." Soul is wealth; flesh is poverty. Miroshnikov sums up the idea that: "The passions are the body's allies and together they go to great lengths to prevent the soul from contemplating the divine realm." He continues: "The Gospel of Thomas . . . maintains that the body and the soul are hostile to each other and thus exhorts the reader to despise the former and take care of the latter. . . . For this reason, we should neither regret nor resist the death of the body. . . . The wise soul longs to escape its imprisonment."

Alfie, a wise little soul herself, was never inclined to leave us for long. She remained a remarkably steady presence. A couple of regurgitated pellets under her roost contained not the white fur of the food we served her but coal-dark fur and the jawbones of shrews, with their blood-orange teeth. Still, Alfie was almost always very nearby in the yard and interested in food. Clearly she knew what hunting was. Clearly she was capable of catching food. But she didn't seem to be catching much.

During these short days I tended the chickens, cleaned their coop, split and hauled wood. Every couple of weeks I went clamming, when the new or full moon's lowest tides coincided with a forecast of "unseasonably mild" temperatures—a phrase used with increasing frequency. We kept the house toasty (and quieted the oil burner) by feeding the woodstove. We cozied the kitchen by cooking chowders with buttery-fat cold-weather clams, thickened with our garden's butternut squash, which lasted for months in storage. In my studio, I wrote and read and wrote more and did email. At the nearby university, a new group of students appeared for the first days of the class I teach. Teaching—and learning, of course—depends on all minds remaining open.

THE GREEKS HAD OPENED MINDS. Now minds closed. The second-century Christian polemicist Tertullian wrote, "After Jesus Christ we have no need of speculation, after the Gospel, no need of research. Once we come to believe, we have no desire to believe anything else; for the first article of our faith is that there is nothing else we have to believe." Christian views against nature hardened as other writers regarded the material world as unworthy of reverence, profane. The spirit world was viewed as the only realm worthy of veneration, sacred. The eighth century English Benedictine monk known as The Venerable Bade lauded the first poet to write in English, Caedmon, for having "stirred the hearts of many folk to despise the world and aspire to heavenly things." Historian Colin Wells comments that this was, "quite simply, the highest praise a medieval critic could offer." Ludwig Feuerbach advised in his 1841 book, *The Essence of Christianity*: "Nature, the world, has no value, no interest for Christians."

Christianity saw the human individual as a house divided. And the human species opposed the house itself. The Western view had become "I am down here; God is up there." Most of humanity's other beliefs flowed from perceptions that, essentially, said, "All is here, with the world." Indigenous, Taoist, dharmic, and various other peoples sought to live within and maintain the interwoven harmony of spiritual and material realms and all the relational networks of existence. Confucians proceeded from the premise that human nature was fundamentally good. Contrasting sharply are writers such as Maximus of Tyre, a Greek Platonist rhetorician of the second century, who called the body "this useless garment." He wrote, "The soul is more valuable than the body" and "Death is indeed a healer that will free you from misfortune and from an insatiable, disease-ridden beast." Earth is merely a waiting room where we suffer life.

The nineteenth-century philosopher Friedrich Nietzsche scorned the Christian yearning for death, writing, "The whole of that fictitious world has its sources in hatred of the natural. . . . In [God] war is declared on life, on nature, on the will to live! God becomes the formula for every slander upon the 'here and now,' and for every lie about the 'beyond'!" The modern scholar Heather Eaton observed, "Although each religious worldview has some perception that life does not end with death, the Christian tradition has potent otherworldly imagery that has both depreciated Earthly life and supported notions that salvation means *from this world*."

———

ON FEBRUARY 5 I WOKE in the dark to find a text message from elephant researcher Vicki Fishlock. The giant known as Tim had died in Kenya, age fifty, of natural causes. When I was in Kenya's Amboseli region researching my book *Beyond Words*, Vicki was my main guide and portal into the world of elephant families and elephant minds. For hours each day, for days on end, we watched elephants being themselves. Often we were quiet for long stretches, brimming with the patience that the elephants themselves inspired. Then one day, after a long absence, the legendary Tim reappeared, like an image from the past, his almost impossibly thick tusks extending nearly to the ground. I had the tremendous privilege of watching him for hours on several occasions. Those tusks put quite a price on his head from poachers and wildlife-trafficking criminals. Farmers and herders posed continual hazards. When I returned home, I followed the news about Tim and kept in touch with Vicki. We always worried for his safety. We were filled with anxiousness when he'd vanish, and felt great relief every time he returned to the relative safety of Amboseli National Park. Tim survived several run-ins with people, requiring the intervention of veterinarians. His passing due to natural causes was the end of an era. But as Vicki noted beautifully and consolingly, "Tim has left lots of sons and daughters on the plains and in the hills beneath Kilimanjaro."

Bodies go, bodies come. Life creates its own salvation from oblivion. The process continues, in the greatest show on Earth.

PLATO HAD EXHORTED, "WE MUST get rid of the body," and two particularly influential Christian writers—Paul the Apostle and Saint Augustine—did much to establish the Platonist animus between body and soul as a matter of faith. Here Paul expresses his tormented psychosexual self-loathing:

> The law [of God] is spiritual. But I am carnal. . . . For what I want to do, I do not do; but what I hate, I do. . . . In my flesh dwelleth no good thing . . . my members, warring against the law of my mind. . . . O wretched man that I am!

Augustine of Hippo was born to a family of North African Berbers in the fourth century of our Common Era. He founded a Catholic monastery in Algeria, wrote voluminously, and was later declared a saint. Augustine detested any form of pleasure and, like Paul, obsessed about lust—which he saw as evil yet necessary for male arousal, a predicament making all human copulation—even in marriage, even strictly for procreation—vile. Sex "is only to be tolerated in marriage. It is . . . an evil which is the accident of original sin." Augustine invented the idea that all humans are born blighted with the "original sin" of Adam and Eve. He believed that God punished us all for Adam and Eve's disobedience by giving us our capacity for sexual pleasure, whereby our soul cannot maintain control. (Augustine doesn't venture into what possible motive such a God could have.) And though this is God's doing, sexual craving "is something to be the more ashamed of because the soul, when dealing with it, neither has command of itself so as to be entirely free from lust, nor does it rule the body so completely that the organs of shame are moved by the will instead of by lust." Augustine seems equally distressed by his occasional impotence: "Sometimes the impulse is an unwanted intruder, sometimes it abandons the eager lover, and desire cools off in the body while it is at boiling heat in the mind. Thus strangely does lust refuse to be a servant not only to the will to beget but even to the lust for lascivious indulgence; and although on the whole it is totally opposed to the mind's control, it is quite often divided against itself. It arouses the mind, but does not follow its own lead by arousing the body." Augustine also rejected essentially everything that induced any twinge of beauty. "I must confess how I am tempted through the eye. . . . The eyes delight in beautiful shapes of different sorts and bright and attractive colours. I would not have these things take possession of my soul." Even sacred singing harrowed Augustine: "When I find the singing itself more moving than the truth which it conveys, I confess that this is a grievous sin." Wrote Augustine, "The Platonists, who approached the truth more nearly than other philosophers, acknowledged that anger and lust are perverted elements in man's character, or soul . . . leading to acts which wisdom forbids, and therefore they need the control of intelligence and reason."

To be fair, engaging intelligence and reason is good advice. More sanely than Augustine's gyrations, the Jewish concept of *yetzer harah* teaches that humans should be on guard against excesses of good and necessary behavior. Food and eating are good and necessary, but too much eating, gluttony, is bad. Sex is good and necessary, but lust can cause trouble. Rest on the Sabbath is required, but too much rest is laziness, sloth. Humans can, by their free will, choose good or bad behavior (in this idea we hear another echo of Zoroaster). This view would find concordance with Chinese and Indian emphases on maintaining moderation and balance.

But Augustine wasn't one to seek balance, and he didn't hate only bodily impulses. "To this," he warns, "is added another form of temptation more manifoldly dangerous . . . this disease of curiosity . . . to search out the hidden powers of nature . . . wherein men desire nothing but to know." Hear echoes of Adam and Eve, whose sin was their God-given curiosity.

Augustine's writings reveal an unbalanced fanatic who denigrated his body, human curiosity, and nature. Yet it's been observed that "Augustine's impact on Western Christian thought can hardly be overstated." Augustine was a major influencer on Christianity's views toward all things natural. The twentieth-century theological writer Francis J. Sheed wrote that Augustine "developed the intellectual framework that allowed Christianity to become the predominant European religion."

HOW VERY STRANGE ALL OF that seemed against the quiet contrast of Alfie's comfort in her own nature, her being so at home in the world. Her sermons were brief, but she was a powerful preacher.

That peculiar Chinese pneumonia reported by the *Times* acquired a name: corona virus disease of 2019: Co-Vi-D-19. In the first months of 2020, Covid-19 found many countries. Too soon, people were getting sick where we lived.

And with incredible rapidity, the life we all knew—of visiting, going out, going into classrooms, going to work, of even funerals and burials, our known ways of being in the world—went away into the indefinite future.

This global pandemic was only the latest in a line of regional epidemics that have appeared in recent decades, several with much higher fatality rates: swine flu, bird flu, MERS, Ebola, AIDS, and others. Almost all came from animals that humans eat and as a result of how we treat them.

Before the first week of March was over, the known world felt suspended in space and time. Life imploded.

In this anguished, disorienting time, I did not expect that a sliver of a silver lining would slowly emerge, a reality parallel to the storm of human events. Alfie's consistent magic could not have been better timed. She was sprinkling fairy dust on an otherwise awful, often appalling year. Being stuck at home had its freeing aspects, delivering to our doorstep an unfamiliar calm, an opportunity to pay attention to the life we all shared.

The relative quiet of humanity's newly constricted existence let the voices of birds come more clearly into the range of many people's hearing. Skies and water cleared noticeably as the gears of human activity ground into a slowdown. Various news outlets announced wildlife roaming nearly deserted city streets. The *Guardian* gave us photos of mountain goats on Welsh sidewalks, jackals in Tel Aviv, raccoons sauntering in broad daylight through an eerily empty Central Park in New York City. In an Argentine harbor town, a sea lion rested on a deserted sidewalk. Deer wandered front lawns in a seemingly de-peopled east London. The BBC showed us dolphins in a much-quieted Bosporus, wild boars with babies on empty Haifa streets, flamingos on a de-touristed Albanian lagoon, pumas in Santiago, Chile—and so on around the globe.

IGNORING THE BURDENS AND DISRUPTIONS humans were suffering, the sun and the Earth honored their understanding that spring would repeat as usual. Sap defied gravity, and buds swelled. Their news reached the endocrine systems of animals, whose messengers sent a memo to all. Subject heading: Spring is in the air.

Going nowhere myself, I watched a living world very much on the move.

Many events that keep the world going are humbly hidden. With two local naturalists I went searching one night for forest salamanders. The little amphibians rouse from burrows in winter-chilled darkness. Making their way across undulating ground corrugated by fallen logs, they somehow navigate to ponds that may yet be rimmed with frost. In that dark, cold universe, the salamanders find and grip one another in procreative acts. How they can accomplish all this while their blood remains near the freezing point of water, in the dark, without a sight line to their ponds, no one quite knows. To have one's headlamp illuminate a dark-bodied amphibian in a shallow pond is to wonder how such creatures experience the moods and sensations that motivate such exertions, such strange and mysterious acts. To walk through a cold nighttime woodland feeling inspired by the million-year devotions of salamanders is to have pierced one's usual bubble and touched the nearby reality. The salamanders reaffirm that beings yet exist who keep the world's secrets.

AS DAWN CAME EARLIER, ARRIVING red-winged blackbirds reclaimed and proclaimed their marshes. Flocks of grackles and robins followed the north-trending daylight. The urge spread, until the planet's subscription to sunlight and the circulation of time delivered to every living thing and to our very doorstep a sense of a year renewed.

Alfie had felt no autumnal urge to leave. Eastern screech owls do not migrate. Heavy snow and prolonged freezes can be hard on them, but it was a mild winter here, anyway. And by staying close to us, Alfie had risked little. That's not to say she risked nothing. One early morning as I went to fill the bird feeders, Alfie was in the chickens' drinking bowl, silently taking a bath. She was constantly making swiveling glances right and left, monitoring the dangerous ground around her. Cats worried me. And always on my mind was the bird-reaping Cooper's hawk, who from unseen vantages might swiftly strike and carry Alfie away.

PART THREE

⬥

Bindings

9

Isn't It Romantic

ON THE MORNING OF MARCH 8, A SUNDAY, ALFIE DID NOT return our calls. Likewise she did not sing her morning hymn. Alfie was not in her usual spot, her Ivy Tower.

Hmm. I wondered if I should be concerned.

In midmorning Patricia again peered up into the deep shade of the cascading umbrella of Alfie's ivy. Looking down at her with ear tufts straight up, eyes squinted nearly closed, and body stretched, was a screech owl.

"That's not *Alfie*," she thought. Patricia circled the tree and saw another owl, fluffed and relaxed as usual. Alfie. "Alfie has a buddy," Patricia called to me.

That evening, Alfie again did not return our calls. No owls gazed back from the tangle of the Ivy Tower. Patricia noticed Alfie sitting in full moonlight in the dogwood that grows through our deck, the same tree she'd shown up in after her disappearance during her first week of liberty.

But this night, Alfie showed no interest in food. She was in owl love.

"It's very clear," I started singing the Gershwin melody, "owl love is here to stay . . ."

Patricia squinted at me.

I considered stopping, but—.

Alfie flew into the woods on the north side of the yard. Owl chivalry early in courtship entails the male getting food and feeding his intended. We still weren't sure Alfie was actually female, but the fact that "she" wasn't hungry suggested she was being fed. New question: Did Alfie realize that she was an owl; could she respond normally? "Normal" would mean that despite being an orphan who bore the imprint of her human upbringing, Alfie would respond appropriately to another owl's signals, calls, and postures in their context.

In the morning an owl began calling from the Ivy Tower. It was Alfie—there alone.

A COUPLE OF NIGHTS LATER, Alfie was calling from a tree next to my studio. On the outside wall, about twelve feet off the ground, I'd hung a nest box, a birdhouse designed for screech owls. It had been made by a dear friend, J.P. Badkin. J.P. was in the last months of a long and beautiful life, and whenever I glanced at the box it seemed like a little blessing from him. Of course, that's what it was.

MORE THAN A WEEK LATER, March 19, I walked out of the studio at nine p.m. I scanned the trees. No luck. Halfway to our house I heard a soft trill behind me. I turned back. *Both* owls were in one of the trees I had just gazed up into.

Alfie wasn't hungry. Alfie's Plus-One flew to the nest box. Plus-One had two darkish marks just below the bottom edge of his feathery facial "disk." Alfie had similar markings but smudgier. Plus-One's markings there were more distinct, gathered into a sort of bow tie. Alfie sported her brown-sweater-open-at-the-neck look.

In the morning Alfie was roosting in her Ivy Tower. There was no sign of Plus-One. I'd have guessed they'd be roosting together either in the Tower or inside the box. But it appeared she was going to take her courtship slowly.

The next evening I was in the studio when Patricia phoned me, excitedly saying, "The owls are in the back-door dogwood—kissing!"

A bit of moonlight aided us in following their movements around the yard (and added to the romantic mood). They both flew to a tree outside the studio. From there one flew into the woods and one, I was pretty sure, disappeared into the nest box. Their evening activities seemed centered about the nest box, but come daylight it was apparently back to separate bedrooms. Alfie continued roosting in the Ivy Tower. Was she unsure of him? Or had she developed some bond of faith that her special one was present somewhere in the landscape nearby?

✦

LIKE LANDSCAPE-BASED PEOPLES elsewhere, original peoples of what is now called Europe believed that conscious presences inhabited every tree, stream, and stone. Ancestors watched the living. Landscapes, animals, fire, cardinal directions, and the winds—all were imbued with spirits. Before a tree could be cut or a stream could be dammed, their spirits required appeasement.

The process of Europe's conversion to Christianity did not immediately deny the varied divinities' and spirits' *existence*. Rather, gods of nature got demoted to demons, effectively demonizing the natural world. Eliminating European animism "made it possible to exploit nature in a mood of indifference," observed the Christian and historian Lynn White Jr. "The spirits *in* natural objects, which formerly had protected nature from man, evaporated. Ancient respect and inhibitions about over-exploiting nature crumbled."

The faith called monotheism requires both the belief in a god called God *and* disbelief in everyone else's gods. Historian Colin Wells observes that Western monotheism is "unique in that it 'destroyed' belief as well as creating it.'" For many centuries—roughly the 1100s to the 1800s—various Inquisitions sniffed out skeptics of Catholic Church dogma, persecuted Jews and Muslims, and crushed Christian reform movements. On behalf of the Catholic Church, many thousands were terrorized, tortured, and executed in the campaign to make everyone believe the same thing.

Explorers and colonists brought Europe's religious fervors to their overseas ventures. In 1532 in what is now Peru, a friar accompanying Francisco Pizarro offered a Bible and conversion to the Inca ruler Atahualpa. Atahualpa's anticipated rejection was their pretext for the next hour's prearranged massacre of two thousand of Atahualpa's accompaniment of unarmed men. Fast-forward and move north, to Cotton Mather, a devout Puritan minister who lived in New England from 1663 to 1728 and is often considered a key intellectual figure in colonial America. Mather's parishioners gifted him an enslaved man, who he named Onesimus. In West Africa, Onesimus had learned a practice of inoculation called variolation, and he taught Mather how to inoculate a person against smallpox. Mather was an advocate for science, and when smallpox broke out in Boston in the 1720s, he introduced the technique to other colonists. He met fierce resistance, including a grenade thrown through his window. Yet the inoculations worked. Mather also advocated in favor of prosecuting women as witches. And he wrote famously of his revulsion toward his natural body by expressing disgust over the similarity of a dog urinating and himself urinating, noting, "How much do our natural necessities abase us."

Wrote Lynn White Jr.: "Christianity, in absolute contrast to ancient paganism and Asia's religions (except, perhaps, Zoroastrianism), not only established a dualism of man and nature but also insisted that it is God's will that man exploit nature for his proper ends." As a Christian himself, White put the blame on Christianity. But Christianity got its dualism from Plato.

As Friedrich Nietzsche noted—with characteristic scorn—in his 1886 book, *Beyond Good and Evil*,

The worst, the most tiresome, and the most dangerous of errors hitherto has been . . . Plato's invention of Pure Spirit. . . . This nightmare . . . amounted to the very inversion of truth, and the denial of the . . . fundamental condition of life.

Nietzsche wrapped up that thought by adding, with emphasis, *"Christianity is Platonism for the 'people.'"* Scholar Maria Popova observes that we inherit a "cultural tyranny telling us there are a handful of valid ways to be human." She calls this a "great hoax" built on "Platonic forms . . . too narrow for the reality of being what we are."

AT DUSK, ALFIE'S FOCUS WAS somewhere past the two people who were watching her, very much into the woods. Soon Plus-One arrived from the tree shadows. They perched near each other for a couple of minutes but seemed tentative. Not yet comfortable. Still getting to know one another.

After a short interlude, Plus-One flew back into the trees. Alfie followed.

10

⁂

Honeymooners

ON MARCH 22, ALFIE MADE SEVERAL SHORT FLIGHTS FROM her Ivy Tower to the nest box and—*in!* She reappeared in the opening, spent a couple of minutes looking out, then flew to a small maple at the edge of the woods. Soon I heard a soft trill to her left. Plus-One was in a nearby tree. He flew to Alfie. They *copulated*.

So, finally confirmed beyond doubt: Alfie is indeed female. Patricia wanted to have "the talk" with her but—events overtook plans.

Alfie remained tame with us. But she knew, after all, how to be an owl. It was exciting to see her visit the nest box, and more exciting to see her responding appropriately to the sexual cues of her suitor.

This excitement brought great relief. Her compromised upbringing and protracted protective custody notwithstanding, she could see an owl as one of her own kind, could see herself as an owl among owls.

Plus-One seemed to follow Alfie's lead that it was okay to be chill with us at close proximity. When Patricia had first seen him up in the Ivy Tower, he'd sleeked and squinted in full cryptic posture, his best imitation of dead wood. But with Alfie paying us no mind, he was becoming more relaxed. This allowed us close and personal views of behaviors we would never otherwise have been able to see. We could watch Alfie and Plus-One as individuals. We could be just standing outside, sometimes talking, even with the dogs around, while Alfie and Plus-One were calling to each other, courting, strengthening their developing bond.

Plus-One flew to the nest box and perched outside the entrance. I turned my head to see if Alfie was still on the branch. When I looked back, Plus-One had disappeared. While I was watching to see if he'd reappear, Alfie disappeared.

Owl watching is *hard*. You simply cannot take your eyes off birds who move with absolute silence. If you believe that a bird you glanced at five seconds ago is still sitting there, you're probably wrong. And keeping track of two such silently moving birds is essentially impossible. It's easier to track events in seventeenth-century Europe.

HALFWAY THROUGH THE SEVENTEENTH CENTURY, René Descartes died of pneumonia at age fifty-three. He is still called the "father of modern philosophy."

Descartes considered the possibility that he was imagining *everything*, that perhaps *nothing* was real in his strawberry fields. But even if all things, people, and his body were figments, he *was* doing one thing. "I think, therefore I am," he famously realized. Thus for him the mind—alone—constituted the proof point of existence. In the history of human apprehension of nature's nature, this seems a new twist.

But it wasn't entirely new. Descartes might have believed that he thought in a vacuum, but he wasn't raised in one. "From Plato onwards, Western philosophy has favored mind over 'mere' body," observes the writer John Banville, "so that by the time we get to Descartes, the human has become hardly more than a brain stuck atop a stick, like a child's hobbyhorse." Actually, René Descartes didn't even need the stick—*or* the brain. He imagined himself an entity whose "whole essence or nature is to think and whose being requires no place and depends on no material thing." This jeté beyond reality stands in starkest contrast to the ancient Chinese concept of *shin*, which recognized that mind and body are fully integrated. (The lack of an equivalent European concept causes *shin* to be translated awkwardly as "heart-mind.")

For several billion years, the world spun without a human mind. But a human mind without the world is impossible. This reality is so intuitively apparent that many creation stories—perhaps all—tell of a world developed before humans make their appearance. That seemed sensible to everyone—until Descartes. Descartes didn't need the world. But one can sympathize with his line of thinking about thinking. Thoughts appear to be immaterial, yet they exist somehow. Thoughts seem, indeed, to have a mind of their own, occurring not only when we are concentrating but in random streams of consciousness and in dreams. They occur when we are endeavoring to remember our mother's voice or unable to get a tiresome pop tune out of our head. They intrude unbidden, sometimes unwelcome.

In Descartes's time, scientific understanding of our integrated body-mind makeup, or of biology generally, lay far beyond future horizons. No one yet fully understands how a mind arises, but because brain damage can damage a mind, we understand at least that the mind and the material nervous system are integrated. The mind appears to function as a subjective sifter, filterer, and manipulator of the tiny fragments of reality that our senses detect. Sensory information, encoded along nerves and interpreted by the brain into sights, sounds, sensations, scents, sentiments, and sighs, gives a mind something to think about.

Descartes believed that our thinking and speaking arise in our eternal soul, which is both immaterial and divinely crafted. "The rational soul," he asserted, "could not be in any way derived from the power of matter . . . it must be expressly created." Pouring Plato through a Catholic filter, Descartes contended that humans *alone* possess such souls and are, thus, the only creatures capable of thought. Thereby did Descartes make his contribution to elevating humans while denigrating the rest of the living world.

MORNING. IVY TOWER. NO ALFIE.

When I reached the door to my studio, I heard the soft whinny that says, "I'm here; where are you?" It was coming from inside the nest box. With her very special ears, Alfie seemed to know the sound of my steps.

I said, "Hi, you."

By midafternoon in a light drizzle, jays, Carolina wrens, and sparrows were mobbing the nest box from a few feet away, scolding and alarm calling. Later, cardinals joined the protesters. I was at my writing table. The nest box, on the exterior side of the wall, was only about six feet from where I typed. The birds were scolding from branches right outside my windows.

At dusk, Plus-One was looking out of the box. I knew it was him because my proximity made him a little uncomfortable; he looked down at me in mild alarm, tufts up and eyes squinted. I presumed that Alfie was still in there, and that they'd been enjoying some time alone.

Alfie and Plus-One were still early in their courtship. Things could go wrong. To reduce the amount of disturbance, I closed the curtains to darken my studio windows. And I put a note on each side of the door saying, "Quiet for Owls," to remind me to close the door gently. Moreover, my writing studio is also my music studio. I would forthwith keep the volume down on recorded music, and I felt compelled to suspend practicing my jazz drumming while the owls were the vocalists in residence on the outside wall.

ALFIE DAY-ROOSTED IN THE IVY Tower for the next three days. Plainly, she had not laid eggs. I did not know where Plus-One was spending his days. But when they got together every evening, this young honeymooning couple went right at it with few preliminaries. A *lot* of sex. Mating is obviously a necessary precursor to fertile eggs, and with so much bonking going on, I expected eggs imminently. No eggs appeared. I would realize only in hindsight that their early-and-often mating was performing a mainly emotional function at this point, tightly solidifying their pair-bond.

I could have walked right up to Alfie with no fear of making her nervous. But in this sensitive period, I did not want to crowd Plus-

One. So I watched from a discreet distance until the lens of dusk closed down my vision. It seemed that much of the bonding occurred when Alfie and Plus-One first rendezvoused at dusk. After that I got the impression that Plus-One would leave to go hunting.

At ten p.m. on March 25, Alfie was in the back-door dogwood but, perhaps too in love and perhaps too well fed by Plus-One, she showed no interest in coming down to me or taking food. I joked with Patricia that I was trying not to feel too hurt or left out. Then I wondered if I was entirely joking.

SHORTLY AFTER DAWN, ALFIE WAS back in the Ivy Tower, loudly singing her sunrise chant. But wait—was that Alfie? This owl was not quite in the usual Alfie spot in the cascading ivy. And this owl had feather tufts up and was squinting at me. Must be Plus-One. Perhaps his bride was just out of sight in the ivy. Or perhaps Alfie was roosting for the day inside the nest box, playing house and getting comfortable.

In the evening they both appeared at the studio. Alfie flew into the nest box, stayed a minute and a half, then came out and flew to a small maple. Plus-One landed next to her. She half-crouched and he hopped on. Then they flew out of sight.

ALFIE AND HER GROOM, PLUS-ONE, knew where their nest box was, where the Ivy Tower was; they knew the landmarks and significant locations in their familiar territory. Most importantly, they knew each other as individuals. And, of course, they distinguished us and the dogs from strangers. In psychology, the concept of "object permanence" refers to the ability to understand that an object exists when you no longer see it. Children develop this understanding at around eight months of age. Some psychologists consider object permanence a uniquely human ability. But many psychologists study only humans, so how would they know? When Alfie was young and loose in the house, she sometimes flew upstairs, looking for Patricia. In fact, most animals show that they have a concept of "object permanence" simply by knowing where things are. They know where home is, where water is, and so on. If we tell our dogs, "Car," they run to the car, quite reasonably expecting it to be where it always is. If I invite Cady onto the bed, she'll circle to the side of the bed where the stepstool is, then hop up. That involves a sense of the permanence of unseen objects, as well as a simple plan: "I'll move farther from him in order to get closer." If we leave our dogs home for an evening, we often return to find them waiting for us in the driveway. Thinking of us and keeping us in mind indicates that they indeed have minds.

Cady *really* impressed us one night. When Patricia and I went out to watch Alfie at dusk, we left the doggies inside the house. I didn't want to risk distracting Plus-One's focus on his bride and their delicate interactions if the dogs started scampering around, barking perhaps at a deer or cat they might see in the woods. But Cady objected loudly to being excluded. Inside the house she kept barking, barking, barking, demanding to join us.

Moments later we heard a bark that was very distinctly *not* coming from behind closed doors. Patricia and I looked at each other: "How'd she get out?" We turned toward the house. Cady *hadn't* gotten out. She'd run upstairs and was barking at us through the screen of the open bedroom window. I'd never even seen her looking out of that window. She had gotten the *idea* of going upstairs for a vantage point from which to watch us at the far end of the yard. Cady showed true insight in realizing that she could go upstairs to see what we were doing. She knew what *she* was doing.

CADY'S BARKS WERE EXPRESSIVE, BUT neither dogs nor other animals speak as humans do. For Descartes, "This proves not only that the brutes have less reason than man, but that they have none at all." Distorting his logic with his dogma, he wrote illogically, "If they thought as we do, they would have an immortal soul like us." For Descartes, animals were animals and humans were not. Humans were specially created. And so, Descartes politely concluded, "a mind should be found in every human body" and "should be lacking in animals."

Adding some nuance, he wrote, "Please note that I am speaking of thought, and not of life or sensation." With a measure of meager generosity, he continued: "I do not deny life to animals . . . and I do not deny sensation, in so far as it depends on a bodily organ. Thus my opinion is indulgent to men . . . not given to the superstitions of Pythagoras—since it absolves them [men] from the suspicion of crime when they eat or kill animals." The ancient Greek mathematician and philosopher Pythagoras had apparently created a sore spot for Descartes. Pythagoras believed that humans and other animals had *equivalent*, reincarnating souls; consequently, he and his followers were said to be vegetarians. Obviously, ancient Greek views, as well as a need to justify and absolve the killing and eating of animals, were very much on Descartes's disembodied mind. Perhaps it bothered Descartes that Pythagoreans operated on elevated moral ground.

As a philosopher rather than a clergyman, Descartes secularized an unthinking, dispirited world. The splitting of mind from body, of humans from nature, now had an intellectual authority accessible equally to religious believers, agnostics, and those who would create the Scientific Revolution. People of modernity would no longer require explicit recourse to theologians or ancient classics to view humans as separate and superior, to view consciousness as strictly human. The only thing on Earth with intrinsic importance: what humans think. Descartes's fellow Europeans, whether sanctified or secular, spiritual or industrial or scientifically inclined, could rally round a unifying modern outlook: an agreeably devalued natural world. But the roots of that irreverence are religious, and the deeper roots of those religious views are Plato's plantings. Descartes's disembodied mind is Plato's invention. His immortal soul is Plato's trapped soul. The woolly world of animists had been shorn of its spirits by Plato, then pressed into faith by Christianity, and released from religion by Descartes, who'd handed a denigrated and de-spirited world back to us wrapped in something resembling logic. When this thickened pour of mental concrete dried, the foundation of Western values was hard-set for the coming centuries. Remodeled for oncoming modernity, the physical world was ready for its role as strip mine and drainpipe.

ALFIE AND PLUS-ONE WERE NOW inseparable. They often roosted together in the Ivy Tower; in the evening they rendezvoused at the nest box, sometimes entering together. I saw Plus-One pluck a moth off a tree trunk and feed it to Alfie. They were in a sort of extended honeymoon, with their own little place, fine dining, and an abundance of physical romance.

They had gone from a period of being very tentative with each other—when I wasn't sure whether their interactions were friendly or hostile—to being relaxed in each other's presence, to calling for and looking for one another as soon as they came out of their roosts at dusk, to the current phase: evening rendezvous with benefits.

These phases, these subtle shifts of courtship activities, and the differing things they were emphasizing became recognizable to me only because Alfie was tame and I was able to watch them almost every morning and evening. Of course, in a normal year of travels and absences, I would have missed not only transitions but whole phases of their unfolding courtship. I didn't feel stuck at home. I had a golden opportunity: to be home a lot.

Alfie no longer came to me. She'd transferred all interest and inter-action to Plus-One. I didn't want to risk skimping on her nutrition when egg-laying seemed imminent, so I continued leaving food on the back-steps banister. It would be gone by morning but probably wasn't necessary. Other than that, Alfie was becoming wild, beautifully.

FOR ANIMAL-WELFARE ADVOCATES AND EARTH lovers, Descartes's disembodied mind, earthly disregard, and disrespect for other living things has positioned him as modernity's patron villain. Yet Descartes was not a cardboard character. For one thing, worry about the church coming down on him greatly affected what he said and wrote. When he finished writing his magnum opus, *Le Monde* (*The World*), he confided—rather monumentally—in a letter to a friend,

I had intended to send you *Le Monde* as a New Year gift . . . but in the meantime I tried to find out in Leiden and Amsterdam whether Galileo's *World System* was available, as I thought I had heard that it was published in Italy last year. I was told that it had indeed been published, but that all copies had been burned at Rome, and that Galileo had been convicted and fined. I was so surprised by this that I nearly decided to burn all my papers, or at least let no one see them. For I couldn't imagine that he— an Italian and, I believe, in favor with the Pope—could have been made a criminal, just because he tried, as he certainly did, to establish that the earth moves. . . . I must admit that if this view is false, then so too are the entire foundations of my philosophy. . . . And it is such an integral part of my treatise that I couldn't remove it without making the whole work defective. But for all that, I wouldn't want to publish a discourse which had a single word that the Church disapproved of. So I prefer to suppress it rather than publish it in a mutilated form.

For centuries the church kept its thumbscrews on European minds. Copernicus and Bruno in the 1500s and Newton and Galileo in the 1600s all saw the church's flashing lights in their rearview mirror. All were called heretics. The Italian Dominican friar Giordano Bruno believed that reality and divinity were the same, that souls reincarnate, that stars are distant suns, and that the universe is infinite with no center. Friar Bruno was arrested and tried for heresy before a panel of cardinals of the Supreme Sacred Congregation of the Roman and Universal Inquisition on behalf of the pope. Unwilling to recant, upon his sentencing he pronounced his accusers more fearful of him than he was of them. On the holy day called Ash Wednesday, in 1600, executioners stripped Friar Bruno, hung him upside down, and then publicly burned him to death. In 1633 Galileo was convicted of heresy for saying that Earth and other planets move around the sun; he was sentenced to lifelong house arrest. Newton wrote to a friend, "When I wrote my treatise about our System I had an eye upon such Principles as might work with . . . the belief of a Deity."

Descartes's *The World* was not published in full until a quarter century after his death. Certain passages of his writing reveal a man of admirable humility, uncertain of himself, searching for truth: "When I look with a philosopher's eye on the various actions and enterprises of all men, there are hardly any which do not seem to me vain and useless. . . . However, it could be the case that I am wrong and that perhaps what I have taken for gold and diamonds is only a little copper and glass. I know how much we are subject to making mistakes. . . . I hope that it will be useful to some people, without harming anyone, and that everyone will find my frankness agreeable."

Though admirably brilliant in many ways, Descartes was in fact often—as he feared—mistaken. But his views were convenient—and safe—so his beliefs were widely embraced. Among his most influential ideas was one particularly convenient notion: animals are merely machines. "It accords well with reason," Descartes propounded in a letter to British philosopher Henry More, "that, since art imitates nature and man can produce automata [machines] in which there is motion without any thinking, nature should also be able to produce its own automata which are far superior in their workmanship, to wit, animals."

11

⁂

Full House

BEING HOMEBOUND SEEMED A GOOD TIME TO AUGMENT our surviving trio of hens. Feed stores usually had chicks at this time of year. But Covid affected that, too, as people stuck at home started backyard flocks and chicks quickly got snapped up. Most places we checked were sold out. One feed store had just gotten some, so Patricia and I jumped into the car and secured six tiny chickens. For variety we brought home two barred rock chicks, two Rhode Island reds, and two golden laced Wyandottes. We set them up in our living room in a dog crate. For added warmth we used a heat rock intended for reptiles, rather than a heat lamp, which would waste energy making unneeded light and glare at them all day and night. They could go under a little open-fronted cardboard box, huddle together atop the heat rock, and dream of their next meal.

Chula and Jude had been through several rounds of chicks. Chula harbors no aggression, just fascination and an occasional urge to lick. I've mentioned that she related to new chicks as helpless babies, as if they were a new litter of pups. When we let our latest brood out for exercise and they scurried around the living and dining room floor, Chula followed and watched the chicks at close range for long periods. Jude was less than indifferent; he went upstairs to get away from them. That was very amusing. It was also interesting. Owing to an old hip injury, Jude almost never bothered to climb the stairs. His effort indicated that he understood where the chicks could not follow.

Cady had never seen fluffy little chickens. I fully expected her to get extremely excited, bark a lot, and try at least to paw and play with them. To my great surprise, she took her cue from Chula. No barking. No aggression. No play. When I held a chick in my hand so Cady could sniff, she actually pulled her head back a bit. She expressed mild fear, a bit bug-eyed, nose a bit down, ears a bit back. She didn't seem comfortable approaching the chicks until sometime the next morning.

A couple of times a day we opened the cage door and put the food container on the living room floor. After some hesitation, the little fluffballs were scurrying in and out, eating, exploring, heading back into the cage for water. Cady, true to her Australian shepherd roots, started prancing around them as if trying to herd them together. When she looked like she was getting a little wound up, I admonished her to relax. She was a good girl, and eventually she'd get a bit bored and go to look for Patricia. The chicks would get full, get tired, and trek back into their cage to nap. I'd clean up, a small price for all the fun.

♦

WE OFTEN HEAR NATURE DESCRIBED by analogy to the dominant technology of the time. In our time: computers. Cells are said to run DNA "programs," brains are "processors," and so on. This is Descartes's shadow. When Descartes began comparing nature with the technology of his time—mechanical machines—he was almost literally squeezing the life out of the world. Descartes pressed the point: "I do not recognize any difference between the machines made by craftsmen and the various bodies that nature alone composes." He gazed upon the vast and fundamental distinctions between life and non-life, human-made and natural, and squinted until everything blurred to a collection of moving parts. "It is not less natural for a clock, made of the requisite number of wheels, to mark the hours, than for a tree, which has sprung from this or that seed, to produce the fruit peculiar to it." Thomas Hobbes echoed this idea: "What is the heart, but a spring, and the nerves but so many strings; and the joints, but so many wheels."

Seeing a thing as solely the sum of its parts is called "reductionism." To see how things work, take them apart. If you do, you will come to understand much. Scientists certainly have. But even if we followed Descartes's and Hobbes's off-base analogies of living things as springs and strings, we might nonetheless see *fine* machinery, worthy of appreciation, of care. A finely made antique table is equally firewood, but we value it for its beauty, for all that went into its creation, and for the character of its journeyed nicks and scratches. A reductionist approach doesn't *require* devaluation of the world. A rainbow understood is no less beautiful, and perhaps more so. Understanding the mathematics of spiral structures can add to our aesthetic appreciation of a snail's shell. Reductionist answers can generate new questions that enlarge the wonders. The sheer complexity of the whole, its scale and improbability and the beauty that fills us; all of these qualities generate an appreciation so profound it feels like reverence—or so I have experienced.

Using a reductionist approach is not what devalues the world. The devaluation comes first.

AT THE END OF MARCH, Alfie was still day-roosting in the Ivy Tower. That meant that despite all the copulating of the last week, she had laid no eggs. A clutch of eggs was the normal next step, but—eggs were not guaranteed.

The air's earthy scent promised spring. I savored it. We are said to have five senses, but we have many more than just sight, sound, smell, touch, and taste. Our sense of molecular motion tells us whether the air is warm or cold. We have a sense of balance. We can sense pressure, which differs from the feeling of texture. We possess many kinds of nerve endings that are each shaped to detect one particular kind of molecule but, together, are capable of detecting all the things we can "smell." Our nerves identify the molecules; our analytical mind types a label that says "springtime," and our emotional mind receives the neurotransmitters that give us the feeling of "Aaahhhh, yes." Some other animals can see light in the ultraviolet or the infrared. Colors that we are blind to can appear brilliant to birds. Pit vipers have a special heat-sensing organ that helps them hunt small warm-blooded animals and might let them visualize warmth. Birds and fishes use a magnetic sense for certain navigations. Some animals sense the faint electrical charges of potential prey. So the scent of springtime; it's not trivial.

I had gotten the impression that Plus-One roosted with Alfie in the ivy on some days and on other days roosted in an undisclosed location. In the evenings Alfie came out of the Tower and often flew to the edge of the yard, where she perched in a tree, calling softly and looking into the woods. Alfie's attention was frequently directed into what seemed like some plane of deep perceptions, some event horizon beyond my light of access. Her gaze coaxes from the very air great stories and a way forward. She can take her time but—chess master that she is—eventually makes her move.

IT WAS DUSK, AROUND SEVEN-THIRTY p.m., when Alfie came out of the Tower, went to the dogwood by the back door, and trilled. She seemed ready to collect her furry supper. But when I came out with a mouse, she was gone. I re-located her in a tree adjacent to the studio. Plus-One soon appeared from the woods. He flew to the nest box. From there, he flew directly onto Alfie's back. Who thinks about food when romance is literally in the air on wings of love?

I noticed something important that I'd previously missed: Alfie did not crouch into the full posture necessary for successful fertilization. In most bird species, males do not have an organ of intromission (a penis). The external port of both males and females is called a cloaca. Successful fertilization requires direct contact, something people who study birds call a "cloacal kiss." Alfie was not moving her tail aside to accomplish the good, firm touch that's necessary.

On another night, when Plus-One appeared with a large bug,

Alfie did not accept his sweet offering. Considering her abnormal childhood and lack of experience, I was beginning to wonder whether she really was responding adequately to him, making the fine-tuned moves and responses that would result in a fertile clutch of eggs.

Alfie flew away from him. She landed in the huge old maple in the center of our yard. Was her commitment to this enterprise wavering? I was becoming concerned.

He followed her, landing next to her. Their calls intensified into short screechy chitters. He hopped onto her back. And *this* time she leaned forward a little and put her tail up slightly. This time they consummated clear, direct contact. Ah, youth. This was a new phase.

TEMPERATURES REMAINED COOL, IN THE Fahrenheit forties. But spring continued advancing. Peepers were singing their full-throated chorus in the little wetlands across the street, behind our neighbor Ann's house. From the woods an occasional peeper would burst out a few notes on their way downhill to join the vernal pool party. For the next two months these little tree frogs would pledge their brief loves and make their couplings and fill the shallows with their promises as they'd been doing for uncountable springtimes. Their persistence through the ages testifies to the immense power of such seemingly humble hopes.

"HUMBLE HOPE" DOES NOT CHARACTERIZE one of the earliest scientists of Europe. One sees instead a hardened cast of callous zeal. Francis Bacon's enormous intellectual contributions earned him the moniker "father of the scientific method." A politically influential and devout Anglican, he called for "turning with united forces against the Nature of Things, to storm and occupy her castles and strongholds, and extend the bounds of human empire." He exhorted the Scientific Revolution to "conquer nature." The implications are even nastier than they sound. Scholar Heidi D. Studer writes, "Francis Bacon's pronouncement that 'Man is the Center of the World' seems to unleash us from all guidance and restraint, providing no grounds for judging any human action to be better or worse than any other." Lynn White Jr. wrote that "the Baconian creed" could be summarized as: "scientific knowledge means technological power over nature." He concluded, "Its acceptance as a normal pattern of action may mark the greatest event in human history since the invention of agriculture."

ALFIE CONTINUED HER MORNING CALLINGS. Her braided trills and whinnies often started well after full light, often *after* the songbirds' dawn chorus quelled. At dusk she'd meet her lover near the nest box. Often he'd go inside. Sometimes Alfie would land on the ledge just outside the entrance while Plus-One was poking his head out. Like that, together, they would sing.

BY EARLY APRIL 2020, THE Covid-19 restrictions were intensifying: Edicts to stay home. Patchwork quarantine requirements. Businesses sidelined like roadkill. People losing jobs, people forced to quit. Schools and universities sending students home, scrambling to move classes online. Parents struggling to invent new coping strategies on shifting sands.

One afternoon I found Patricia in tears. The bad news and the struggles of people we knew, worries about extended family—a close family member's income abruptly ceased—and the withdrawal from all things social: it weighed on everything and everyone like heavy fouling on the hull of an abandoned boat. Friends who worked in hospitals went to life-threatening jobs, facing shortages of the simplest safety gear while being told they were heroes. People who worked in slaughterhouses and meat plants were told their grim, miserable work was "essential," but clearly their lives were not; at least fifty-nine thousand meatpacking workers came down with Covid. Nearly three hundred died.

ADOPTION SHELTERS BEGAN EMPTYING AS many people decided they needed pets to get them through a year when humanity could not keep up, could not quite cope, could not quite rise to the grinding occasion. Pets kept the heartbroken and the struggling rest of us connected to a remembrance of normality. They remained full of beauty and innocence. They bade us to survive, to recover our smile. They modeled a zest for living, in case we'd forgotten.

Maintaining a zest for life was a challenge. Merely getting prepared to go to a food store—mask, gloves, sanitizer—felt like entering a hazardous hot zone of potential infection, because: it was. Meanwhile, the frantic were wiping down bags of groceries as the heedless, the hapless, the heartless, the helpless, and the hacks helped spread the sickness.

Various friends caught the virus. Most had fairly mild cases and prompt recoveries. Then the grandfather of a close friend died. By the time my aunt died of Covid, funeral homes were so overwhelmed that her daughter, my cousin, had to cold-call various funeral parlors to find one willing to put her mother on ice until she could advance to the front of the burial cue. For a while, we lost a relative or acquaintance about once a month. The usual grieving rituals became a thing of the past. No coming together. People were simply gone. When Uncle Tony died of his suite of other ailments, the only good-bye available to my grief-stricken mother was to watch on my phone as burial workers lowered his casket into the ground.

COVID, THE ECONOMY, RACIAL RECKONINGS—THESE were problems for us. Our owls, dogs, and chickens, blissfully unaware of human turmoils, helped save our sanity. Sometimes when I went outside to breathe a dose of the sane and consistent natural world, Alfie and Plus-One were visible together in the Ivy Tower. When he saw us looking up at him, he'd still stretch into his best imitation of a branch, tufts up and squinting. Alfie would just look down at us, feathers poofed, thoroughly relaxed.

Our baby chickens, still crate-based inside our house for warmth, were growing apace. To get them relaxed in our presence I'd often sit on the floor, spreading a big towel across my legs, then putting their food on the towel. They showed little fear and came right up on my legs and arms. Sometimes I'd do this with my computer in my lap, tapping out emails while chicks came and went, pecking out meals.

Whether or not Alfie and Plus-One had roosted together during the day, Alfie's first evening move was usually to fly across the yard to the nest box and call softly. Plus-One would soon be with her. They'd usually visit the box together, then fly to a nearby branch and quickly mate. Then sometimes he'd leave and she'd wait. Within perhaps ten minutes he'd return with a sacred offering, usually an insect such as a moth, occasionally a mouse or shrew. I got the impression that he sometimes simply retrieved food he'd stashed: a vole, perhaps a bird. The "what" mattered less; it was the thought that counted. No, not the thought—the *feeling*. The feeling was: "You are mine, I am yours, we are what we are." These love offerings showed her that he could provide well. Providing would be crucial if Alfie laid a clutch of eggs. Eggs would require her near-constant incubating, and small chicks would require brooding. During her maternity leave from the surrounding world, hunting would fall to Plus-One.

But there were no eggs.

Meanwhile, Plus-One ran an increasingly efficient food-delivery service. Alfie was showing no interest in coming to me for food. To further help her "fledge" from me and focus on Plus-One, I stopped calling her. But if I left food out at night, it would as usual be gone by morning. Owl nests sometimes become repositories for a couple of excess meals to ensure against bad weather or bad luck; that was one reason an owl who wasn't hungry might take food.

AS THE OFFSPRING OF PLATONIST-ABRAHAMIC de-enchantment of nature, science bears the birth scar of a world unvalued. Through a kind of emotionally detached childhood, science grew strong but felt little love for its mother, Nature. Consequently, science has had a brilliant career, but as it matured it has tended to deny paternity for two unintended twin offspring: sufferings inflicted and damages done.

I BEGAN BRINGING THE CHICKEN chicks outside on warm afternoons. They took naturally to being loose. They could enjoy the grass, scratch in the soil, and lie in the sunshine. They stuck close together and did not go far. The doggies were very enthused that the chicks required a little extra watchfulness during this new outdoor stage. And when the downy little ones got tired, they'd usually return to the familiar safety of their crate, and nap.

12

Bloomings

THE FIRST WEEK OF APRIL CLICKED THROUGH ITS DAWNS and dusks with our owl neighbors continuing a slow, unhurried courtship. Too slow. Weeks had passed since I first saw them mating. So I wondered again whether Alfie was well enough tuned in to the whole cycle to actually breed. She was sexually mature but—. Had her artificial childhood and delayed freedom tweaked something fundamental in her ability to produce eggs?

I'd been trained to see birds' breeding cycle in three stages: courtship, incubation, chick rearing. The more I observed, the more I realized that their courtship was not simply a category but rather a work in progress, still unfolding, a nuanced romance. She seemed to be investing more faith in him. Each evening she seemed more patient while waiting for him to bring something to eat. One night around dusk I saw him launch toward a tree about thirty feet away and pluck from the trunk a dark, thick-bodied moth; his eyesight in low light was incredible. When he went hunting deeper into the woods, Alfie stayed at the nest box until he returned with takeout. After their dinner date, mating would follow.

If gifts of food might convince her that she could rely on him, it appeared to be working. As we moved into April's second week, their interactions flowed more smoothly. Mating came ever faster and more easily. Sex was their first priority as soon as they came down from the Ivy Tower; no more waiting for a food exchange. Mating now routinely involved her experienced posturing, moving her tail aside to achieve an effective cloacal kiss. Often they'd fly to the nest box and do it again. Only then did he go to hunt. Alfie was suddenly more adult. She seemed more skillful, more confident, more procreative. They were no longer just courting. Now they were committed, bonded, and in breeding mode. They had a life, and were living fully in it. It seemed to be working.

◆

THE SCIENTIFIC REVOLUTION GENERALLY PROCEEDED with this straight, narrow view: everything is a sum of its parts. But despite the power of that approach, "reductionism" has crucial weak spots. The biggest: some things are more than the sum of their parts. Approaching everything as a pluckable widget in a Lego cosmology overlooks *relational* dynamics. And reductionist approaches miss "emergent functions" that are not in the parts. A toolshed made of wood and nails and shingles could be said to be the sum of those parts. A lamp is hardware and wiring and a bulb, but there is no light in the parts; light is an emergent function of relationships between the hardware and energy. Speed and motion emerge from an automobile's engine and drive train but are not to be found in the hardware. So let's say you understand and can explain every piece of an automobile. You are the perfect automobile reductionist. Still, you cannot say much about the vehicle's emergent properties during its career in the world. Where will it go? What dents and indignities will occur to it? What music will it be tuned to? Who will make love in it? How many dogs will it carry; will they enjoy riding with their heads out the windows? How many smiles per mile? How will it end? Where will its components go? The car creates possibilities. Which of those possibilities will happen is not to be found in a list of its components. Multiply that by infinity and you have the world. You won't find the world in just its parts. You would miss much that matters.

A forest is not just a bricolage of trees; it is an immensity of functional relationships and feedbacks whereby each thing makes other things possible within dynamic and constantly adjusting suites of entities and behaviors. A tropical reef is not just coral polyps plus fish but thousands of finely inter-depending life forms in their sunlit fluid environment. A species is not just a pool of DNA; it is all the relationships that create and maintain its node in its network, even as its existence influences the network. A mind is not just the brain; a mind is a feeling experience arising somehow out of the brain's matter and energy. A mind is an emergent entity, perhaps the universe's most complex emergent function.

NEARING MID-APRIL, and still no eggs.

Alfie continued roosting in the Tower over the next few days, clearly visible just a few feet away through the ivy veil. The recent routine was maintained: At dusk Alfie comes out first. Soon they rendezvous. They mate enthusiastically. They visit the box; both enter. In a few minutes they come out. He hunts. She waits. In five or ten minutes he returns with an insect. Occasionally he has meatier fare. Alfie was so well fed that she ignored not only my food offerings but even some of his. One midnight, Alfie was in the back-door dogwood. I showed her a mouse and she just looked. I tossed it and she just looked. I'd never felt so pleased to be so ignored.

April 15 dawned chilly, around fifty degrees Fahrenheit. I saw only Plus-One in the Ivy Tower. On a hunch, I walked to the nest box. Alfie returned my calls from inside the box.

No longer was she roosting in her Ivy Tower; she was spending all day in the box. Each evening of the next few days she flew from the box to the Tower to collect Plus-One, and together they'd fly to the driveway cedars and copulate. Then together they'd fly toward the nest box—where more was going on than met my eyes.

EVEN IN OUR OWN BACKYARD, where I was trying to observe the major changes, the accelerating springtime was outpacing my ability to keep track. Daffodils, pear and apple trees, forsythias—things were blooming. Birds were restless. The juncos had departed for points north. White-throated sparrows were still singing "Oh Canada, Canada, Canada." Soon they would sift northward and resettle in breeding territories in Canada's vast remaining boreal forests. In the lengthening days, our three older hens were laying more. Our garden was again producing enough kale to join our eggs at breakfast. A chipping sparrow, an early spring migrant from the south, showed up. Other birds moved through in a subtle shimmer of color and song.

Our young chickens were getting bigger and more feathered. I was offering them a varied diet of millet, suet, grass, and—most quirkily—diced clam. They liked it all, but for the clam they properly rioted. On nice days I'd bring them outside for half an hour. They'd spend that time eating grass tips and bugs. The capture of a plump earthworm would spark a crazed chase for possession around the bushes and along the rock wall. When they were full they'd scratch and shimmy in the dust, then doze while bathing in warm shafts of sunlight.

THE CONCEPT OF LIVING THINGS as machines met a spirited resistance called vitalism. The idea: living things are more than machines, due to a mysterious "life force." A rock has not been deprived of anything, but from every lifeless bird, something has been subtracted. Sometimes beneath a window we hold a bird's warm carcass, wondering how life could withdraw so thoroughly from so perfect a body. The unseen reality has to be complex. But we sense simply that whatever force animated this soft creature has stopped or gone away. Vitalism arose in antiquity but flourished among scientific thinkers mainly in the 1700s and 1800s. The reasoning: What makes things alive cannot be their non-living parts. It has to be the "vital force" that *coordinates* the parts and *enlivens* the organism. But vitalism failed to *find* the vital force. In essence, a reductionist proof was demanded for something beyond the sum of parts, as if someone dissecting a brain should be able to find therein a person's thoughts and fears and the image of their mother's face. So even though no one yet has the full answer to what enlivens a cell or a complex organism such as a rosebush or a parrot, vitalism did not take hold. The recent recognition of "emergent functions" is essentially vitalism's heir. Nevertheless, in the twentieth century the machine metaphor crushed vitalism and proved powerful enough to ascend to overwhelming dominance.

IN THE EVENING ON APRIL 15, Alfie and Plus-One quickly found each other and mated. Nothing unusual there. But when he disappeared into the woods, she seemed unusually "antsy." Anxious for him to appear with food, she flew to several vantage points around the yard. She was now an owl in a hurry. Her recent patience was gone. Soon she abandoned her vigil, flew to the box, and slipped in.

That was new. I happily suspected she was incubating. But they were still copulating. So even if she had laid an egg already, she likely had not finished a full clutch.

On April 19 Alfie was in the box again all day; she sweetly called to me every time she heard my footsteps going in or out of the studio.

"Hi, you," I'd say.

◆

A BLOCK FROM OUR HOUSE, an opossum has been newly killed by a car. This death, made ugly by its uselessness, will be consigned to the category of common carnage. We exculpate ourselves by thinking it "accidental." Its routineness makes it acceptable. Its acceptability makes it routine. This time, we stop. We pause not to honor the dead but to inquire of the carcass whether we might be of some help; females can have live babies in their pouch. This road casualty is male. Suddenly from just inside the road's tree line, a crowd of blue jays erupts in frantic calls. Their attentions converge on the ground beneath them. A yearling Cooper's hawk has ambushed one of the jay family. The hawk lifts off, carrying to denser seclusion the limp jay.

In one sense, its death will be momentary, life transferred from jay to hawk. But try telling that to the bereft jays, who have permanently lost a member to this perennial terror.

IN THE EVENING OF APRIL 21, Alfie popped out of the box at around eight p.m., flew to the driveway cedars, then to the birdbath. After bathing, she flew to a branch, where she scratched her head with the talons of one foot, wiped her beak, and looked around attentively. She seemed to be waiting eagerly for her lovebird.

Plus-One appeared as if from nowhere. With the familiar ease of a human couple kissing hello, they copulated. Their relationship thus far had entailed a surprisingly protracted time of mutually shared sexual energies, practiced with increasing ease and competence. And they were still going at it strong.

With his tame mate occupying his attention, Plus-One seemed to accept me and Patricia as part of his scenery. He and Alfie were acting completely naturally in our presence, behaving as they would.

But only Alfie was inclined to approach us. She would occasionally land on us when there was no food in sight, even after she'd eaten. Did being next to us make her feel safe? Did she feel a fondness, an affection? Fondness and affection seem to be things owls understand; they frequently preen each other, and they are among the few birds who invite (by bowing their heads) preening by a trusted human.

IN THE EARLY 1900S, A book titled *The Mechanistic Conception of Life* asserted, "Living organisms are chemical machines possessing the peculiarity of preserving and reproducing themselves." In one sense, that is true; there is a lot of sheer chemistry going on in living things. But the book said that self-preservation and procreation are mere "peculiarities" of these chemical machines. Yet no machine self-preserves or procreates. A living thing is capable of growth, procreation, and self-repair. These are not mere peculiarities; these are stark distinctions, defining characteristics, extraordinary things.

Consider what that book's assertion ignores. All of life on Earth is one lit candle that has maintained itself and proliferated for nearly four billion years solely by the process of living cells dividing. A living thing can die, but non-living things cannot be brought to life. A living thing is enlivened only because it is part of the unbroken flame. The flame is sometimes called metabolism. This involves chemistry but it is not *just* chemistry. The difference is that aliveness is an emergent property, not just a sum of its parts. A carcass is a sum of parts.

I WAS OUT IN THE gathering darkness. The low light caused uncertainty. Who was whom? The who whom I thought was Plus-One vanished. Who I thought was Alfie suddenly appeared on a branch, yanking mightily on the head of a wild mouse, severing its spine. After decapitating the mouse and swallowing said head, the hunter walked about two feet along the limb to stash the headless carcass at a widened fork of the branch.

The one I thought was Alfie, now mouseless, flew to the studio and went straight into the nest box. But when I checked a minute later, the mouse on the branch was gone. I went back to the nest box. The bird I thought was Plus-One appeared outside the nest box holding a mouse, called softly several times, looked in, deposited the mouse inside the box, and flew into the dark woodland. I was confused. But the owls knew exactly who was doing what.

ON APRIL 22 AT DUSK, around eight p.m., I went to the Ivy Tower to watch Plus-One emerge from his day roost. While I was gazing up at him, Alfie tapped my head during a flyby from the nest box to the driveway cedars. It seemed remarkably cheeky of her. Do owls have a sense of humor?

They perched close together. But this time they did *not* copulate. This marked a new phase shift in their relationship. Once again the gears had subtly turned.

Alfie again seemed very antsy, looking right, left, up, down, sideways. Alfie's restlessness seemed to reflect feelings of conflict: between being drawn outside and a pull to get back into the nest. The cool air meant that if Alfie had eggs, she'd be feeling anxious to get back to them.

After Alfie was out of the box for just ten minutes, she flew toward the studio, accompanied by her husband (husbird? mate?). Plus-One went into the woods. Alfie scrambled into the nest, where, I presumed, the most complex and profound of all life's processes was under development.

◆

"A FEATHER MAGNIFIED AND THE whole image in distortion," the naturalist Henry Beston wrote, alluding to how proponents of reductionism, with their focus on parts, lost sight of Life's big picture. In the 1940s, the Nobel-winning physicist Erwin Schrödinger tried to convey the profound complexity of Life by saying that the difference between atoms and a chromosome was like the difference between "wallpaper in which the same pattern is repeated again and again and a masterpiece of embroidery, say a Raphael tapestry." Schrödinger noted that a chemist can tell you what percent of molecules will react during the first minute of some particular interaction. But whether any *particular* molecule will have reacted is "pure chance." The chemist's law is only a statistical average. A radioactive atom might last a short time or millennia. But all during that time, the chance of it blowing up in the next second is always the same. The "law" of the rate of radioactive decay is an *average* of lifetimes of a large number of atoms. By starkest contrast, in every living cell every single gene, though itself composed of atoms, "produces events which are a paragon of orderliness." Schrödinger points out that this astonishing situation is "unknown anywhere else except in living matter." He says that the chemist and physicist, accustomed to investigating non-living matter, have "never witnessed" the self-ordered happenings that life exhibits. "And so our theory did not cover it—our beautiful statistical theory of which we were so justly proud."

What could Schrödinger have meant in saying that many chemists and physicists have "never witnessed" aliveness? The kinds of equations that physicists and chemists use to express the predictable behavior of gravity, light, atoms, and the statistical averages of quantum processes cannot describe or predict living organisms, ecosystems, and evolution. Aliveness is not purely chemical or physical—it is emergent. Schrödinger, sounding both daunted and inspired, added, "We must therefore not be discouraged by the difficulty of interpreting life by the ordinary laws of physics."

These "laws of physics"—with that phrase's Mosaic intonation—are not really laws but, rather, human descriptions of observed consistencies in the known universe. Some appear very consistent indeed. Other such laws work only in certain domains (Newton's laws of mechanics don't apply well at the quantum level), and scientists debate possible limitations and apparent exceptions. The Second Law of Thermodynamics is commonly understood in simple terms as meaning that the universe tends toward disorder. But hang on, not so fast. The universe brims with spontaneous order-forming atoms, molecules, gases, stars, galaxies—. Most flagrantly, something happening on one particular planet has been breaking the law for these last few billion years, and getting away with it. A unique spontaneous chain reaction arisen from simplicity and inert matter has created its own intensifying, self-proliferating complexity—the magic we call, of course, "Life." It has somehow created a conscious awareness of itself. In religion and sometimes in literary fiction and film, the word for something that disrupts the laws of physics is: "miracle." The top headline for this planet is that Life on Earth creates the most unique and extreme complexity yet detected in the universe. Our existence is a cloth of woven miracles. Perhaps gratitude is what miraculous feels like to itself. When something is more than the simple sum of its parts, we might think about what matters. And everything that matters—*all* meaning—is more than the sum of parts.

◆

OVER THE NEXT WEEK, WE found three very young, no-longer-living opossums right outside our house. One near our back steps. One in the driveway. One near our front steps. All half-eaten. Who did this? They're generally nocturnal, so probably not a hawk. On several occasions the dogs had either abandoned or carried small dead mammals; they never ate them. A cat or fox would have taken these little possums somewhere secluded. The evidence indicated a hunter at the edge of their abilities, able to tackle and subdue such targets, but not able to move or fully consume them. Small but lion-hearted, screech owls kill birds up to the size of mourning doves. I didn't know the maximum size of their mammalian prey. But I thought the baby opossums, though small, were too big for our owls. I'd never solve this mystery. However, subsequent events revealing Plus-One as a boldly competent hunter would make him my main "person of interest" in this serial whodunit.

By the last week of April, with their sexual ardors abruptly culminated, Alfie and Plus-One shifted gears again. Their new groove was a slower rhythm to their months-long dance.

Alfie stayed in the nest box. Whenever I first let the dogs out in the morning, Alfie would call from inside the box. I'd call back. And satisfied that we'd said, "Hi, you; good morning," she'd keep her quiet peace for the rest of the day. Throughout my comings and goings from the studio door beneath the nest box, she kept silent. She was sitting tight.

Plus-One was day-roosting in the Ivy Tower. In the evening they'd meet briefly in the driveway cedars. Alfie would go to the birdbath and take a drink. Within ten minutes she'd fly back to the box for— as far as I could tell—most, maybe all, of the night. I was pretty sure she was incubating, caring for living eggs by providing the warmth and occasional turning that their development required.

LIFE WIELDS A CHEMISTRY THAT not only makes more of itself; it makes different *kinds* of itself. Life does unpredictable things: acts, responds, self-adjusts, proliferates, diversifies, adapts to changing surroundings, and creates dynamic relationships. That is what living things do.

For a computer, say, to be alive, it would need to grow itself, either from sunlight, air, soil, and water, as does a plant, or perhaps by eating e-waste or hard drives. Maybe it would begin in a larval stage, a pocket calculator, say, before metamorphosing into a tablet, laptop, desktop, or mainframe. At this point it might compete with other computers for the attentions of a potential mate. After joining their docking stations and exchanging perfectly complementary halves of their individually unique operating systems, one or both would emit computer seeds or spores; or lay a clutch of thumb drives; or split into two halves of the keyboard and screen, each capable of growing into a full-sized computer.

This complicated proposition is improbable. In fact, Life is the most improbable thing in the universe. People who make computers know everything about how they work. No human can fully explain a living cell or a functioning being. A computer is merely complicated. Living organisms are *complex*. A cell's components function with feedback loops subject to intracellular conditions and influence from the outside world. The whole organism is an interaction of genes, history, situation, nutrition, environment, competitive stresses, predation pressures, and luck. Complexity creates unpredictability.

OUR CHICKEN CHICKS CONTINUED GROWING rapidly. The weather would soon be warm enough to move them to the coop. Meanwhile, they remained mostly in the house, with long stretches of exercise and daily trips to the backyard. Growing so fast had made them thin. So I greatly boosted their food. The six of them were daily eating: a bunch of romaine lettuce, three to four plates of rice and beans, two large chopped clams, plus seeds, suet, freeze-dried mealworms, and occasional other items. Collectively, they were eating far more than I. They possessed fathomless appetites. Let loose outside, they immediately took to scratching, pecking, and hunting the occasional and wildly popular earthworm. When outdoors they were less prone to wandering than when loose inside our house, more prone to staying close to each other and us. They seemed, correctly, to sense the danger of this realer world. Outside, they would freeze in response to loud blue jay calls or geese flying overhead. Indoors, they never wanted to go back into the crate; we'd have to herd them off their preferred resting spots on the sofa and dog bed. But after a while outdoors, they were more likely to return together to the crate's safer haven.

Our elder hens exhibited no interest in the chicks. I'd have thought they would be curious, maybe even protective. But they showed as little interest in hanging out with the young chicks as we might have in joining a group of teenagers walking home from school. Even chickens, it seemed, feel generational barriers.

THE SPRING SONGBIRD MIGRATION CONTINUED its *crescendo accelerando*. Faster came orange-bright orioles, plush catbirds, startling redstarts, and rose-breasted grosbeaks. The orioles and catbirds stayed in our yard; the redstarts and grosbeaks departed. Whip-poor-wills arrived in weakened numbers. Formerly, they were abundant enough to keep us awake, their night-long chanting coming from all points of the dark pitch-pine woods. Now just one or two constitute a slightly reassuring presence. Their reliance on large night-flying insects is suspected in their decline. Insects amalgamate much of the living world, but insects too are declining.

Meanwhile, the white-throated sparrows who had been at our feeders all winter lingered into May's first days, still singing longingly of the land of their birth. They would soon depart toward the North Star, joining the hundred or so avian species frantically foraging by day in our region, their flocks at times detected on regional weather radars by night as they powered themselves into the black of northward. Birds by their thousands enliven our shires and shores. Only a fraction receive notice from any human eye.

LIFE IS *ALWAYS* MUCH MORE than meets the eye. Life is: self-organizing, self-perpetuating, self-proliferating; capable of growth, self-repair, procreation, and diversification. Every living thing: metabolizes, self-maintains, self-regulates, and is a member of a self-adapting, self-evolving lineage. All living things *behave*, taking initiative and responding to their surroundings. Animals exert complex agency, choosing where to go and what to do, not only sensing but perceiving, often having thoughts, experiencing emotions. And sometimes dreaming. In sleeping male finches, neurons of their brain's song system undergo spontaneous bursts of activity. Even cuttlefish dream.

Components of a cell act on their own to create the concert of the functioning cell. This is what Schrödinger meant by "events which are a paragon of orderliness." By self-propagation and self-differentiation, cells themselves diversify into tissue and organs and organisms. Organisms make up species, which exist within and because of community interactions and dynamic dependencies. Life helps to create the planetary conditions necessary for its own survival, from altering the atmosphere by producing oxygen, to plants and fungi creating soil, to creating regional weather as do rainforests, to the madness of a coral reef, to animals busily building nests and storing food. Living things can respond to contingencies by exercising options, using chance encounters to their advantage. Even the very concept of advantage and disadvantage applies only to living things.

Machines do not create conditions suitable for their functioning, do not create themselves, make their own parts, do not self-propagate, do not form communities, do not self-evolve or self-diversify. A more basic difference distinguishes the living. Living things have purpose: to stay alive, to create more life, to adapt to a world that likewise adapts to their presence in the world. Cedars or spiders are always busy doing things for themselves, in their own interest. No machine has purpose or self-interest. A machine has merely a use. Only aliveness creates conditions for meaning.

THE LITTLE CHICKEN CHICKS WERE finally big enough—and it was finally warm enough—to let them spend their first night in the coop. At dusk, a bit confused, they wanted to go "home." The large and airy coop was entirely unfamiliar. To alleviate their distress, I brought their home—their crate—to them. They happily entered their accustomed abode and snuggled in as the natural light fell. The older hens roosted as normal on their perches above. In the morning we let the hens roam as usual. The chicks spent the day protectively confined in the open-air screened coop—Alfie's former suite. Though getting big, they continued squealing and cheeping, their voices not yet changed to the various clucking calls that constitute an adult's vocabulary. At dusk of that first full day, the chicks would not voluntarily enter the shadows of the inner coop, nor stay when I placed them inside. I went inside, turned on the light, and called them in. They hesitantly explored the coop's inner recess, moving up to some of the perches before returning to the ground to spend the night in their crate.

Over the following days, they continued eating and eating, growing rapidly on their copious and diverse diet. I amused myself by digging from the lawn a daily piece of sod and putting it in the coop, whereupon the chicks ate the grass down to the roots. Later I dropped the sod back into the hole where I'd gotten it so it could regrow. It was certainly an economical and sustainable food. The chicks loved it. They'd grown so fast, they were already molting their first set of feathers.

PLUS-ONE CONTINUED ROOSTING IN THE Ivy Tower most days. Alfie tucked her time into the nest box. Days got T-shirt warm. In the late afternoons, Alfie began giving herself a break and some fresh air by looking out from the box entrance. She came out only around sunset, flying directly to the driveway cedars and then quickly returning to the nest box. Elapsed time about five minutes. In those swift minutes, Plus-One did not always show up for a rendezvous. The romance of their honeymoon had morphed into the differing responsibilities of a parental partnership.

I still had only circumstantial evidence that she was incubating eggs. I was reluctant to intrude. I did not want to upset her or make her feel insecure or, by checking while she was inside, risk causing her to accidentally break an egg. So on May 2, I readied a ladder and waited. At sunset Alfie launched out of the box and dropped low, shooting through a gap in the bushes and crossing the yard toward the birdbath and the cedars. I propped the ladder against the studio wall alongside the nest box, quickly climbed, stuck my phone in the entrance, fired off three photo frames, and came down before Alfie returned. I was fast enough to avoid confronting her with the unexpected sight of the ladder at her most secure redoubt, her most private site.

I took a few steps away from the studio and checked the images and—eggs!

I was not just delighted; I was *elated* by the photos showing three white, nearly spherical eggs. (White because camouflage isn't necessary inside a dark cavity nest, and spherical because there's no danger of eggs rolling out of such a deep nest.) In 1862 the American abolitionist, soldier, pastor, and women's rights activist Thomas Wentworth Higginson wrote, "If required on pain of death to name instantly the most perfect thing in the universe, I should risk my fate on a bird's egg." He championed liberty, so perhaps his admiration was partly metaphorical; every wild bird's egg is dedicated to the eventuality of a splendid freedom.

In the short minutes that Alfie was leaving her nest, she continued showing no interest in coming to me for food. Plus-One had stepped competently into his role of hunter and provider while his mate was incubating their potential offspring.

LIFE IS AN ENTERPRISE. IT has undertaken a mission to persist and perpetuate and has developed its modes—procreation, adaptation, diversification—for advancing its mission in the face of change. Life is always on the move, flowing, altering, self-interested. If that evolving process looks frozen to us, it's because we are walk-on, bit-part actors in one frame of one scene. Try to watch the whole movie.

Science has given us a lot of that movie. It's a magnificent picture of space and time. Even the non-living universe is more than a sum of parts, subject, as it is, to the complexities of infinite randomness creating this or that atom, forming a nebula here, a galaxy there, subjecting swarms of suns to the gravitational influence of a black hole.

But Life is the art of parts guiding their own parts, taking themselves into new and unimagined ventures. Life is music that composes itself, a play that writes its own story. No railcar has ever decided what train to join. But billions of times a day a bird chooses a flock, a fish goes to school. Life is spontaneous. Irregular. Unpredictable. Life is *turbulent*.

I CERTAINLY FELT IT. THE first week of May speedballed past in blossoms and bud bursts, waves of flying migrants, new choruses of frogs and toads. We had a surfeit of springtime, too much of Life's vernal frenzy to see, to absorb, for any human mind to grasp.

My worst nightmare is that one day, all the wild animals of the world are gone—and no one notices. Most people notice none of them now. We are all more or less strangers in our own homeland. This is a very modern malady.

For the first billion years or so of Life's 3.5-billion-year history, single cells continually traded genes. There were no lineages, no lines of descent, no *species*. Only promiscuous gene swapping in the community pool. The kind of evolution Darwin wrote about—descent with variation, sifted and sorted in a struggle for existence—did not yet exist. For the next billion years or so, all cells continued living as singles or connected in mats or strings. How did simple life manage the balletic leap across the seemingly unbridgeable chasm from a single cell dividing to many cells in the different organs of a complex organism that could procreate? The challenges are almost unimaginable. The hurdles were precipitous, but rather than vaulting the ramparts in one leap, the ascent to multicell complexity was more like rock climbing. Slow. Tiny steps. A year. A million years. A hundred million years. During the climb, cells developed regulator molecules that turned genes on and off. A thousand million years. As more cells began sticking together, some genes got turned on and off in different ways, places, and times, helping cells to specialize and differentiate into organs and structures. Two thousand million years. Trillions of generations of cells. The most primitive animals, sponges, didn't get going until more than 2.75 billion years after the first living cells. More than 3 billion years after Life began, about 470 million years ago, from algal forebears the first true plants arose.

The advent of separate lineages—species—created an enormous transition in Life's trajectory. A being such as a sequoia or a whale pulses with the tidal networkings of hard-to-imagine cellular multitudes. A mid-sized animal—a human, for example—is a galaxy of thirty-seven trillion cells.

Somehow this planet's living things grow and probe, seeking, striving. Evolution generates outcomes that are actually less and less likely, creates the increasingly improbable, until the utterly implausible and absolutely fantastic become commonplace and matter acquires the capacity for conscious sensation, for active appraisal. We see workings of awareness across a broad swath of the living world, from a spider trying to get out of a tub to an elephant rescuing her niece from a raging river. And through that capacity for consideration of circumstance, a mote of the cosmos becomes a cosmos aware of itself, capable of wonder.

◆

ALFIE POPPED OUT OF THE nest box at eight twenty-five p.m. and flew to the driveway cedars. Plus-One, coming from somewhere near the southeast corner of our yard, immediately met her. They softly vocalized. In this intimate proximity, each whinny was barely a remark, a whispered acknowledgment. He tried to preen her. She backed off a bit. They indulged only in a quick bill touch. He melted back through the cedars. She sped back to the nest.

The chicken chicks were getting big enough that I started letting them out for a few hours before dusk. They'd move around the yard a bit, scratching away fallen leaves, pecking at newly exposed bugs and seeds with obvious satisfaction. Around sundown, of their own volition, they'd head inside. To do such simple things requires, of course, complex things: intentionality, senses of place and of time, a mental map, and a simple plan.

I began letting them out for prolonged, supervised periods of exercise and exploration a couple of times a day. They were so big that I'd occasionally do a double take to ascertain whether I was looking at a chick or one of our older ladies. I accustomed them to understand that when I tapped two pieces of wood together, food had been served inside. So even at midday I never needed to herd them back into the coop. I'd just tap a few times. They'd scurry up the ramp, chow down, then laze around in sunbeams, dozing it off. I was proud they'd all come so far, looked so healthy and lustrous, and seemed so content in their life with us.

LIFE'S GRAND CREATIVE ENTERPRISE HAS something we individuals lack: unlimited time for exploring options and trying new twists. Life flows along, filling the passageways of opportunity. In a sense, it's one river. But it flows through many braided channels. If intelligence facilitates solutions to new problems, then this is Life's intelligence.

Genes, cells, individuals, and populations work at different scales to survive long enough to pass the torch. Coordination, cooperation, and competition all affect the success of individuals, populations, and species. In Life's theater, cells have the briefest role and the shortest programmed life span. Individuals the next briefest. Species, which get the starring roles, stay onstage the longest, often "disappearing" by slowly morphing into what we call a "new" species, a lineage's next act of survival. Dinosaurs as such breathe no more, but birds—including Alfie—are the direct descendants of so-called avian dinosaurs that never went extinct.

The challenge of survival on planet Earth has been met; survival won so handily that life has thrived, prospered, proliferated, and infused the world so thoroughly that I was looking up and an owl was looking down at me.

ALL DAY ON MAY 14, Plus-One and I could trade glances while he dozed in the Ivy Tower. In the evening Alfie appeared in the back-door dogwood. Patricia got some food and Alfie took it from her hand. I had not hand-fed her for several months. I was quite surprised that despite her wild mate and clutch of eggs, despite her life as so normal a free-living, free-loving owl, Alfie remained thoroughly tame.

By rough calculation I estimated that Alfie's eggs were due to hatch on May 16. That night, she did not take the mouse I'd left for her on the back banister. The preoccupation of her attention was total.

So on the evening of May 17 I readied the ladder and waited. If Alfie was going to make her usual brief sojourn from the box, I was going to climb and check on developments. She did. I did.

The box was littered with wren and catbird feathers. And—no eggs. Three *tiny*, snowy-fuzzed chicks lay huddled in a ball.

I was staring at a kind of organic karma that involves the continual rebirth of a species incarnating its own next generation. Life's most crucial miracle. The owlets were so minute that the whole huddle of all three hatchlings was smaller than the white-footed mouse carcass lying in the nest. Alfie hadn't touched the mouse; her competent, determined mate, Plus-One, was delivering plenty of food for her *and* their new offspring.

PART FOUR

·≡·

Nursery Days

13

◈

Nursery Days

A COOL, DAMP, PROTRACTED SPRING CAUSED VARIOUS warbler species to linger, delighting birders. An ocean slow to warm delayed migrating fishes, testing the patience of fishing birds and fishing people.

We were all savoring the longer days. The afternoon sun struck the nest box directly; it must have gotten quite warm in there. Alfie started poking her head out of the nest at around four p.m., hours before sundown. At dusk, she would drop from the nest box and shoot across the undulating contours of the vegetation, as if relishing her skill. She'd cross the yard and land on one of her favored branches in the driveway cedars, scanning for her able mate. He seemed in recent days to often stand her up at this time. But as Patricia said, "They've got the whole night."

There might have been a good reason for Plus-One's no-shows. During the last couple of days of May, I finally tuned in to something Patricia was very good at: listening for scolding birds. Alarm calls of cardinals and wrens meant they'd located a murderous mortal enemy in their territory. The first time I followed, their protests revealed Plus-One situated in a cedar next to our mailbox, adjacent to the street's stop sign. I suspected he was noting where small birds were tucking themselves in to roost for the night.

Alfie was in a driveway cedar, so I rushed back to the studio, put up the ladder, and shot two photos. I was still on the ladder, hurriedly checking the images, when—as I'd feared—I heard Alfie calling from behind me. I had not wanted her to find me at the entrance to her nest, like some kind of common predator. I scrambled down.

Usually when coming back from the driveway cedars, she'd fly right in. But now she called a few more times. Then—she flew into the woods.

I worried greatly that I'd upset her sense that the nest box was a safe place. I'd frequently sat in a chair right below the nest, working on my computer as she looked out, unperturbed. But the strange transgression of the ladder right at the nest itself, with her babes in there, might have constituted an unacceptable breach, an incursion into her most private chamber.

A while later, I heard her calling softly near the box. Or was that Plus-One, wondering where Alfie was?

I decided I'd better leave the area. I could see from the photos I'd just gotten that the growing chicks were now covered with thicker down and tiny feathers and should be, I thought, able to stay warm enough for a short while without their mother. But it was a damp evening. How long could they survive the night's chill?

I went to bed thinking, "They're probably okay."

That is, of course, a terrible way to go to bed.

I READ A LITTLE AND tried to sleep. The first time I woke to look at the clock, it was only one a.m. The remainder of the night, I felt wide awake.

Just after four a.m., I slipped out the back door. I was met immediately by Alfie's soft calls. This was a surprise because it had been months since I had stepped out in the morning twilight. It wasn't clear whether she was really there for me; it would make more sense if she wasn't. No way to know. The food I'd left before going to bed was gone. She was facing away, calling, then flew to the tree outside the studio. By the time I got there, her hind end was just disappearing into the nest box. And for the first time I heard, from outside the box, the chitters of the little ones therein.

So as with all mornings, the tint of dawn started the day off with a bit of magic. And this particular day began with great relief. The kids were alright.

REGARDLESS OF HOW OBVIOUS IT is that creatures with eyes and ears see and hear, feel calmness or fear, and use information from their finely tuned senses to make decisions favoring their comfort and well-being, many people still choose to see merely a sum of components, running like a washing machine.

Richard Dawkins is a prominent, strident advocate of biological evolution and also of atheism. Ironically, as a science evangelizer, he puts forth arguments that reverberate with the dualism whose provenance is religion, shaded with creationist rhetoric, delivered with the case-is-closed zeal typical of fundamentalists. Bombast is popular; Dawkins has many acolytes.

Dawkins writes, "A bat is a machine, whose internal electronics are so wired up that its wing muscles cause it to home in on insects, as an unconscious guided missile homes in on an aeroplane. So far our intuition, derived from technology, is correct."

How could he know that a bat is "unconscious?" Why would he think so? Bats are mammals; humans are mammals. Bats and humans have eyes and ears, and recognize the individual babies we take care of. Especially if he's such a fan of evolution, doesn't Dawkins understand that these shared vertebrate systems are inherited from shared ancestors? Deriving explanations for life by analogies to technology is not evidence-based scientific logic. We're no longer living in the times of Descartes and Hobbes—are we? Dawkins can't get farther than "machine," because that's where he's parked.

Dawkins begins one of his books with this astonishing assertion: "Our own existence once presented the greatest of all mysteries, but it is a mystery no longer because it is solved. Darwin and Wallace solved it." Our *existence* solved? And by Darwin and Wallace? No.

Darwin and Wallace did not attempt to solve existence. Their quest was to unveil a process by which life diversifies into so many species. Dawkins's open-and-shut certitude that our existence "is solved" reverberates with the tonality of early fundamentalists such as Tertullian bellowing, "We have no desire to believe anything else; for the first article of our faith is that there is nothing else we have to believe." Because no one in Darwin and Wallace's time knew how heredity worked, their ideas about the process of diversification were brilliantly informed guesswork. Subsequent discoveries affirmed that Darwin and Wallace had identified a major process of diversification: individual variation followed by descent with modification in a world where procreation produces more individuals than there are opportunities to survive. Discoveries in genetic inheritance put muscle on that skeleton. But our existence remains abundantly mysterious.

TEMPERATURES ROSE SHARPLY DURING THE last few days of May. At two weeks of age, the chicks no longer needed brooding. Alfie often looked out of the box all day.

The ocean surface's temperature jumped eight degrees Fahrenheit in a week. So I went in search of fish. Terns recently arrived in their breeding range from wintering areas in South America were spread out over a broad, blue, tranquil ocean, hunting. When packs of migrating bluefish sporadically erupted, the nearer terns swiftly converged on the white explosions and the sprays of fleeing anchovies. Those terns who first got to the action managed a plunge or two and often came away with an anchovy struggling in the needle tweeze of their bill. Sometimes they'd stop in midair, flip the wriggling fish, and swallow their prize headfirst. High speed and high stakes—everything seemed Olympian. My lure landed amid a sudden frothing commotion at the sea surface, and I wrested up a bluefish as long as my leg, who would provide quite a few meals of the finest kind: meals with a story. In deep dusk I switched on the running lights and turned the wheel for the harbor. Chula had waited in the driveway at the house till well after dark. When we greeted, I explained that I had some very nice fish trimmings for her.

THE NEXT EVENING, ALFIE FLEW across our view while we were on the deck enjoying a meal from my catch. It was still light, so I used her exit to quickly check on the owlets. The fast-growing little ones had gotten bigger than I expected over the few days since my last check. All looked great, all growing steadily.

Alfie called from the driveway cedars for many minutes. Plus-One didn't respond. But we knew where he was. Mockingbirds, catbirds, and robins alerted us again to Plus-One's presence in the cedar near the mailbox and the stop sign. I guessed that at this stage he'd deliver food when he had it; until then he would focus narrowly on hunting. Their long romance and honeymoon had morphed into working parenthood.

Alfie moved to the back-door dogwood. When Patricia rested her hand on the banister, Alfie flew down and tagged her fingers, then swooped up just above our heads. She must have felt intense motivation to feed her babies. She continued calling. Perhaps she was asking both her mate and her adoptive parents for food she could take to her nestlings. I went inside and carved off three small pieces of bluefish. No sooner had I put a slice on the banister than Alfie snatched it up and freighted it straight to the nest. I walked over and could hear the youngsters chittering as she fed them.

Alfie returned to the back-door dogwood. I laid the other two pieces of fish on the banister. In a quick and clever assessment of a situation she'd never faced before, Alfie took one in her bill, one in her foot, and flew to the nest.

I was conflicted about having intervened in the flow of food so early in the night. I preferred to give Plus-One time to bring prey. At nine twenty-eight p.m. I was sitting on the deck, typing in the dark on my computer. I was just about to note that the owls had all settled down when Alfie materialized in the back-door dogwood, calling for more. I thought that she should resume doing some hunting as her nestlings outgrew the need for her to brood them. I didn't want to enable her slipping back to heavy dependence on us. Overhead, the moon was billowing toward full; Plus-One would have plenty of light by which to hunt. He had the whole night to do his job. On the other hand, a few months ago, there had been just Alfie. Now our back-yard hosted a family totaling five owls in need of food. So I relented and brought out a mouse. Alfie immediately took the meal into the cedars. She'd fed her children first with the fish; now it was her turn to eat. Still worried about "spoiling" her, I had to admit that it really wasn't so bad to risk the possibility that our owl family might have a little extra food. I could never be certain where—or even if—to draw the line. Certainty was seldom part of the Alfie equation.

"LIFE IS JUST BYTES AND bytes and bytes of digital informa-tion," insists the always-certain Richard Dawkins, equating life with a computer's memory board. Our purpose, he tells us, is to function as transport packages for his favorite thing: "selfish genes." The English philosopher and novelist Samuel Butler anticipated the inanity of such thinking more than a century ago when he quipped that a chicken is just a way an egg makes another egg. Dawkins's book *The Selfish Gene* catapulted him to fame in the me-first 1980s. His picture of life driven by ruthless genes with selfish motives furnished an irresistible excuse for ruthless people to act selfishly. It's a secular variant of "the devil made me do it" but without the guilt or contrition.

Reality check: genes cannot be selfish. Selfish genes would be dead ends, speeding their lineage's extinction. A gene that makes fur white, say, is valuable as camouflage in the Arctic but lethal to an individual who needs concealment in the emerald tropics. Sex evolved to mix and stir genetic notes, to recompose and try out new genetic melodies, retaining genes that work well in concert, that keep the beat of the rhythms of a changing world. "To consider genes as inde-pendent units is meaningless," wrote the great biologist Ernst Mayr. Former National Institutes of Health director Francis Collins and his colleagues pointed out that genes "do not function independently, but participate in complex, interconnected pathways, networks and molecular systems that, taken together, give rise to the workings of cells, tissues, organs and organisms." That's all the "selfishness" genes have: none.

JUNE ARRIVED DURING A CHILLY night, with temps dipping under fifty degrees. We had the windows open, expecting, well, a June night. What we got was another blanket from the closet.

Because Alfie had been so food-oriented the previous night, I set my alarm for four forty-five a.m. It was already light enough for a dawn drenched in birdsong, augmented by a couple of wild turkeys calling, one from the squeezed little wetland across the road and one to our south, where a few meager woody patches remain.

As soon as I waded into the chilly, song-threaded gloaming, Alfie started calling from directly overhead in the back-door dogwood. But I could not discern her in the shadowy leaves. She clearly was right there—somewhere—ten or fifteen feet away.

She was calling with a soft but insistent high whistle whose tone arced downward, no vibrato—though ending with a slight quaver. This seemed her lowest-intensity version of a whinny. I didn't know whether this relatively unwavering version was particular to her. Few people get the chance to be spoken to in confiding tones by an owl at such close range. I answered. We continued corresponding.

To feed? Or not to feed? I continued debating myself. I wanted to leave the whole job of feeding to Plus-One. But that argument was tempered by recalling that our yard had always seemed unable to support screech owls for long. I'd occasionally hear one, but never for a whole season. In previous years, the nest box had never hosted occupants.

Alfie's heightened hunger stood in stark contrast to the months during courtship and incubation when she seemed rather uninterested in us. She was now urgently motivated to bring food to her three fast-growing chicks. And what about her own needs? I'd given her three finger-sized pieces of fish plus a mouse last night; she'd immediately shunted most of the incoming food to her chicks. No one ever said motherhood is easy. My summation: If this isn't great habitat, and she has growing owlets, and she is so hungry—. I lost the argument with myself. I fetched more food.

I still could not see her, but she sounded as though she was right above me. Suddenly she was on my hand. Whoa. So stealthy are these owls that *while I was looking directly toward where she was calling from*, I did not detect her silent approach.

She airlifted the food straight to the nest box.

And quickly she was back, calling again.

Now I said no. Three pieces of fish and two mice between dusk and dawn were enough for the full span of a single night shift.

Alfie went to the driveway a couple of times, calling for Plus-One. She seemed insatiable.

I was hoping to see my owl son-in-law appear with a mouse or sparrow. But he was absent. What he might have brought during the night, I couldn't say. But clearly it wasn't enough to satisfy our owl daughter.

Alfie twice focused on the ground and planed down to pounce. Both times she seemed to eat something. I could not see what tiny bugs she might have grabbed. Her prowess with snack bugs notwith-standing, she instantly continued calling.

Patricia appeared in the doorway. Alfie had effectively called her out of bed.

"Why so much vocalizing?" she asked

"Well, she's got three hungry kids. And she's gotta eat, too."

Alfie landed on Patricia's hand, nibbled at the eyeglasses she was holding, determined that they were inedible, and hopped off.

Patricia disappeared back into the kitchen. Meanwhile, Alfie landed on my empty hand.

Patricia reappeared, holding *another* mouse. Alfie instantly took the mouse and flew to the nest to feed her chicks.

"Okay, well, I'm going back to bed," Patricia said.

Alfie might have echoed that sentiment; she did not reappear.

❖

THE NEXT DAY AT AROUND ten-thirty a.m., I happened to hear scolding songbirds and an owl's screechy defensive threat sounds. That was no longer surprising. But when I saw Plus-One on a bare maple branch in broad daylight, I was shocked to recognize what he was holding—a chipmunk!

If anyone had asked me, "Do screech owls ever hunt in broad daylight; do they ever catch chipmunks?" I would have answered, "No. And no." Apparently the correct answer to both questions is "Never; except when they do." I could hardly believe my eyes. I ran inside for my good camera and longest lens.

Eastern chipmunks weigh about four ounces and, including their tail, can be about twelve inches long. Eastern screech owls weigh about six ounces and, because their tails are short, measure merely eight inches or so in length. I suddenly had a whole new respect for Plus-One's hunting capability. He was a big-game hunter, devoted to whatever it took—and *doing* it—to provide. He was willing to forsake the safety of daytime cover, to hunt round the clock if necessary. And he could *fly* carrying fully two-thirds his body weight.

After a long ten minutes, he headed, chased by several harassing birds, to the driveway cedars. I didn't see whether a bird hit him hard or he just lost his grip, but when he landed he had dropped the chipmunk. To see whether he'd be back to retrieve it, I set up my motion-triggered camera next to the fallen rodent.

I had recently set the camera up at the nest box, so in the process of resetting it, I checked the card. To my amazement, Plus-One had delivered a different chipmunk to the nest a few minutes before noon two days earlier.

Alfie's heightened urge to feed her owlets was matched by Plus-One's heightened efforts to hunt and deliver prey. Did this daytime hunting reflect a scarcity of prey at night? Years before, at the edge of a system of salt marshes, I'd watched a pair of barn owls bringing meadow voles to their large chicks. All night the parents returned with food, reappearing about every ten minutes. That's my idea of what good habitat provides. Well-fed owls should not feel compelled to hunt large and difficult prey, much less hunt at noon while suffering the wrath of owl-hating birds. And speaking of large prey, had scarcity motivated Plus-One to tackle those three baby possums I'd found half-eaten in late April?

At seven p.m., scolding birds alerted me to the fact that Plus-One had returned to pick up his dropped chipmunk. The motion-activated camera I'd placed got some images of him on the chipmunk, facing the scolding birds. But it had also recorded, hours earlier, several frames of a live chipmunk coming to investigate the carcass. The visitor sniffs the fallen one's head. A friend? No way to know. But poignant. Hard to shake the images from the mind. Chipmunk empathy has not been studied. But mouse empathy has been. Mice "experience the pain and the relief of other mice," scientists have found. When mice responded to the distress or the alleviation of pain in their cagemates, "the same brain areas involved in empathic behavior in humans were activated in the mice." My camera's briefly framed moments opened a window on deeper and wider questions.

I sat with a close view of the nest until ten p.m. The adults added two moths and an earthworm. Alfie added the white mouse I'd put out on the banister. I went into the studio. Soon a June bug came to the window screen. I wondered if the owls noticed. Moments later, an owl strafed the screen. The bug was no more. With chicks in the nest, the owls considered many different things fair fare.

◆

OWLS HAVE, OF COURSE, BECOME masters of the times between daylight. Experiments have shown that barn owls can perceive and catch mice using hearing alone, in completely darkened rooms. Our own brains, operating as they do in the darkness inside our skulls, cannot perceive their own complexity. So they—meaning we—often cling to simplistic analogies in an attempt to grasp who and what we are. A few years ago, a speaker at the World Economic Forum proclaimed, "Organisms are algorithms." The speaker wasn't merely claiming that our bodies were built from a set of instructions—he was saying that we *are* a set of instructions. But an individual is not instructions any more than an automobile is an owner's manual. Organisms could not exist as "algorithms" because living beings are shaped through discourse with the world. But if one has not been raised to inquire about relationships, one might see a living thing as nothing but a product model. One would miss that living is a correspondence with the surroundings, a matter of taking in and putting forth, as exemplified by breathing and eating. Each species is in continual conversation with other individuals, various species, and the land- and waterscapes of their time and place. In the conversation that carries across many generations, each individual life is but a word in edgewise. We are *many* things, functioning flexibly in various ways, playing different roles, acting our bit parts and cameo appearances and nudging the plot along.

THE FOLLOWING EVENING, ALFIE WAS in the back-door dogwood, begging with her soft descending whistle. My new appreciation of Plus-One's prowess allowed me to resist Alfie's entreaties. I decided I'd just get up early, in the dark, and see how she seemed after a night without my interference.

At a quarter after four, I stepped out beneath a low and overcast sky just flooding up with birdsong. Alfie was right there in the back-door dogwood, as though she'd waited there all night.

I showed her a mouse. She looked at it for a few moments. She could take it or leave it. Eventually, she deigned to take it.

At a quarter after five, she was back asking for more. She went briefly to the birdbath, then to a cedar, calling. Last time I'd looked, the nest box had contained enough songbird feathers to indicate that she or her mate had been stalking the bushes for roosting sparrows and the like, perhaps raiding nests.

She returned to the back-door dogwood and began looking intently in the direction of the deck table. I'd never seen her land on the deck chairs, but she hopped onto the back of one, staring directly at an emptied birdseed bag I'd just placed there.

I thought, "How odd," until I realized that there was a photo of a small bird on the bag. Alfie must have thought the pictured nuthatch a vulnerable individual, worth a try. She jumped on the image. The bag's crunch startled her; she returned immediately to the dogwood. There, despite the onset of a misty intermittent rain, she continued calling softly for half an hour, until she finally flew to her nest.

AT NOON I WENT DOWN the back steps to feed the chickens. I often call them by rattling their seed in a container.

Bang! Alfie knocked the seed container out of my hand.

That rattled *me!*

She had never come looking for me in the middle of the day. Well, this said something about her being hungry. But *what* did it say? It was possible that Alfie was doing what a responsible mom in her situation (being an owl) should do: not seeking "enough" but, rather, seeking "as much as possible."

How much prey were the owls catching? Somewhere between too little and more than plenty. That uncertainty always weakened my resolve to let them go it entirely on their own. Tough love is often more tough than it is love. Alfie had me wrapped around her sharpest talon, because I wanted her to succeed. In purely natural settings, chicks sometimes starve. If I was going to err, I preferred to err on the side of helping her raise all three chicks at their healthiest and plumpest. So even though it was midday, I got some food and spoke some words, and in moments she was calling unseen from the foliage of the back-door dogwood. I put the food on the banister, and in a raking instant she was swiftly air-hauling it toward the chicks. Perhaps I was nothing but a softy. But we'd gotten to this point, and life was nothing but good.

LIFE IS NOTHING BUT ALGORITHMS; we've heard that said. Nothing but selfish genes. Nothing but digital information. A mind is nothing but nerve cells. The universe, nothing but particles and energy. It's all so simple—for the self-aggrandized. Certain they have the right answers, what they really need are the right questions.

Flowering is about opening. Humanity at its best is about wondering even more than knowing. Real understanding generates further curiosity. Some of us are not threatened by realizing the immensity of how very little we know, are awed that the universe is at least partly accessible. We're inspired with the humility required to comprehend more.

Like most people, Alfie seems to act on things at face value. I used to share her apparent presumption that face-value perceptions are sufficient sensors of reality. I did not know enough to question whether they are. Now I do. Now I understand that the greatest thing one can learn is that learning is a process, that in the great ocean of understanding, we have barely wet a toe. To come to know less than one knew: that is the key that unlocks the universe. When you hear someone say that life is "nothing but . . . ," note the location of the exits.

ALFIE'S GROWING FAMILY AND THEIR behavioral gear shifts— both subtle and startling—were increasingly compelling. So it was no hardship to again launch myself out of bed the instant I heard the first cardinal's whistle at a quarter after four.

Alfie was—no surprise—in the back-door dogwood. But rather than feed her or watch her there, I went to the studio and sat beneath the nest. I could still hear her calling softly from the dogwood, about a hundred feet away.

With no advance notice, I heard her hit the nest entrance; I had no inkling of her coming—she was just *in*.

Had there been a food exchange? Was she bringing something she'd just caught? The silence of flying owls continued to startle me. Trying to observe them, I sometimes felt as ambushed as any mouse.

Inside the nest, she vocalized softly. I heard the chicks chittering. After maybe ten minutes, she popped her head out.

"Hi, you," I said. "What's it all about, Alfie?"

She seemed never to need to *look* at me. Big eyes—yes, she had them. But she knew I was there. Opportunities and dangers yet unseen might prove more important to her. And her world was largely heard. Often she'd come within companionable proximity but focus her attention into the listening distance. Is she accessing some plane of deep perceptions beyond my ken? Certainly. She is a seer of things, a holder of deep innate knowledge. But to what extent our perceptions differ, and whether this is a difference of degree or of kind, I don't know. Clearly at some points, like while we are directly interacting, we function in conjunction; our worlds merge. At other times—.

What does Alfie know that I do not? The black bear specialist Ben Kilham—who happens to be dyslexic—has told me that language took us from being knowers to being believers. Non-humans, he says, are knowers. Believing makes us followers, even of people with mistaken beliefs.

Alfie launched from the nest box and returned to the back-door dogwood. I walked there. It had rained during the night. Still air. Dense new foliage. Lots of birdsong. Just beautiful.

She continued softly calling. I tossed a fat mouse onto the grass. She snatched it away toward the front of our house. It was her turn to eat, in private.

At five a.m. Patricia opened the side door and our three doggies bolted out to skirmish around checking the signs, piecing together the story of what happened during the night. I imagine their headlines read something like "Two Deer Went This Way; A Raccoon Sniffed the Coop; The Same Two Cats Were Here Again . . ."

As for many people, more Covid-induced time at home meant that our garden was the best in several years. We had kale and lettuce, basil, mint, and sage, some peas, and we'd gotten a good start with cucumber and butternut squash seedlings. Patricia had planted her most ambitious dahlia garden (in memory of her mother, Delia). From those bulbs the first green spears were piercing the soil of what was to become a spectacular flowerbed.

ALFIE AND PLUS-ONE'S OWLETS WERE getting big. On June 6 one poked a head out of the nest for a first glimpse at the world, looking comically bewildered. I sympathized. Alfie remained relaxed with me. But when the dogs she'd grown up with strolled directly under her nest, she showed a protective mother's tufts-up reaction of mild alarm.

I wondered how well the youngsters could see. Young owls spend a lot of time waving and bobbing their heads. It's often described as learning to focus. But perhaps, as studies have shown with young barn owls, they must learn how to synchronize their vision and their pinpoint hearing.

Alfie herself seemed far less hungry than a few days earlier. She called less loudly, less insistently. The chicks' growth was leveling off. Patricia and I continued to provide a mouse most nights. That was enough for at least one owl. But not five. We were helping to take care of a family that could take care of themselves.

14

⬩⬩⬩

On the Loose

I WENT TO MY BOAT AT TWO-THIRTY A.M. SO THAT I could live up to the boat's name, *First Light*. I drifted tight to the shore of a dark cove where the black sweep of tide would float me over an underwater bar at the cove's far end. That bar has been a place of gathered fishes.

A whip-poor-will chanted from somewhere up beyond the beach. The world enveloped me as if it knew I was there, and I wrapped the night and the waters tight. Unseen wavelets hissed as they expended their final energies along the pebbly shore. Trees on the shore outlined a sky pulled low. Stars in the distant stillness of their sidereal vault tracked the rolling arc of Earth. The tides that swell and swirl, the chanting bird, the fish that feed me: we had convened. The tide led my mind seaward. I had merely a lure to cast, but the moment cast a spell. I know this place well, but never before had I quite realized what it means to say that place and time are one thing. The mostly unseen scene evoked a bone-felt sense that, out of continuity, possibilities arise. Here, close at hand, were the encompassing realities. Of all animals, humans can best record their own stories. But the plants, birds, fishes: they *are* their stories. I cast my lure, my way of seeking evidence that the authentic past survives in the urgent present. If a fish rose, I'd be reassured. The excitement quells my nerves. "To wait was to pray," wrote Sylvain Tesson in *The Art of Patience*. "And if nothing came, it was because we had not known how to look."

By the time dawn put the light back into my eyes and the magic of night opened into the majesty of morning, the only thing I had caught was a vision of how the entire world had been. Uncluttered. Populated by voices not our own. Its air freely breathable. The wide horizon a reminder of how it once felt to be human and alive.

TO BE HUMAN IS TO ask questions. What kinds of questions we ask depends on what answers have been provided by those who preceded us, who instructed us. We can let our mind loose among the stars or narrow our view to nuts and bolts. The options are unequal. The latter misses everything that is neither a nut nor a bolt, obscures all networks, fails to detect all that is not sum-of-parts. "As long as we think of living systems as machines," sums up Oxford University professor Amia Srinivasan, "we are guaranteed not to understand them."

If living things are not machines, what metaphor better serves? We've seen that living things involve chemistry but that aliveness is more than sums of atoms. A molecule does not have a lineage. But each cell is a living runner in a relay unbroken through eons since Life's earliest inception. As is each organism.

"Organisms," wrote the towering microbiologist Carl Woese, "are resilient patterns in a turbulent flow." Materially and mysteriously, living things are a bit like a whirlpool in a river: all the water that forms the whirlpool moves through, but the whirlpool remains. Unlike a whirlpool, living things work to keep the process flowing for themselves. And they do it against tides of odds.

The molecules that have composed our body have each been like raindrops in a stream we call our "self." The drops flow through and pass on and still we wake and stretch and rub our eyes and see the world we recognize. Energy and matter constantly create and then leave us, but we remain recognizable. We sense ourselves as individuals—and we *are* individuals in the same sense that a raindrop is an individual while it is falling, and a wave is an individual while it is rippling. We are raindrops falling into waves in the great ocean. But mainly we are energy in a package, matter of a moment, a little puff of breeze that will whirl away while everything around it continues. When I pay attention, I feel wonderment at all of this of course, and a touch of melancholy, and gratitude that I've participated.

ALFIE WAS CALLING LOUDLY AT eight-thirty p.m. on June 8. Her calling stopped abruptly. Hmm.

I'd set up my motion-activated camera at the nest box. I had close to two thousand ghostly green-white images that the camera had captured after dark. But many had been triggered by branches waving in the wind or Alfie or an owlet simply looking out of the box and moving their head. Later that night, I started going through the latest frames, deleting, deleting, deleting—until I was stopped by an image that surprised me. Several frames showed that at eight fifty-five p.m., a short while after Alfie had stopped begging and disappeared, one of the parent owls brought a chipmunk to the owlets. Chipmunks sleep at night. I could only presume that Plus-One had caught this chipmunk in daylight and stored the body somewhere safe for retrieval and delivery after dark. Perhaps his résumé as an impressive hunter should include mention of him being a foresightful provider.

OUR YOUNG CHICKENS HAD GROWN nearly as tall as our mature older matrons, but were far trimmer, youthfully slimmer. We were letting them out for exercise before summoning them inside for their breakfast. Hawks had their own chicks to feed now, too. We did not want a hawk to feed our chicken chicks to their hawk chicks, so we kept ours in the screened coop all day. (Our older hens roamed during the day as usual, bulky enough and savvy enough to be of little interest to local hawks at this season of easier, less seasoned prey.) At around six p.m. we let them out. They enjoyed a couple of hours of stretching, running, scratching, and pecking until, around sundown and of their own accord, they commuted back into the coop for the night.

IN THE MID-1970S CARL WOESE discovered an entire, previously unknown realm of life. It is now called the "archaea." The consequently triggered "Woesian revolution" reclassified all of life on Earth into three domains: bacteria, archaea, and organisms whose cells have a nucleus. The latter include many single-celled organisms as well as all complex monumental life, right up to the great whales. Archaea turn out to be everywhere, capable of surviving extreme environments; they live intimately in vast numbers on and in us. One could say they were hiding in plain sight, but of course they're invisible.

In 2004 Woese, who'd won the National Medal of Science, wrote a razor-edged article titled "A New Biology for a New Century," in which he delivered a scathing critique of the path his own discipline had taken. "Biology today is at a crossroads," he challenged, "a choice between a biology that solely does society's bidding and a biology that is society's teacher." Woese warned, "A society that permits biology to become an engineering discipline, that allows that science to slip into the role of changing the living world without trying to understand it, is a danger to itself."

Woese passionately believed that humans need to live both in and *with* the world, and that to make this possible, science must ask big questions in a vast quest to understand Life. Without insisting upon that inspired guiding vision, science becomes enslaved to shortsighted masters. There lie great perils. In the twentieth century, physics—not biology—was seen as the paragon of real science.

Woese almost echoes Schrödinger in observing that classical physicists worked as if "The living world did not exist . . . reality lay only in atoms, their interactions, and certain forces." In essence, most physicists assumed that Life could be ignored until it could be explained with formulas for jostling particles. Classical physics saw a purely cause-and-effect cosmos in which, as Woese put it, "the endless deterministic jumble of bouncing atomic balls" was so law-abiding that if—hypothetically—one knew the position of all atoms at any moment, one could predict all things past and future.

Rather than challenging that simplifying assumption taken by physics, many biologists envied the pace at which physics was moving and the status it was achieving. They wondered why they could not "predict" living things as physicists and chemists could predict actions and reactions. Biologists somehow failed to appreciate that the living things they were exploring were far more complex and networked than atoms and molecules.

Imagine: A physicist and a biologist, each carrying a small bag, take some students to the top of a tall tower on a mountain. The physics students measure the ground elevation and the tower's height and factor these adjustments into standard acceleration. When their professor reaches into the bag and releases a brick from the top of the tower, they feel triumphal that the brick's acceleration and the split second it hits the ground match their calculations. The biology students are impressed and even a bit intimidated by such precision and predictive power. When it's the biologist's turn, the biology students note the temperature, humidity, and wind and hope to measure whatever might happen next. Their professor reaches into her bag and releases a pigeon. The bird circles twice and flies away toward a distant unseen nest and mate known only to the pigeon herself. The physics students mock the biology students, who feel shamed and humiliated that their chosen discipline has no power to measure the pigeon's motivations and agency.

Rather than envying the "hard sciences," biologists might instead have congratulated themselves for having the courage and curiosity to enter a field of inquiry that was in fact tougher, less tractable, its complexities more difficult. Mix sodium and chlorine and you'll get table salt, every time. No reliable formulas exist for the instincts, urges, love, rage, compassion, fear, trust, and hope of living beings—. You can chase them to the moon and back in an evening; you won't make them in a test tube. Nevertheless, casting the uneasy eye of physics envy over their shoulder, many biologists sought to quicken their rate of discoveries. They focused on easily defined biological problems that benefited from a crisp, professional, white-coated laboratory approach. Focus in biology shifted to the kind of reductionism that had hugely rewarded classical physics and chemistry. DNA's co-discoverer Francis Crick said as much, writing, "The ultimate aim . . . is to explain all biology in terms of physics and chemistry." But some of the biggest-picture questions—the living world's emergent properties—were not amenable to physics-like cleanliness. Too complicated and seemingly of less utility for growing the human enterprise anyway, they largely got sidelined in funding and shrunken in prestige.

Now, if your approach cannot handle the big questions, the likely problem is the approach, not the questions. Wrote Woese, "The most pernicious aspect of the new molecular biology was its reductionist perspective," which "came to permeate biology, completely changing its concept of living systems." Details could have enlarged the big picture; no trade-off was required. But some biologists aggressively demanded that the big picture be ignored. The twentieth-century experimental biologist Lancelot Hogben devoted himself to "the elimination of holistic concepts by the ruthless application of mechanistic logic." In other words, he believed that the power of opening an eye to mechanistic logic was worth blinding the eye that sees the whole. Woese absolutely disagreed, writing, metaphorically, "Molecular biology could read notes in the score, but it couldn't hear the music." He concluded with exasperation, "It is impossible to discuss modern biology without the cacophony of materialistic reductionism."

He was particularly vexed by the way modern biology's magnifying glass has focused almost exclusively on the workings of DNA and molecules inside cells. When I was a graduate student, my university split molecular biology (the mechanistic details) away from ecology (the big picture of living relationships). The two no longer shared a building, or seminars, or much hope of a conversation. "Anyone who would hire an ecologist is out of his mind," railed DNA's notably nasty co-discoverer James Watson, who derisively called Harvard's famed ecologists "stamp collectors."

Woese graphically pressed his point, writing, "Not seeing the forest for the trees (and not caring what a tree was in any case) molecular biology took the only approach open to it: it clear-cut the forest. In other words, it dispensed with all those aspects of biology that it could not comprehend or effectively deal with." He saw two kinds of biological puzzles: easily defined problems of genes and cells, and more difficult inquiry into the complexity of biological origins, living forms, dynamic patterns, and evolutionary trends. In other words: Where have we come from? Why are things as they are? Where are we headed?

Woese wrote scaldingly that a heavy price had been paid in the reductionist scramble for financial grants and social gravitas. This approach to molecular biology isolated the entity we call an "organism" from its environment, stripped it of its history, revoked its citizenship in the evolutionary flow, and dismantled it such that its wholeness—the whole cell, the whole organism, the whole living world—sank out of sight. In university laboratories, in medical research facilities, in classrooms, and on the desks of funding agencies, much of the big picture of the only known living planet slipped from view. "Biology today is little more than an engineering discipline," Woese noted acidly, "a distorted and incomplete reflection of the world."

ALFIE AND HER FAMILY, ON the other hand, offered a beautifully balanced image, and their young ones were growing fast. During the second week of June, owlets of slightly differing sizes peeked out from time to time during daylight, bobbing and waving their heads as they acquired their fix on an entirely new realm. In contrast to Alfie's thoroughgoing tameness and Plus-One's developed tolerance, the nestlings responded to my approach with a measured level of fear. Usually they'd simply withdraw. One responded to me by clacking their bill, a threat owls issue when they feel threatened.

Also new was another phase of parenting. Rather than have the kids move out, *Mom* moved out. Alfie and Plus-One were *both* in the Ivy Tower on the morning of June 12. As if to underscore her renewed sense of independence—and her ability to continue to find ways to surprise me—at about two-thirty in the afternoon I saw Alfie "at the spa," on the ground dust-bathing luxuriously in the sunshine. If you'd asked me whether a screech owl would take a midday dust bath, I'd have said, "I doubt it." I was still learning things that I could learn only from an owl literally at home in my presence.

As day was rolling toward evening, I watched the young chickens file up the ramp into their night coop. I sat outside the studio, almost directly beneath the owls' nest. One of the owlets was sitting in the nest-box entrance. That one soon got knocked off-balance by a sibling and wound up hanging comically upside down from the little landing platform outside the entrance before quickly righting and regaining composure. I had expected the youngsters to remain in the box for several more days. But new things were happening. Fledging might be imminent.

So I decided to stay where I was sitting until something happened or I got too sleepy. Alfie arrived empty-footed and went into the box for a while. When she jumped out, she flew to the edge of the woods and uttered a three-note call that—for lack of a better syllable—I described as three low but clear *hoo*s. I noted this as a "strong contact call." The call says, "I'm here, where *are* you?" A question in the form of a strong interrogative demand for an answer.

From the dimmed woods, Plus-One answered.

I wrote "*hoo.*" But screech owls don't hoot like great horned or barred owls do. The closest screech owls come to *hoo* still sounds a bit whistled, as a human might try to *whistle* a series of short, low *hoo*s. Try it; you'll see what I mean.

To date, I'd known Alfie to use three main calls. She sang the whinny and the tremolo at various volumes when advertising her presence, calling during courtship and when maintaining contact. I'd more recently come to know a long series of low staccato notes, a sort of *ooh-ooh-ooh-ooh-ooh* . . . used during very close contact, usually at the nest. Each *ooh* in that call sounds a little like rubbing your thumb across a balloon. I have never come across a written description of that call, probably because no human would be privy to hearing it unless they were in a relationship with a tame, free-living owl who had a nest just a few feet over their door. She would, for instance, utter, "*Ooh-ooh-ooh-ooh* . . ." from inside the nest if we called up to her or when she seemed to be inviting approach and preening. It seemed her call of bonded intimacy and explicit deep trust. I thought of it as her cuddle call or her "cozy call." When directed at us from inside the nest box, it seemed to underscore what an odd little life she had, split between her intimate confidence in us and her innate competence as a female owl who had acquired a mate, incubated her eggs, and could raise a family. Our worlds overlapped; she, as I liked to say, with a wing in ours, I, with a foot in hers. But what that really meant was that our bond was mutually enriching. A parent and a child neither approach their relationship from the same perspective nor get the same things from it, and neither did Alfie and I. But we both knew we could rely on each other. Our capacities to relate reached out in their ways and intertwined; we were entangled in each other in the most constructive way. Perhaps she understood what this meant more simply—and more fully—than did I.

THE LAST TRICKLES OF THE light of June 12 drained quickly down the western sky. In the enclosing darkness, something hit the metal awning over the studio door, just one giant stride from the nest. I heard nothing further. Then Alfie called from the adjacent tree. Had Alfie landed on the awning? She never had, but she often did things I'd never seen her do.

I heard bill clacking.

Cady showed up and started barking very excitedly. Now the clacking clearly came from the ground.

I went for a flashlight.

I was suddenly looking down at a wad of cotton candy staring up wide-eyed. The first fledger was on the ground! Neither of us had expected to meet quite like this, and the surprise was quite mutual.

Cady was transfixed. Because helpless, flightless birds are part of our family culture, Cady knew what category to place this strange new chick-thing in. She showed intense interest and good manners. "Good *girl*, Cady!" I purred. "*Good* girl." Cady kept her eyes on the owlet while half her body wagged her excitement.

Alfie as I first met her; rescued near death.

Alfie in her first summer.

Alfie in fine new adult plumage.

Left: Alfie in the back-door dogwood. Right: Alfie dozes in her Ivy Tower, as seen from our bedroom window.

Jude, Chula, Patricia, Cady.

"I turned . . . and got an owly kiss."

Top: Plus-One feeds Alfie early in their courtship.

Left: Alfie watches as Patricia walks by the nest box.

Bottom: Plus-One remains vigilant while Alfie, right, is relaxed in our presence.

Top: Alfie's eggs.

Right: All three newly hatched owlets together were no bigger than a mouse their father delivered.

Bottom: The owlets in the nest at seventeen days old.

Plus-One proved himself a highly capable provider when his growing chicks were at their peak need of food.

Top: Plus-One hunting chipmunks at midday.

Right: A hungry youngster greets Plus-One as he delivers a sparrow.

Bottom: Moths were often on the menu, too.

Top: *Alfie and a babe.*

Middle: *Watching the world a couple of nights before fledging.*

Left: *First morning out of the nest, looking up at where they came from.*

Top: A jay knocks a fledger out of a tree on their first morning out of the nest.

Middle: A fledger walk-flutters straight up a trunk.

Bottom: The Hoo say hi.

Alfie sometimes ended a photo session by landing on the lens.

Alfie the successful mother, healthy and free.

I called Patricia. Chula and Jude came running from the house to the studio. Chula immediately started nosing around in the vicinity of the clacking. She abruptly confronted the owlet and jerked her head back. Then Jude came blundering in and, but for my intervention, might have stepped on the little owl. Imagine the owlet's impression of their first minute on the surface of planet Earth: The world consists of dazzle and a herd of dogs!

Alfie was calling nearby. I wondered whether she felt distressed by all the activity or reassured by the presence of those she knew and trusted.

Patricia and I decided the owlet should be off the ground. She picked up the fluff-jacketed cutie, who instantly sank some talons into her arm. I put a towel on the awning for traction, then placed the fledger there.

Within a couple of minutes, the fluffer landed on the ground again. I picked the little adventurer up. A fat ball of a baby. Good parenting.

I returned the owlet to the awning. Alfie landed next to her errant youngster.

I went to cut some green branches to give the fledger some cover on the awning. I heard a rustle and a thud. The owlet seemed to have missed an attempt to land in the tree and was again on the ground. Not good.

I put the fledger on the awning again. And again this impatient explorer leapt, then began hopping on the ground. Put back on the awning yet again, the fledger leapt into the tree and caught a branch.

Alfie again landed right next to her youngster, softly whinnying. The little one seemed content to stay put on the branch. Good.

Patricia wanted to go to bed.

Me, too. But. "I don't want to miss this."

It was ten p.m. A few mosquitoes were patrolling. I sat in the chair beneath the nest, opened my laptop in the dark, and went through the motion-sensing camera's new photos. Several images showed a *midnight* delivery of another chipmunk. Wow, Plus-One was hell on wings.

———

AT NEARLY ELEVEN P.M., I heard strong contact calls.

The little fledger had stayed still for about an hour. I went and put a white mouse on the banister, in the usual spot. I wanted to see if Alfie would directly feed the fledger. She went right into the nest. She made no attempt to feed her wanderer. Around eleven-thirty, one of the parents brought a sparrow into the nest. The fledger had now missed two feedings. Freedom extracts a price.

The young one tried to move along the branch several times, but each time slipped and wound up hanging upside down. I expected a fall. But after thrashing a bit, the youngster self-righted. Between these little mishaps, the fledger spent most of the time looking around, attempting with much head bobbing to bring this bewildering new world into some sensible order. Good luck with that; I've tried.

SHORTLY AFTER MIDNIGHT, THE FLEDGER jumped off that branch and landed—no surprise—on the ground. Feeling vulnerable, the little one crawled under the studio's wooden landing. I returned the youngster to the awning. But our adventurer was going places. In a few minutes a thud alerted me that the babe had again come to earth, this time on the deck. This owlet seemed to understand the idea of "spread your wings," but not yet "learn to fly." No flapping attempted. Thus, no flying achieved.

I wasn't sure what to do. It's not all friendly doggies out here. Dogs go to bed, and then there are cats, raccoons, foxes, opossums, horned owls; night can be deadly for a blundering youngster.

I heard Alfie announcing her return with her high, soft whinny. She acted anxious. She was a new mom who had never before seen a babe out of the nest. Perhaps, as for some human parents, it has never occurred to her that a child would want to leave home. After all, home is the place of Mama and Papa and all the food. Why leave?

This owlet needs a name. I placed Fledj on to the awning yet again. I didn't want to do this all night. But I was caught in this cycle between gravity and salvation. With each return to the awning or the tree, Fledj rescheduled departure within a minute or two. And, wow, this little baby's talons were sharp and their feet owl-strong. Getting stabbed is a little unpleasant. And a bit worrisome. Talons are coated in bacteria. I've seen talon piercings create some nasty infections.

HAZARDS ARE, OF COURSE, A major feature of existence. But, hazards notwithstanding, what stuns me is that the sediment of broken stars and little sparks of time find each other and agree—somehow—to do what it takes such that beings arise and become aware of all the shining stardust gathered around us, that they see and sense. And that we are among those who find it beautiful.

IT WAS NEARLY ONE IN the morning, and I couldn't believe I was still out here. At one point when I put Fledj in the tree and let go, our floppy adventurer hung upside down. Not very dignified. But when Fledj decided to get right side up, achieving the upright position seems to require little effort.

Fledj began walking upward on a slanted branch, while fluttering. That was good and necessary exercise for a bird who, since hatching, had been a babe in a box. This baby's legs were strong and toning up quickly.

I didn't know how much longer I'd be able to stay awake in my chair on this pleasantly eventful June night. I guessed I'd find out.

A FEW MINUTES LATER, I was working to erect a mosquito-mesh sleeping shelter I'd retrieved from the shed. I was making a bit of noise with the fabric and poles, but I wasn't too concerned about bothering Alfie. She and I were so familiar that it seemed nothing I did—from climbing to her nest to accidentally accomplishing a deafening bang—bothered her. But there was another parent involved. I soon heard two sharp notes. I didn't know if this was warning or alarm—or how much difference there might be—but I imagined Plus-One coming with food and, seeing me wrestling with this billowy dark mass, feeling too wary to deliver it to the two youngsters in the nest.

So I abandoned my effort with the sleeping shelter. Enough of a breeze had come up to disperse the few mosquitoes that had been a bother. I put a quilt on the ground, covered myself with a blanket, rested my head on a pillow, and let our owls do their thing for the three remaining hours of night. I slept lightly, half-listening for rustlings in the tree above, for arrivals or departures from the nest.

AT FOUR-FORTY A.M., THE FIRST birdsong sparkled the darkness. As usual, the cardinals' whistles and the robins' flutes came on first. Fledj, having survived the most dangerous night of a bird's life, uttered a scratchy little begging call from a low branch just overhead. Alfie replied with a soft whinny from a few feet away. So my all-night vigil seemed worthwhile. The fat little fledger had not spent the night on the ground; I had. The fledger had not gotten eaten; I'd suffered only modest extracted meals from hungry mosquitoes. A worthy trade, I thought.

The complement of Alfie's brood remained in the box. One was looking out, seeming a bit awestruck. When Alfie tried to go in, her child would not cede the entrance.

Alfie repeatedly landed right next to Fledj, close enough to touch. Fledge kept up a scratchy begging call. But during these concerned check-ins, I didn't see Alfie offer any food to her outbound babe.

Fledj decided to seek altitude with a couple of hops and wing-assisted climbing, finding a protected foothold in the tree's leafy canopy. I hoped that the light of morning would convince our traveler to rest for the duration of the long June day.

Alfie managed to squeeze in with her other two kids. But all the kids cared about was crowding the nest entrance to maintain their vigil of the unprecedented world as daylight flooded this astounding scape of colors and structure, of heights and breadths and the spreading ground below. Bobbing and waving their little heads, absorbing all directions, they endeavored to focus their astonishments.

CAPACITY FOR ASTONISHMENT MAKES A superior being. Radio host Robert Krulwich interviewed two students of biology from the Massachusetts Institute of Technology who were transferring genes from plants into bacteria. He asked, "What does it feel like to make something that's never existed before?"

One student answered, "It just feels like basic engineering."

"Yeah," echoed the other. "We're building stuff."

At the same institution, by contrast, the Nobel-winning physicist Frank Wilczek reflected that he was "wonderstruck" by science.

The wonderstruck expand human knowledge and consider its implications; the builders expand power and seldom consider the consequences.

As with everything, the difference is in the values. And then there are proponents of "transhumanism," who seek to enhance the human condition by permeating humans with technology, enabling one to, say, mentally upload thoughts to a computer. Admittedly, that would save a lot of typing. But whether it enhances humanity depends on what kind of thoughts one is uploading, eh? Thoughts don't improve because you've been impregnated with software and circuitry; they improve if life has inspired you to add some increment of beauty and compassion to the world.

Carl Woese wanted biology to investigate Life's origins and complexities. He asked us to "try to imagine a biology released from the intellectual shackles of mechanism, reductionism, and determinism."

At this point, that's easier to say than to do. But the time may be right to see things differently. The programmer and writer James Somers observed in 2022, "It was easy to imagine that progress in biology was a matter of zooming in further—seeing what parts the parts were made of. But, having seen to the bottom, we've found that reductionism is a dead end."

Carl Woese had understood all this. He wanted to "put the organism back into its environment; connect it again to its evolutionary past; and let us feel that complex flow." What might that be like? DNA is a set of instructions that *cannot* by itself tell you how the world will affect an individual, a species, or an ecosystem in the coming days and generations. For instance, a mother's stress affects how her offspring develop. And whether a mammalian fetus lies next to male or female fetuses has lifelong effects on hormone levels, masculinization or feminization of adult traits, aggressiveness, and so on. Then, of course, there is everything that happens out in the world. Water temperature can affect fishes' rates and timings of growth, maturation, breeding, fertility, and migration. Experiments with certain minnows demonstrated that the water temperature a mother lives in becomes the water temperature in which her offspring grow fastest. Studies in more than sixty species, from bacteria to plants to lizards, show that levels of temperature, humidity, light, and so on experienced by parents affect growth and behavior of their offspring. And, quite surprisingly, wolves infected with a parasite that commonly infects cougars (and house cats) leave the packs of their birth sooner and become pack leaders sooner than do uninfected animals. The interactions between genetic blueprints and the wider world is not just complicated; it's *complex*. Chance happenings create consequences as the flow of life adjusts, finds new channels, and carves new bends—as our little owls were on the threshold of discovering.

But for humans to discover such causes and consequences, the research culture must encourage such explorations where the world meets living beings. Obviously, some of it has; that's how we know about those developmental effects. Much of it hasn't; that's one reason we have such problems.

You cannot search for big answers if you aren't asking big questions. Enormous mysteries remain. We don't yet know enough to even formulate some of the biggest questions. Nigel Goldenfeld, who'd been a close colleague of Woese's, wants science to explore such questions as Why do systems capable of evolving and reproducing exist? How does a planet sustain life? *Why* does life occur? "Remarkably," he notes, "we don't have an idea even in principle of how to address that question."

"Biology's primary job is to teach us," Woese concluded with a seemingly disarming simplicity that veiled so major a call to action. "In that realization lies our hope of learning to live in harmony with our planet."

Will we ask science to teach us into coexistence, as Woese envisioned? Or to continue only to exploit unlocked secrets? Darwin and Wallace did not explain our existence. But how we answer those questions will determine it.

———

THE SUN WAS FREE OF the horizon. Fledj had not moved. Alfie was looking out of the box. Plus-One was in the Ivy Tower. All accounted for. All calm. All safe.

Around seven a.m. the dogs noticed a black cat prowling in our yard, a direct danger to a naïve youngster like Fledj—to say nothing of the carcasses they bring to doorsteps. The mice, chipmunks, and birds that cats kill not only constitute a waste of lives; their deletion helps starve hawks and owls.

At just past nine of the inaugural morning out of the nest box, Fledj got a first lesson in the harshness of the world. Three blue jays went directly at Alfie, who was still looking out of the nest box. She withdrew, and they veered away. They quickly discovered Fledj. The jays were not happy with the appearance of this additional danger to their lives and nestlings. Two of them tried repeatedly to strike. But Fledj was now ensconced within a leafy umbrella canopy. It was difficult for the jays to maneuver for a good blow.

Still, their persistence worked. They made contact, striking hard with their bills, yet failing to knock Fledj to the ground. Fledj turned to better face and threaten the attackers, but flinched when a jay strafed.

Alfie watched intently, feather tufts raised in intensified alarm.

Two of the three original jays departed. This bettered Alfie's odds. When the persisting jay landed a direct strike on Fledj, Alfie launched an attack straight at the jay, coming in with a high, scratchy growl. The jay withdrew to a nearby branch and reconsidered.

Alfie returned to her nest box and her two interior owlets. The jay seized the unguarded moment, smacking Fledj hard. Knocked over and dangling, Fledj barely maintained a grip on the branch.

The jay next menaced the nest box. Alfie withdrew into its protection.

If this wasn't Alfie's decoying tactic to draw the jay away from Fledj, it functioned that way. The jay left Fledj alone after that. And calm returned. Temporarily.

15

✺

Down Town

EVENING, MORNING: ALL REMAINED WELL. PATRICIA AND I set up that little mosquito-mesh tent outside the studio on the afternoon of June 14. The idea was that this night was to be our vigil, as we waited for the next owlet or two to fledge. We went to make dinner.

When we returned before dark to take up our positions with a close view of the nest entrance, I was dismayed to spot all three owlets in nearby trees. We had missed seeing both of the latter two leave the nest!

They looked like little snowmen, like holiday ornaments somehow pranked into the leafy greenness of June, or like sprites, enchantments, ghost spirits. The youngsters were little spheres of fluffiness, each body shaped like a down pillow between parentheses; their heads, otherwise round as a generous scoop of ice cream, bore the subtlest hint of tufts. In countenance they appeared to be old souls, as if envoys from a more original world, yet also new and innocent. Notice their ashy-gray down, so finely edged in darker barring. Bills, toes, even talons matching their ashy gowns. The feathering constituting their facial disks shows palest beige. Their big eyes' large, round pupils are their only dark spots, stark as two charcoals in a bed of snow. I was delighted that each member of this trio of delicates had made it to the verge of new horizons in such good health. It felt wondrous to be amid owls fledging in the presence of my trusting little friend, their mother.

Now I was most curious about how the two newest fledglings got into the trees. Had they actually flown? One of the youngsters soon tried to join a sibling in a maple at the edge of the woods, a gap of perhaps thirty feet. The owlet flapped valiantly through the air but attempted to alight on leaves, which gave way, and the fledgling fluttered to earth. We resisted an impulse to help.

Hopping to the base of a tree, the little fledger *walked* straight up the trunk, wings aflutter all the way. Yesterday I'd thought that any flightless baby owl on the ground would be completely, perhaps fatally, stranded. I was entirely surprised that, literally out of the box, a baby owl comes equipped to invert gravity, operating from the premise that what comes down must go up. Mere moments after emerging from the confinement that had been their world, they have the inclination and muscle tone to walk up tree trunks, immediately tapping into their inner bird and seeking the stars. That felt amazing.

I guess—in retrospect—I needn't have worried so much about Fledj the previous evening. I didn't need to sit vigil and play shepherd through the night, or keep returning the owlet to the awning after each departure. I should have left the choice of desired destinations and the available means of getting there to Fledj. Had I done so, Fledj *might* have made a life-threatening mistake. We *all* do. Living is life-threatening, death-defying—and thrilling.

Sometimes what's most needed is to know when we're not needed. The owlets have begun to free themselves, forcing me to free them from my desire to hold on to and protect them. The security of the nest was time-limited and a dead end; there was no choice. I was forced to accept what is. It was a Buddhist lesson from the owls, who know only their Buddha nature.

The sky was still blue, the clouds still white. But here at ground level where we sat, deep dusk was rising toward night. One lone firefly—the very first of the year—prickled the new shadows of night.

The fledged trio was at the edge of the woods. They absorbed all of Alfie's attention. And ours.

Alfie abruptly went back into the nest box, quickly turned around in there, and looked out, calling softly. Maybe she needed to confirm its sudden emptiness, the starkest gear shift of recent months. Then she streaked across the yard in the gathering darkness and was gone to us. All three fledgers continued uttering scratchy begging calls from the leaf-shadowed woods. But soon all callings quieted.

We had the dogs with us for our intended backyard vigil in the mesh tent. Cady would not settle down or accept the confinement of a zipped-up entrance. She didn't relate to the mesh as a wall—quite sensible of her—and kept trying to push through.

Eventually we came to a negotiated settlement. We would leave the side unzipped. Cady lay directly on the opened flap of screen. Fortunately, the night air quickly chilled enough to still the few mosquitoes. Chula immediately understood that this was a campout and lay on the deck a few feet away. When Jude is outside, he assumes the job of sentinel and bouncer at the edges of the yard, barking at (a) deer, (b) raccoons, (c) cats, (d) opossums, and/or (e) humans in the street. So for the sake of quietude we let him sleep inside the studio, where he had gone to lie down earlier. The tent was adjacent to the studio doorway.

Twice during the night Cady leapt up and ran barking into the ink of darkness, followed by Chula. But to my surprise, both quickly returned. And both came inside the tent, with little fox-sized Cady tucked in just north of our pillows and sixty-pound Chula down by our feet. Restful it wasn't. But the novelty and the cool, breezy beauty of the owled night made it fun.

Restfulness can be overrated, especially if what's keeping you awake are some oscillating atoms of the world's long rhythms, life's whispered promises, and a dream you are living. A good night's sleep has its place, but not while so much is happening.

Turned out, late in the night not much was happening. We managed a few winks. It got chillier through the night and was only fifty-five degrees when we rose. I won't say we woke; I was awake most of the night, listening to occasional chitters of the young and the soft whinny-whistles of the adults, trying to cipher whether there'd been a food drop. In the gathering daylight, the amplifying sound of owl chicks and owl parents and birdsong made me force my sleepy bones from the cushions.

At every moment an eyelash of the world is just rolling out of night. And in that eternal dawn, birds are welcoming first light in a chorus that lasts only a few minutes wherever you happen to wake, but has been going on without interruption for tens of millions of years.

Rachel Carson worried that there might someday come a "silent spring" without songbirds. But she did not imagine that songbirds might not learn to sing because they lacked mentors. An Australian bird called the regent honeyeater is now so rare that many young males never hear adult males from whom to learn the song of their kind. Females refuse the untutored males' garbled advances, accelerating the species' slide into deeper danger. Analogously, young humans cannot speak cogently of Life if untutored in its mysteries and amazements. On his blog, James Somers observed, "I should have loved biology but I found it to be a lifeless recitation of names. . . . In the textbooks, astonishing facts were presented without astonishment. Someone probably told me that every cell in my body has the same DNA. But no one shook me by the shoulders, saying how crazy that was."

College biology majors taught the wonders of a cell in preparation for an industrial career seldom encounter a mentor who speaks to the mystery of why cells even exist, about their profound ancestry, of the beings cells build, or how those beings weave themselves into the world's fabric and create the tapestry. Though their *major* is the study of life, "Half of our first-year students in biology can't name five British birds and 20 percent can't name one," University of Oxford professor Andrew Gosler told BBC News. "When you say to students, 'Did you know that this species has declined 70 percent in the UK?,' it means nothing to them. They say 'Why should I care? I didn't know that bird existed.'"

ACT I. THE SETTING: June's halfway mark.

This beautiful morning opens with Alfie flying around carrying part of a white mouse I'd put out at two a.m. All three owlets are alive and accounted for. For our whole little tribe, a great start to the day. But then—.

Jays and robins soon find the owls. And right away, things get very rough.

In fast-streaking attacks they make contact sharp and hard, smacking one fledger to the ground. The youngster immediately hops to the trunk and walk-flutters up to a branch—only to be slammed off again.

On the ground after this second knockdown, the owlet does not move. I wait a few excruciating minutes, then go to check. The fledger seems somewhere between astonished and stunned. But physically probably uninjured.

Alfie, again in the entrance of the nest box, has her eyes on her downed fledgling. After about five minutes on the ground, this chick starts walk-fluttering up the trunk. Partway up, the owlet gets knocked to the ground yet again, and now Alfie shoots out of her wooden fortress and rushes the jay, who turns the tables and makes a flying lunge at Alfie, causing her to streak back to her box and disappear within its safety.

Again the grounded chick seems hesitant to move.

And now two jays slam a second owlet, partially detaching the fledgling's foothold on this first morning in the new world. Hanging upside down and fluttering vulnerably, the youngster suffers several added smacks, gets knocked loose, and plummets like a falling apple, hitting the ground hard.

Alfie seems startled by the severity of the attacks. But conflicted. The bills of the jays are a danger to her, too, especially her eyes. And these jays of daylight show no hesitancy about using their bills on Alfie.

The just-fallen owlet starts hopping, not back to the tree trunks at the woods' edge but toward the studio, a distance of perhaps twenty feet, during which the little one endures two strikes from a female robin. This second owlet under siege nestles up against the ladder lying on the ground alongside the studio wall.

The first babe who got knocked down has decided yet again to trunk-walk up into the tree. And in a few moments we realize that the one up against the ladder—isn't. That little one has disappeared. We search along the wall, behind the studio, expecting a ball of down to be looking up at us. Nothing. No slyboots cat or flash-snatch Cooper's hawk, certainly no hard-flapping crow, could have pulled a fast one at such close quarters without so much as a scream from the fledger and with none of the dogs noticing. Could they have? But how might a little snowball of a grounded owl have disappeared in the few short moments when we were focused on their bewildered sibling?

We walk around the studio fine-combing the groundcover. I say, "Chula—where's the chickie?" Chula deploys her most intense quick-sniffing method, her nose audibly thumping. I don't *think* the chick could have wriggled under the deck right here. But Chula does. Her sniffing is intense and insistent at one spot. We look with a flashlight. We see nothing, and Chula could as well be sniffing, say, an opossum, tucked way back.

Meanwhile, the fledgling who'd come under the first and most intense aerial bombardments gets knocked to the ground a fourth time. Whenever that owlet tries to make any move, the female robin attacks. When the owlet does nothing, she attacks anyway.

Detecting a short break in the assaults, the long-suffering one on the ground again begins another climb.

And again gets knocked out of the tree, and falls. First few hours in the big world. Wow. Harsh.

Alfie, observing, does not exit the box. In the long, sometimes grim economy of evolution, a mother who loses one chick out of three might yet raise the other two, and breed in years to come. A mother who gets killed is a death sentence for all her chicks. Prudence pays.

To underscore that point, a robin streaks in and tears a feather from Alfie's head.

PATRICIA RETURNS FROM AROUND THE back of the studio with—a baby owl! A great relief. Now all three—. Wait; the one who'd been in a tree overhead—isn't there. We are again missing someone.

Patricia places the owlet she's found onto the ground. Not so simple because the little one is vise-gripping her hand with needled talons. This chick and the one who's been repeatedly knocked down hop to the front of the studio. Together they stop directly under the nest box, which was until a few hours ago their secure redoubt from the cruel vicissitudes that now envelop them.

They are trying to climb the wall.

I place them on the awning above the door, about six feet from the nest box. I know, I know; but I can't think of anything better. The cut branches I'd put there remain for cover, and the towel for footing. But neither little one wants any part of being there. They soon hop into the adjacent tree. Then one goes into an adjacent euonymus bush. Though the fledgling is now only five feet from the ground, this many-branched, densely leafed bush offers secure, cagelike cover. Let the jays and robins try to bother them; they can't.

So at seven a.m. one owlet was in that dense bush, one had managed to get into a good spot in a tree under lush canopy cover. The third was—somewhere.

AN HOUR LATER, A CONVERGENCE. Alfie and the fledger who'd been in the tree canopy move into the euonymus with the other youngster. They huddle up. Alfie is guarding. When would-be attackers approach, she threatens. When attackers withdraw, the mood eases.

Tenderness. Alfie preens one of her babies, who returns the gesture. Their bills gently rake through and nibble feathers around the head, eyes, bill, and neck. A palpable affection pervades their mutual attentions.

Alfie leaves her chicks a little after nine a.m. The protective vacuum left by her departure seems to make both youngsters uneasy. One assesses a move into the adjacent tree. A blue jay is skulking there. The blue jay utters the sharp call that summons an accomplice. They're ready. The appearance of two jays affects the owlet's decision. The fledgling reconsiders the move up and out, instead going deeper into the bush's protective branches. Having already learned of an ancestral enemy, the young owls seem to be making strategic choices based on this understanding.

Alfie is now uttering threats from the bunker of her nest-box entrance.

The blue jays exit the stage.

End of Act I.

AT THIS AGE, THE ONLY vocalization the owlets utter is a descending rattling screech. They drone this call with roughly the duration and cadence of Alfie's whinnies, but the timbre and tone are very different. Both these calls—juveniles' and adults'—mainly say, "I'm here." But the youngsters imply, "so feed me."

As holding hands is reassurance by touch, Alfie's whinny often functions as reassurance by sound. Loud whinnies (and shouted contact calls) are inquiries uttered when the caller believes the intended recipient is far away: "Where are you?" The soft whinny is murmured when the answer is quite obviously, "I'm right here, and you're right there; for now we're together and I acknowledge your presence."

Context modulates the meaning of the calls, within the range of meaningful things in an owl's life. "I'm here—and I don't want to be alone." "I'm here—and I'd like food." "I'm here—where are you?" "I'm here, too—be reassured. " They may have only a few things to say to each other. But when they say it, the message is clear.

USE YOUR WORDS. I'LL USE mine. In 2007, the Oxford Junior Dictionary began dropping words such as "heron," "leopard," and "oyster." Not being spoken enough, they said. Added were words like "bandwidth" and "chatroom." Famous authors wrote an impassioned letter urging that the language of the natural be retained. They opined that a dictionary "should help shape children's understanding of the world, not just mirror its trends." A concerned public petitioned likewise, to no avail. "Almond," "blackberry," and "clover" were out in favor of "analogue," "block graph," and "celebrity."

Oxford University Press replied that older versions of their children's dictionaries included many flowers "because many children lived in semi-rural environments and saw the seasons." "Hamster," "herring," "kingfisher," "lark," "lobster," "magpie," "minnow," "mussel," "newt," "otter," "ox," "panther"—all deleted. Author Robert Macfarlane stated the obvious problem: We cannot know what we cannot name; we cannot care about what we do not know. As we erode the natural, we lose our desire to know, and then we forget how to remember.

THE MISSING OWLET REMAINS MISSING. We worry all day.

At the edge of the yard, Jude begins barking. Cady joins him. Chula stands silently, focused intently. The black cat we have seen before is stalking chipmunks in the woods only about eighty feet from where the little owls were hopping around on the ground this morning. The cats, like the deer who come and go, are shrewd observers. They well know the limit line of the dogs' movements. The dogs were trained with a buried electric perimeter wire and collars that deliver warning beeps and then may deliver a mild shock. I can personally attest that the shocks are unpleasant; I tried the device on myself. After one or two such experiences, the beeping alone becomes sufficient. The dogs quickly learn the whole perimeter. Then even without the collars—which we seldom put on them—the dogs don't cross the property line, not even to chase cats.

The cat, confident that these dogs will not pursue, utterly ignores them. The cat remains so focused on hunting that my own sneaky approach goes undetected until I'm close and the cat startles. "That's right, Cat—and don't come back!"

Alfie rests in a nearby pine. A meteoric blue jay from nowhere hits her hard enough to knock her from her perch. I wince as she tumbles downward a few rungs in the branches until she catches herself. No mystery why she's been reluctant to tangle with them in daylight— they're dangerous.

Had she come out from the cover of the nest box to search for her lost fledgling? I'm not sure an owl thinks this way, or could afford to. But her visit with her other two chicks in the euonymus bush this morning shows that there are felt emotions at work here.

What felt emotions are at work in us? Does what we feel emotionally enhance or impede our rational thinking? We have created generations "without any imperative to know about the rest of the living world," writes Melanie Challenger. Indeed, many of us cannot see the stars in our washed-out skies; most people scarcely notice the moon's cycles. Like our pets at their bowls, most of us know nothing of where our food and water come from. We know less than they about where our waste goes, little of where our pipes drain, where our garbage ends up, how and where our electricity and combustible energy is generated. We know, in other words, little about ourselves, less about our context. Each generation, more remote from the sources of our lives, tutors less knowledge forward. The learnings and teachings built on contact with wild things and natural rhythms over thousands of years of human experience and tradition are breaking up like warming shelves of polar ice. With those bergs of knowledge dissolve the care, respect, and empathy that made humans social animals in strongly bound communities. Asks Challenger, "What kind of creature are we who know so much, yet value so little?"

We're the kind we have chosen to be. Operating in the world we have chosen to see. Self-deprived of our desire to know, we rob from ourselves the motivation to care.

NEARING NOON, I FOLLOWED A minor racket of scolding chickadees to a cedar adjacent to the studio. I saw Alfie and one fledger lying next to each other along a tree limb, relaxed and dozing. Until a jay arrived.

Plus-One did not come to defend his wife and children. They could have used some help. He was still in the Tower on the far side of the house. He might not yet have known that the youngsters were out of their nest, and that there was trouble.

And so the fledged owlets endured their first morning out. The

world can hurt, can be a real killer. But these adorable balls of fluff—
if luck favors them—will come to rule the night so superbly that all
the small furred and feathered become defenseless targets for their
silent pluckings. Each time our sun grazes the horizon on either end
of the Earth, the tunings of fortune and the tables of favor turn a
one-eighty.

16

⫸

Out and About

AT SEVEN P.M. ON THIS FIRST DAY THAT ALL THREE OWL-
ets were out of the nest, we resumed the search for the lost owlet. It
was difficult to keep track of all the little owls around this place—
but Patricia proved astute at finding them. Patricia heard and saw an
agitated robin and followed the calls into the edge of the woods. She
soon summoned me.

The owlet was only about twenty feet from where Patricia had
found the other lost fledgling this morning. After hiding all day, this
one had emerged in the softening evening light to seek some altitude.
Patricia had located the little one about five feet off the ground in a
spindly sapling, feet gripping the trunk, a bit sideways, legs spread
apart. The selected sapling offered little cover, little height, little
safety; and the worked-up robin had blown what scant secrecy the
fledger had. We did not hesitate to pluck this baby for relocation to a
safer place.

The fluffy foundling promptly fell asleep in the safest place they'd
been all day: Patricia's arms. We went toward the euonymus bush to
position this babe alongside one of the siblings there. Patricia walked
slowly, not wanting to wake her bundle—and to tell the whole truth,

she was in no hurry to let go of the enchanting snowy baby. We sat for a few minutes, savoring this precious creature, the relief we felt in the moment's safety, and all the terrible beauties of the day's events. I tried hard to fully fathom that the morning's attacks and detached feathers were only the latest skirmish in a conflict these species have been waging for millions of springtime mornings since some time in the Miocene. Despite the planet's transformations, that deep and direct history was part of this day. With luck—which they will need—their squabbles might continue for perhaps another fifty million seasons of nest building and chick raising.

Taking the fledgling gently from Patricia and reaching up to the top of the bush, I had to release my hands very slowly, making sure the babe got a grip, because for all appearances this newbie remained asleep with the exhaustions of a tough first day.

Alfie remained with the third, marginally larger sibling where they'd been resting most of the day, in the cedar next to the studio. The lowering sun now stirred them into a little relaxed preening.

I would again spend the night out, minus restless dogs—and with a better pillow. Patricia demurred. I went into the house to get a heavier shirt. When I returned, the euonymus was empty of owls. I looked all through the bush's dense and leafy branches, only to suddenly notice that an owlet was on top of my screen tent, watching me with interest before hopping back into the bush.

The second little one abruptly launched from the adjacent tree and, in an impressive feat of early aviation, flapped heavily across the very short gap to the studio cedar.

So two of the fluffy fledgling owls were in the studio cedar, one in the euonymus bush. Alfie was—. Where did she just go?

AMPLE LIGHT REMAINED WHILE THE sun sank. Plus-One landed between two of his fledglings in the dogwood adjacent to the nest box. Alfie and the third youngster stood in the studio cedar. It appeared to me that Plus-One was just now realizing that during the night two young had fledged.

Patricia and I wanted to name each fledger. But we couldn't tell the three apart. So, how about a group name for the trio? I had a few ideas. But Patricia's suggestion was best: the Hoo.

The Hoo showed a strong proclivity to remain together, to affiliate. When two were in the white pine, standing on the same branch, and one was in an adjacent crab apple ten feet from the other two, that proximity represented anything but random wandering. Their homing instinct kept them close to home, and they acted magnetic with each other. They were sticky.

Graceful, they were not. Their hops remained awkward. When moving to another branch, they often barely acquired—or missed— their intended target. If they missed, they'd either flutter to the ground or catch a branch and right themselves. If they fell to the ground, they'd still climb straight up a trunk, but they were also realizing that crossing distances involved flapping their interesting upper limbs. In a way, they were finding their inner owl.

WE CONTAIN MULTITUDES, SAID WALT Whitman. Perhaps we are all populated by a small menagerie of characters waiting to be found or demanding to be fed. Some are benign, and some, perhaps, are mayhem makers. Which of those characters dominate a culture depends on which ones the people of a culture have chosen to feed.

Most of us live a story we were taught, a story we've learned to tell ourselves. We were taught that humans exist above and in opposition to other creatures and to a natural world that we should forcibly subdue. It's an ancient story whose deepest cultural origins we have largely forgotten. But it's the story we recite, the play in which we star, and the legacy we pass along. Without remembering why.

TOWARD DAYLIGHT'S END ON THE Battle of June 15, robins, joined by jays, launched another offensive. All three owlets had accumulated themselves within a ten-foot radius in maple branches at the edge of the woods. The owlets' tight mutual proximity seemed to inhibit the attackers. Though highly agitated, the jays and robins abstained from physical contact. They'd shown no such hesitation during the morning's persistent violence. But at that time the chicks had just left the nest and were widely separated. Perhaps, too, the low light was making the songbirds wary. The tables would soon turn in favor of owls. And sure enough, lengthening shadows overruled the songbirds' objections, ending their protests.

In the last draining light, the black cat we'd seen a couple of times shadowed directly over the area where the two owlets had been temporarily lost to us on their first fraught morning. A clear and present danger to any small creature on the ground.

Plus-One arrived. He uttered what I'd termed the strong contact call: *"Ow. Ow. Ow."* He and the three chicks gathered in maples by the raccoon tree. Alfie answered from the back-door dogwood. Vocal attendance taken, they'd accounted for one another. With all owls present, I relaxed.

The cardinals and mockingbirds quieted, and the robins sang vespers before settling nearby into their hidden night roosts. Harassed by day, the owls got enveloped into their prime hours.

In the gathering dusk, one of the fledglings fluttered fifty feet or so across the gap between the woods' edge and the big central maple. Mom was there. The owlet missed the targeted branch, caught themself, and began calling and climbing upward along the trunk toward Alfie. This counted as flying. Not well. But they'd discovered that as leaving the nest got them a new earth, wings could let them access new heavens.

Plus-One disappeared briefly and returned dangling a wild-caught white-footed mouse.

AFTER THEIR DUSK FLURRIES, ALL begging stopped. From the unseen adult owls I continued hearing occasional "strong contact calls." One thing was certain: Alfie was not hanging around us bumming food. A stark contrast from her maiden winter. A few months ago, whenever we opened a door in the dark or when we came home late—she'd be there. But now she was with her family.

I welcomed that development. I needed to be less important in her life. I did not want to feed her daily for, say, the next fifteen years. Ideally she'd be able to live a truly wild life yet choose to visit regularly with us. I wanted her to continue to consider me an option—because I enjoyed her thoroughly and learned from her constantly—but not a necessity.

Still those lingering questions remained: Could she hunt with sufficient skill and success to be independent of us year-round? Had her unnatural upbringing, the developmental problem that delayed her ability to fly—and my decision to hold her for those months of that first full year—ruined her ability to truly become wild? Had we simply created a free-living dependent? Seeing her go to the ground for a moth had counted for something. But until and unless I saw her catching major meals—with fur or feathers—I just wouldn't be sure.

Then again, the more I thought about it, the less it mattered. The situation was: Our little rescue was free-living. She'd survived the winter and stuck around. She'd found a mate. She'd courted, bred, laid three eggs, lost none of them, and fledged three chicks. Together we'd helped put these new owls into the immediate future of the world. And they'd helped save my psyche in this otherwise disorienting year. Pretty darn good to this point.

We are taught to "pursue happiness" as though happiness is a state to be attained, a plateau, like a promotion. Patricia long ago taught me that even temporary happiness is authentic. Perhaps all happiness is temporary. Perhaps, despite everything and regardless of what might happen next, we'd achieved here during this difficult year a little bit of heaven on Earth.

"AND I SAW A NEW heaven and a new earth: for the first heaven and the first earth were passed away; and there was no more sea." So says the New Testament's Revelation 21:1. In that new world, "there shall be no more death, neither sorrow, nor crying, neither shall there be any more pain." Many Christian preachers—particularly evangelicals—read Revelation 21 as saying that the world's depletion will coincide with the replacement of this faulty world by a new and very different world wherein will exist no suffering. Many counsel that not only may humans use the Earth, but they may in good faith use it up. They follow Peter's admonishment that the faithful should be "wait-

ing for and hastening the coming of the day of God." It's the hastening that must concern us. This exhortation to help speed the world's
destruction: What could constitute a more pathological thought? The
combination of its dissociation from reality and its recklessness has
helped bring it within sight of being achievable. The man who has
been called "the most influential evangelical anti-environmentalist
in the United States," Calvin Beisner, told an interviewer in 2016
that people should be concerned with the fate of their eternal souls,
not about the state of this merely temporary planet—as though it's
somehow necessary to choose. Many of us are enrolled at birth in a
lifelong program based on the idea that: *I am more important than
the world itself.* Could any thought be more self-serving? Could any
belief license a more abusive relationship with the world? Several hundred million people live by this perspective. And, thus, perpetuate it.
Seeking to hasten the passing of "the first earth" is surely dualism's
ultimate psychosis.

"OW. OW. OW," PLUS-ONE CALLED from the direction of the
driveway cedars.

"*Ow. Ow. Ow,*" Alfie answered from the vicinity of the studio,
where she was keeping an eye on the Hoo.

Shadows grew in the woods like dark water rising. A strong contact call came from the cherry tree in the yard. Alfie had moved. A
response from deeper in the woods. The adults were staying in contact
with one another.

Alfie and Plus-One traded contact calls a couple of times a minute. Any call was usually answered within a few seconds. Then a
pause, then someone gave another strong contact call. Back and forth.
Keeping tabs as they advanced their night.

The leafy canopy blackened against the darkened sky. The curtain
was closing on the light accessible to human eyes.

"*Ow. Ow. Ow.*"

"*Ow. Ow. Ow.*"

Alfie's form appeared. No whinnying at me, no begging to me. But
not relaxed. Alfie was on high alert. Keeping close track of the kids?

Hunting? On guard for dangers? She flew into the woods, beyond my ken. Whatever she was up to, she was in command of herself.

Two young ones began rattling their screechy calls from the central maple.

One of the adults flew into a heavily leafed part of the tree, possibly delivering food.

"*Ow. Ow. Ow.*"

"*Ow. Ow. Ow.*"

Ten p.m.

I crawled into the mosquito-mesh tent. Then for hours the most noticeable thing was: silence. Only one or two of the strong contact calls all night long. No chittering from the Hoo. And so the rollicking, momentous events of June 15 blended into something new, as all nights do.

End of Act II.

SEEING OURSELVES AS SEPARATE FROM and superior to other species has been called "a good candidate for the originating idea of Western thought. And . . . a good candidate for the worst." Summing up several thousand years of thinking, in 2021 philosopher Crispin Sartwell wrote, "It's astonishing how relentlessly Western philosophy has strained to prove we are not squirrels."

Sartwell elaborated: "The devaluation of animals and disconnection of us from them reflect a deeper devaluation of the material universe in general. In this scheme of things, we owe nature nothing; it is to yield us everything. This is the ideology of species annihilation and environmental destruction."

Like shaking off a bad hangover, he offers, "I'd like to publicly identify this dualistic view as a disaster . . . I don't feel myself to be a logic program running on an animal body; I'd like to consider myself a lot more integrated than that. And I'd like to repudiate every political and environmental conclusion ever drawn by our supposed transcendence of the order of nature. I don't see how we could cease to be mammals and remain ourselves."

Well, right; we are what we are. As for being a logic program on an animal platform, perhaps that might be an improvement. As Herman Melville so resonantly penned, "There is no folly of the beasts of the earth which is not infinitely outdone by the madness of men."

Owls and other non-human animals know things, as Ben Kilham has said, while we believe things. We are the only animal capable of absorbing centuries of illogic; of perpetuating delusional thinking; and of acting out fervently and violently those things for which there is no evidence, or that evidence, with blinding incandescence, refutes. For millennia the main project of Western thought has been to labor to be who we are not, to loathe our natural selves, to designate and denigrate all "others," and to disregard our world.

Plato's idealized abstractions valued the mind above matter, made disembodiment divine, and injected an estranged revulsion about flesh and physical existence. Abrahamic scribes incorporated Plato's dueling duality, making dissociation between body and soul, between human and the world, matters of faith. In this desiccated ground, Westerners nursed the seeds of their dogmas. Modernity's faithful philosopher Descartes wiped spirit away from all creatures and body away from all mind, offering a world devalued for the secular as well as the sanctified. He and Bacon gave us a mechanical world to pull apart. Thus through the mural of modernity shows the pentimento of Plato, the Roman Catholic Church, and the Industrial and Scientific Revolutions' congenital estrangements and aggressions. That the world spins deconsecrated and disrespected is a religious stance; the devaluation of existence is a value judgment. On the foundational faith that the world is inferior to humans, Europeans erected their castles and cathedrals and constructed their intellectual and engineering revolutions. Plato pushed a psychedelic trip. We took a fatal overdose. Yale Divinity School theologian Willie Jennings has written, "An attitude of separation is reflected in all Western education, which is built on the idea that the world is . . . an object that doesn't interact with our psychological or spiritual lives." The tragedy is: dualism is just an idea. Dualism is "a metaphor based on deception," writes Tyson Yunkaporta, "and in an Aboriginal worldview this is how curses work. You take part of a system . . . then you sing a false pattern into the whole. The curse is a deception made real."

EARTH CONTINUED SHRIEKING TOWARD THE solstice of our orbit, due a few rotations hence. Meanwhile, our planet again spun the sun's streaming photons into view. More prosaically stated: it was June 16, four-fifteen a.m., and I needed a mouse. As the first robin tuned up I rose, fetched the mouse, and placed it as usual on the—. I had hardly touched the banister when a blur named Alfie silently snatched the meal and ghosted.

In the crystal stillness, through the just-lightening sky, an owl's silhouette traveled the gap between the central maple and the woods' edge. I heard the briefest of tremolos, followed by a softer, velvety cadenza—*"Ow ow ow ow ow . . ."*—of about twenty notes.

At ten to five, although it was difficult to hear through the robins' chorus, I detected the youngsters' low, growly voices. It was quite as if they, too, were just waking up. Alfie called from the woods' edge. Robins descended to the ground and began foraging. A hop, a tilt of the head while listening; another hop, and so on. Cardinals were whistling so emphatically, they sounded as if they just wanted to celebrate another day of living, another day of life. Their time—and ours, they reminded us—had come round again. And what could be better?

Alfie, now in the white pine, issued a whinny about every ten seconds. She was monitoring one owlet, who was hopping from branch to branch toward her while uttering growly calls. Alfie flew closer to her young one, who turned toward her. They were vocalizing much more—now that it was getting light—than they had all night.

What happened to "nocturnal"? I'd surmised that the early and late ends of daylight were social, for taking attendance, for greeting, for convening. Night, I also surmised, was used by the adults for watchful, patient still-hunting; listening, changing position; scanning and listening again; flying deeper into the woods or over to the wetland or across adjacent yards. I imagined them staking out neighbors' bird feeders and picking off mice who came rummaging around the ground for seeds dropped during daylight. But that was indeed imagined. Their actual activity pattern was perplexing. I always thought that screech owls are dozy by day, nosy all night. But their lives play a more complex rhythm. They were all more active in the brief gloamings around sundown and daybreak than in the middle bulge of night, more "crepuscular" than nocturnal. In the central stretch of night, their activity seemed to soften, just as many songbirds relax during midday.

Plus-One landed next to Alfie.

One of the little growlers jumped into the leafy canopy of the crab apple, fluttering mightily to get a good grip on things.

Acting very much the proud and protective father, Plus-One buzzed me, clacking—twice.

A mockingbird approached them, setting a hostile tone. *"Chuk! Chuk!"*

Plus-One moved into the tree currently hosting two of his fluffy youngsters. The young ones walked along a branch toward him until they were almost touching.

A robin joined the mockingbird.

Alfie moved in and called sharply, *"Ow. Ow. Ow!"*

Plus-One called out a strong *"Ow. Ow. Ow."*

I had the impression that with the whole family in sight, these strong calls were telling the third fledger to come close.

The third fledger left the foliage and moved out onto a sparse branch, endeavoring toward siblings and father while uttering the growled call. But this owlet was fluttering awkwardly, calling too much attention while remaining too exposed.

Alfie began whinnying.

A streaking robin struck the fluttering fledger, who managed to hang on to the branch.

Alfie called sharply, *"Ow. Ow. Ow!"*

The fluttering fledger was getting more and more exposed. A catbird and a pair of orioles arrived. But the presence of both adult owls together may have dampened their enthusiasm for pressing hostilities. They soon left.

The growling flutterer gained the studio cedar. Better cover, better protection. Mom arrived. The two other fledglings sidled alongside their father in a young maple.

The light stayed soft-filtered through tree trunks, the sun not yet over the forest canopy. High above, gulls glowing gold flew through the slant of early morning. The Hoo were safe in parental presence as Alfie and Plus-One whispered their softest whinnies to one another.

Throughout the day, scoldings by blue jays and robins erupted sporadically. At dusk, an agitated mockingbird joined an upset catbird. But that was all.

Yesterday was a morning of violent surprise. Today, far less so. The attacks would never again be as intense or physical as that first morning of all three owlets' new and delicate freedom.

DANGER. VIOLENCE. THE WORLD CAN seem cruel. But it has its balances. Humans can be cruel, but some had long balked at heartlessness toward our fellow beings. Francis of Assisi (1181–1226) is reputed to have said, "If you have men who will exclude any of God's creatures from the shelter of compassion and pity, you will have men who will deal likewise with their fellow men." In the 1700s, Jean-Jacques Rousseau disputed Thomas Hobbes and also elevated the natural world in his *Confessions*, designed explicitly to counter Augustine's loathsomeness. Two centuries after Descartes told us that non-human animals are thoughtless machines, Charles Darwin jotted this searing note, as if feeling a need to dissent directly: "Animals, whom we have made our slaves, we do not like to consider our equal." Darwin observed that the difference between humans and other animals is one of degree, not of kind. He and Alfred Russel Wallace showed their fellow Westerners that all life is one. Yet the churches insisted, *No no no; it's all been put here for us to take and break*. Studies of DNA have confirmed Darwin's and Wallace's insights about relatedness. Yet millions insist on estrangement from the family of Life, unaware that they are Plato's disciples. Plato and likeminded theologians and philosophers set the stage for nearly unbounded abuses. On this stage over many centuries have danced a veritable carnival of apologists in a multimedia parade of brutality.

The thinking of many sounder, saner ancient Greeks, such as the insightful Anaximander, the humble Socrates, the worldly Aristotle, and the incisive Lucretius, could have oriented humanity to step along any of several better-grounded ways. We could have traveled a very different path.

In fact, the world did travel different paths. Indigenous peoples everywhere and traditional Asian belief systems had long venerated the world, supporting stability through attention to connectedness and balances. They sought great wisdom. The West sought great power. But power in the hands of the unwise is danger.

AS SONGBIRDS VOICE A DAWN chorus and then quiet down, owls seem to have their own "dawn" chorus. But their dawn is our dusk.

At a little after nine p.m., Alfie and Plus-One began strong-calling about twice a minute. *"Ow. Ow. Ow."*

Sometimes a minute passed in silence. *"Ow. Ow. Ow."*

Sometimes less time passed. *"Ow. Ow. Ow."*

Back and forth. *"Ow. Ow. Ow."*

And then I heard something new: one *much* louder *"OW!"* A sharp-edged note, it seemed designed to pierce summer's sound-dampening foliage and night noise. I jotted it as an *"emphatic* contact declaration."

The Hoo had been very fidgety. But I continued to be surprised by how very crepuscular a fidget it was. Now they'd already gone silent. No longer moving around, not doing much of anything.

I got into my mosquito tent, settling in for another night of . . . I wasn't sure what. In the darkest hours, strong contact calls—and the new "emphatic declaration"—occasionally punctuated the prevailing quiet. Many lives went on around me, as usual, inhabiting the neighboring mystery beyond the limits of my civil senses and my all-too-human mind.

17

❖

All Together Now

PART OF THE BEAUTY OF TRYING TO FOLLOW THE MOVE-
ments of silent birds in the dark was in the mystery. And part of the
challenge was in the difficulty. But all of the frustration was in the
impossibility of following them well, of really keeping track of what
they were doing.

At around four-thirty a.m.—it was now June 17—I heard an
adult whinnying the dawn song. I began hearing softer calls too, and
youngsters begging. Soon I could make out all five members of Team
Alfie and the Hoo, sitting together.

At five a.m. I tossed some food to Alfie. She swooped it off the
grass and flew it to the edge of the woods.

For the first time now, I was watching Alfie feed one of her youngsters. She tore pieces from the small carcass in her grasp and offered
those pieces so gently she seemed tentative. The owlet delicately took
each morsel from her beak tip.

After feeding this chick, Alfie flies to another fledger. She tears off
a piece. Offers it. Youngster takes. Youngster swallows.

In many bird species, parents often appear to preferentially feed the most vigorous and competitive chicks. The smaller, weaker chicks, who most need food, can get the least, fall behind, and starve.

And yet here I was watching Alfie moving from one chick to another, apportioning the single item of food in her grasp. It seemed— it could only seem—like a sense of fairness, of indulgence. How did these impulses arise in her? The architecture of instincts emerging and behaviors converging so flexibly with the continually changing situation blew me away.

Eventually the third chick approaches. They all have a healthy appetite, but they're not famished. Not fighting for food. Alfie and Plus-One have seen to it that they've remained well fed. Alfie always seemed a bit of a magician, but the trick of making this mouse disappear took her about twenty-five minutes.

Alfie settled herself into a small maple alongside the old raccoon-den tree. But moments later, she hopped down low. She and I were now eye to eye. Alfie turned her gaze directly to me, briefly. Then she began scanning the ground.

Her attention got disrupted when house wrens found the young owls and started calling them names. Alfie flew up into leafy obscurity and began whinnying. Plus-One answered from nearby canopy shadows. This close-knit family knew who they were by who they belonged with. Finding each other posed no trouble at all. All three chicks converged. Alfie returned to them carrying a fat caterpillar. The scolding wrens dispersed. One owlet took the caterpillar.

At this moment all round the northern globe, the rite of spring was playing out through woodlands, suburbs, and every wild enough place where life faced the challenges and triumphs of its freedoms. Mother owls and uncountable others feeding their offspring were busied in the prosaic and profound transfer of life from one generation to the next. By the end of the day, billions of birds would be feeding billions of young ones. To the degree that they succeeded in their work, the world would be preserved for at least one more generation.

Alfie began gently preening one of her other babes. And so, in filtered light in the moist air of June, under the shadowy forest canopy, I ended my morning with Alfie, Plus-One, and the Hoo.

✦

AT SUNDOWN, ALFIE AND ALL three owlets remained where I'd left them this morning. The youngsters were making short hops, branch to branch. If they didn't like where they landed, they walked up the trunk toward a spot they preferred.

Alfie flew across the yard toward the driveway, where she whinnied softly, apparently trying to locate her mate. She quickly returned to her owlets.

"*Ow. Ow. Ow,*" came from the woods.

Alfie replied, "*Ow. Ow. Ow.*"

The fledgers had not yet moved more than about a hundred feet from their nest. Thirty or forty feet above the ground they sat; they preened, waited for their parents, and begged and begged.

Plus-One arrived silently.

The adults began zooming back and forth through the tree canopies. It seemed they were catching moths and beetles off the trunks.

Darkness closed in. Every now and then one of the adults uttered a strong contact call or the loud, emphatic *OW!* It seemed that if the owls believed in anything, they believed in the importance of being together.

ALL HUMAN BELIEFS HAVE HAD their weaknesses and unhelpful superstitions. But those of the West created history's most sanctity-subtracting culture. Separation and estrangement remain the original sins of the Western view of nature, and of peoples. That's how we live.

Indigenous people plan for future generations. For land-based peoples, for rainforests and reefs, for all life-forms in need of room to live and for descendants near and distant, the Western worldview is an eraser of futures.

Worldview is the West's most consequential high-volume export. Western views dominate the globe now, not because they are an improvement over the insights and intuitions of land-based peoples and other thinkers but because Europeans ruthlessly colonized and monetized the world to feed the West's imbalances, crushing Indigenous peoples of the Americas, Australia, Africa, much of South Asia, and the world's oceanic islands.

Countries with the ability to resist the pressures of exploitation tended to adopt the Western approach in a defensive "if you can't beat 'em, join 'em" strategy. Mao's Cultural Revolution turned China against its own wisdom traditions, blaming Confucius's focus on family and community for causing the country's backwardness. Ironically, Mao's Communist reforms eventually helped propel China into the current globally Westernized economy.

Confucian scholar Tu Weiming has written that Western ideology "is now fully embraced as the unquestioned rationale for development in East Asia." Tu sees in Western ideology "aggressive anthropocentrism . . . the conspicuous absence of community . . . and the disintegration of human togetherness at all levels from family to the nation." He says that Western "willingness to tolerate inequality, and the faith in the salvific power of self-interest . . . have greatly poisoned the good well of progress."

The originating traditions of Asia and Indigenous cultures worldwide leaned decidedly into a world of natural harmonies, dynamic balances, and mingling spirits. They tended to perceive humans along with other living beings as enmeshed in the same cycles. Disenchantment of the world, disenchantment *with* the world—that is Western.

Three griffins of apocalypse—the extinction crisis, the climate crisis, and the toxics crisis—flow from this self-inflicted spiritual impoverishment, with its paradoxically faith-based core. With our sheer numbers on the accelerator, the results are, to say it generously, mixed. To speak plainly, it's a catastrophe.

◆

I WAS CHILLY ALL NIGHT and rested poorly. Birds had been singing for upwards of half an hour on June 18 when I rose at a time that had come to feel shamefully late, about four-fifty a.m.

"Ow. Ow. Ow." Alfie seemed to direct her strong contact call at me, asking, "Where's my morning supper?"

To make the point, she planed down onto the grass where *yesterday* I'd thrown her meal. Was this her businesslike way of reminding me that my job was to help raise her youngsters? She flew back to the fence. Feeling pressure to comply, I tossed a defrosted mouse. But the way it landed, it was partly hidden by a leaf.

Alfie immediately came in, low and quick. She landed in the grass but couldn't find her food. She was looking, looking. She returned to the fence, and I moved her meal. She zoomed right for it and took it directly up into the trees. From where I'd left them last evening, the unseen owlets erupted with raspy voices from a younger planet.

Alfie began pulling off pieces and gently offering them to one eager youngster. The other two did not crowd. They seemed surprisingly polite. They were probably already well fed.

Alfie flew to a nearby branch to feed another kid. Again she was moving deliberately to feed her different young ones in turn.

The third fledger came to Alfie's branch but didn't want any of the food. Merely a social visit with Mama? Two feet from Alfie this owlet sat, a fluffy Buddha. Alfie still had food to give. The youngsters were—done. Sated. Stuffed. But do young birds ever stay full for long?

When I studied terns, some years brought to these seabirds abundant fish and prosperous nesting throughout their colonies on the beaches; other years brought hunger. By the middle of a food-sparse nesting season, all around me lay beautiful carcasses of tiny baby birds who'd starved. So I've carried the deep impression that food can exert lethal limits on birds who must hunt, that life can be harsh.

But Alfie and Plus-One's good-fortune family were not facing famished chicks competing for morsels. Plus-One was a fantastic hunter, Alfie was doing her share, and I was Alfie's patron and patsy. So Alfie's final feeding of her young ones before their daytime bedtime was more like her saying, "Eat your peas."

Some part of an hour unwound before Alfie finally distributed the last of the mouse by handing the hindquarters to one of her over-fed children, who chugged it down until the tail slowly vanished like a pink snake slithering down a hole.

Soon, about twenty-five feet off the ground, they packed onto a branch within ten inches of each other. A branchful of fluffy matry-oshka dolls. Alfie preened one of her babes. One of the fledgers toyed with a leaf, grasping it in a foot while tearing at it with their beak. Another gripped the tip of a splintered branch with both feet, twist-ing and biting pieces from it like a puppy, as if they'd just completed a great hunt and a triumphal catch. Watching, you might have thought they were famished. But they'd just demonstrated that they were full. They were playing, toning muscles, practicing their 3Ms—the moves, manipulations, and maneuvers that would help maintain them. This young time of plentiful provision was the right and crucial period for building the skills they would need when true hunger ate at them. As it surely would. For now everyone seemed settled in for the day in leafy young maples around the old raccoon tree.

Except—. A couple of hours later, Alfie was in the Ivy Tower. Why such an abrupt and isolating move? I hoped everything was still okay with her kids and mate. It takes but a moment for a Cooper's hawk to create the terrible arithmetic of minus one. Yet as usual, my worrying mind was overwrought; the Hoo were fine. They'd hardly moved. So I had a fresh question: Did Alfie's presence in the Tower, her departure from her family this morning, indicate yet another phase in the cycle, another shift of the gearing? Later in the afternoon when I checked on Alfie, Plus-One was *also* in the Tower. So it would *seem* that a new phase had begun. My human thinking was inclined to impose categories. But owls don't live by a rigid rule book. They're freer than that. I avoided jumping to conclusions, made a note, and just kept my eye on developments.

Of course, whatever my fear of Cooper's hawks, owls themselves hunt the food they and their babies need. It can be difficult to con-template them as killers. Yet on the planet where plants make and ani-mals take, this fraught and awful give-and-get has worked through the ages, creating the quickened beauties we see. For that matter, it has created us. Our way is no improvement over the talon and the beak, to say the least. Our rapaciousness has no competition. We, uniquely, deplete the world. Truth is, we have become an existential danger to planetary life on par with the last major asteroid strike. Other creatures take what their circumstances compel, seeking what they need. We alone seek more than needed, pardoning our impulse to take what we want, whatever the cost inflicted on peaceful roosts everywhere.

Other cultures achieved organization and power. Many experienced conflict, some built empires. Guns were invented in China, whose ships were superior to those of Europe. What Western colonizers excelled at was their proclivity to view new landscapes and Native peoples as "other," and to morally dissociate themselves from their impulses to perpetrate extreme violence. What made Westerners inclined to dominate and colonize was not a more advanced approach to the world—but a more brutal one. The problem is not that modernity requires brutality. It's that the West chose to create a brutal modernity.

The rocking cradle of us-as-opposed-to-them nursed a defining horror within Western thinking: a willingness to harm the other animals we call "animals" and the *peoples* whom Westerners have called "animals." In the 1700s, Immanuel Kant expressed the standard Abrahamic self-justification that "animals are not self-conscious and are there merely as a means to an end. That end is man." Such callous malice toward the soft vulnerability of living beings is a short step from the most appalling kind of thinking, and Kant landed there quickly. "Savage nations," he wrote, "can never grow accustomed to the European way of life," because "the animal in this case has so to speak not yet developed the humanity inside itself." The philosophical destination: to excuse from moral consideration his entire continent's violent impulses toward oppression in pursuit of desires.

WHEN PEOPLE SPEAK OF MORALITY, as did Kant—and as will I—we must ask what they mean. Here is what I mean. The Golden Rule is golden because it touches this most simple, most universal truth: all people seek to avoid pain. This truth extends far beyond humans. The backstop of what is "moral" is that all complex living things seek to avoid suffering and confinement. All living things exert themselves to continue living, and all seek well-being.

No one would wonder about the morality of giving water to an animal. But to kill an animal seems to require prior consideration about whether killing is justifiable. For many people, and certain entire religions, killing animals is morally constrained, sometimes forbidden. Even if you believe that your God sanctions killing, you've felt the moral need to check with God on this point. In many Indigenous cultures, as we've discussed, hunting requires ritual preparation. Kills necessitate respectful demonstration of gratitude to the hunted. In the modern industrialized world, people annually kill roughly 50 billion chickens, a billion and a half pigs, three hundred million cattle, various other creatures, and trillions of fish and other aquatic animals. A few centuries ago, virtually all birds, mammals, and fishes were free-living beings in wild places. Now, humans, cows, pigs, and other domesticates make up 96 percent of all living mammals on Earth. Wild mammals, only 4 percent. Some 70 percent of all birds on the planet are captive-born "poultry." Essentially all animals factory-farmed nowadays endure truncated lives and are made to live worse than they are made to die. Along for the ride are dehumanized and devalued workers whose routine injuries result from the demanded pace of production. This, too, has deep roots. Plato had written, "In many ways [nature] shows, among men as well as among animals . . . that justice consists in the superior ruling over and having more than the inferior." Aristotle wrote in *Politics*, "In the case of those whose business is to use their body, and who can do nothing better, the lower sort are by nature slaves, and it is better for them as for all inferiors to be under the rule of a master." Thomas Hobbes believed that people need "a common power to keep them all in awe." In the West, this counts as philosophy. These crude excuses for cruelties don't merely fail to elevate us; they sanctify our most demonic devices. For Plato, Aristotle, and Hobbes, humans without government are savages in immoral anarchy; people under a political state are civilized. But what does their modern political state accomplish? Not peace. Not justice. Rather, hierarchy. Echoes of their thinking continue to reverberate in how people get paid for their labors. Well over half of the people in the United States live paycheck to paycheck; half of Americans don't have enough savings to cover three months of expenses in an emergency. Slaves don't get paid a living wage; neither do many workers.

Dualism doesn't work both ways; it works one way. Gears of division crank wheels of domination. Domination of peoples, of other animals, and of the natural world have all emanated from posts whose officers believed themselves, as Kant wrote, "morally independent of animality," meaning: superior.

A mind-set of hierarchy and denigration—embraced heart and soul across Europe, perfected on its soil, and then exported—has generated, sanctified, and venerated centuries of mayhem, murder, and misery inflicted on humans and the rest of nature alike. The consequences for our planet's thin film of life, its contours and fragile cultures, have mounted for centuries, globalized by conquistadors and colonial ravagers, traders and slavers, industrial polluters and factory farmers, ocean depleters and atmosphere destabilizers, right up and down to the present-day's you and me. "Western technology and the people who have employed it have been the most amazingly destructive forces in all of human history," opined a group of noted Native American writers. "What we're seeing now with the biodiversity collapse and with climate change," Columbia University anthropologist Paige West observes, "is the final stage of the effects of colonialism." Throughout it all, Platonist dualism has consistently whispered urgings of encouragement.

◆

OUR SPRING CHICKENS WERE PRETTY well grown now, and eating ravenously. They came companionably around my feet while nipping the growing tips of grass blades. Grass eats sunlight; it makes life from non-life. The chicks make it all prosaic, going clip, clip, giving me an excuse to put off mowing our scruffy lawn for another few days.

We were into the season when our untidy little garden, suburban yard, errant hens, the harbor, and the sea provide a large share of what we eat, as fresh as it gets. Our three adult ladies were laying enough to keep up with our demand, barely, while we waited for our spring chickens to start laying. I stretched our omelets with garden kale and wild greens. I was pleasantly surprised to discover that dandelions lose all bitterness when sautéed; what started as an experiment became a regular part of some nice breakfast omelets. And for tea I plucked spicebush leaves from the woods' edge and mint from our garden. I'd been prevented from getting out on the water by a run of foggy days, typical here in June. But when the fog ghosted away and the wind quieted to a whisper, I ventured out on a foraging mission along the coastal shore. Food—what it is, how we get it—reflects the relationship one has with the world. A meal with a story is a good meal. We knew where our food was coming from. And in the case of our eggs, *who* they were coming from. We had many good meals.

WHILE PATRICIA AND I WERE having one of our storied dinners on the deck, some crows in the woods raised an unusual racket. I thought the crows' agitations would be momentary, so we didn't interrupt our meal. But they remained excited for several minutes. We should have gotten right up to investigate. Whatever had just happened, we missed it.

I didn't hear anything from the owls during the night. By dawn I realized the night had been too quiet.

WHEN THE LIGHT CAME UP on Juneteenth, I could not locate any fledgers. Alfie and Plus-One were much in evidence, calling and traversing gaps in the canopy. Any young ones—if they were around—should be noisily begging, as they'd been. I started wondering about those overexcited crows. Alfie flew into the woods' edge, calling with her soft whistle, looking toward the tree where I'd last seen a fledger. She seemed to be searching for lost children.

I turned and noticed a crow circling tightly, scrutinizing the area where I'd last seen an owlet. The crow returned three times within the half hour. Ominous. Crows eat a lot of baby birds around fledging; we've often seen this. Could crows have wiped out Alfie's brood while we were eating dinner—is that what happened?

I called. Alfie answered, but she'd moved; I didn't see where to. Perhaps Alfie could now lead me to whatever chicks might remain alive. So I held out a bit of food—not a whole meal—on my flat palm. Alfie was instantly on my hand; I'd neither heard nor seen her coming. She flew with the morsel to a tree, looked into the woods, then flew deeper in. But I heard no owlets.

Alfie returned so quickly that I suspected that she was still feeding at least one youngster. I gave her a bit more. She flew farther into the woods, about a hundred yards ahead. Picking my way over old storm-felled trees, I hurried forward as best I could. In moments a brick-colored blur was headed my way. She landed on my hand, grasped more food, spent about ten seconds looking cautiously around, as if concerned about being watched, then flew high into the leafy maples. This time I distinctly heard a fledger begging. My ploy had worked. Through binoculars I located one fledgling chattering at Mom's arrival on a nearby branch.

A crow came through, cawing. The crow's patrol put an immediate chill into the owlet, who stopped chattering until the crow's calls faded in the distance. Was this pure instinct? Or had this baby owl witnessed crows carrying away their siblings?

Wait—maybe not! A *second* fledgling popped into view from behind some foliage. And then the *third* fledger moved into view. I was watching the rematerializing of a lost brood coming out of hiding.

Plus-One joined his family, giving the tremolo call. Whatever had happened, whatever the crows might have attempted, the Hoo was whole. If the game was Crows vs. Owls, this time it was Crows 0, Owls 3—actually, five. I left them in their green sea of tranquility and, feeling happy, went to let the doggies out.

◆

FOR ABOUT TWO HUNDRED THOUSAND YEARS, the human mind developed with a sense of belonging. The last few thousand years have been a much stranger trip. Various examiners laid us out and opened our skulls, excising our fresh impressions and original reflections and implanting instead their own ideas. They sewed us up and sent us on our way, off to teach, off to preach, off to kill and conquer. No wonder we can no longer think straight and we struggle to love ourselves, while fear of "others" comes easy.

Alfie can be viewed as very much "other," inhabiting a reality alien to human experience. *Or* she can be seen as a kindred spirit in a shared world. But that's just philosophy. We have evidence to consult. She and I share expectations and understandings—as when we call and respond to one another. Despite the purity of her physical freedom, our perceptions and our affections overlap enough to keep us in relationship. What brings and holds us in our bond is not perfect symmetry but sufficient similarity, not even quite a yin-yang unity of necessary opposites but an even more integrated wholeness of overlapping distinctions. We live as biological kin in a blended existence. And to a meaningful extent, we've been sharing a life. We contain enough of each other that similarities define us more than differences divide us. She enjoys getting her head scratched. She is another, not an "other."

18

⁂

Into a New Day

AT HALF PAST EIGHT IN THE EVENING, THE YOUNG OWLS remained remarkably subdued. One chick rattled briefly from somewhere up in the leafy shades and shadows.

Owl silence notwithstanding, the air trucked plenty of sound. Robins from here and there flooded the forest's quiet corners with soft good nights. A deer stepped slowly through the woods. A mockingbird chucked a territorial reminder. At the stop sign, a car with a loud engine slowed only slightly before lurching along.

Alfie flew up to a high branch and started whinnying for her significant other. Plus-One flew in through the trees swiftly, silently, precisely. I lost him in the foliage, but suddenly from two directions I heard owlets growling and clacking, and the sound of one youngster intensified. Their father had delivered takeout. But seeing into the leafiness of these maples? No. I couldn't.

Over the treetops quite a bit of light remained. Yet the forest, their world of shadows, began filtering me out.

"Ow. Ow. Ow."

"Ow. Ow. Ow."

Deeper in the woods, there was activity. Of course there was. But it was beyond my vision and my abilities. I had to leave them to it. I had no choice; they'd left me.

THE YOUNG OWLS WERE OPEN to whatever their new world brought. The openness of our own toddling child mind is not too difficult to recall. It's easy to behold in young children. Unguarded and inquisitive, the young human mind seeks connection with every creature and holds no prejudgment against any person. But the adult mind sees what it has learned to see, knows what it has needed to know, remains receptive to only a few channels out of the whole array. Many become hardened by harshness received. Some of the latter achieve high positions in our tilted society. Others have learned an ideology of plunder. When nations are referred to as "economies" and human beings are reduced to "consumers," the eclipse of all values for the profits of a few is nearing totality. As Wade Davis observes,

> The American cult of the individual denies not just community but the very idea of society. No one owes anything to anyone. All must be prepared to fight for everything: education, shelter, food, medical care. What every prosperous and successful democracy deems to be fundamental rights—universal health care, equal access to quality public education, a social safety net for the elderly and infirmed—America dismisses as socialist indulgences, as if so many signs of weakness.

◆

BEFORE DAWN ON THE YEAR'S "longest day"—or, if you're an owl, shortest night—I watched the livestream of Paul Winter's unique Summer Solstice Celebration. This annual event is the only human concert I know that is timed to do what countless birds do routinely: usher in the day. It was time to go outside.

I stepped into a dawn of sacred bells and holy chimes. The lungs of feathered beings trembled, and the air around us gently thrilled. These were not just "birds." That label had fallen. These were the most recent players, the latest starring cast, in a long-running pageant of voices that has been chanting sun into ascendance for something like fifty million summer solstices. I savored them all, and put aside the question of the next fifty million. That question hinged on whether we would break the promise that the world had made to us a billion years or so ago. Of the past, I'd learned a few things. Of the future, all bets were off. Compared to those singers and most of our other kin, we are recent arrivals. Yet someone rather prematurely named us *Homo sapiens*—"man, the wise." That label too, no longer resonates. Something is wrong. How long has it been since wisdom was our working aspiration? Were we born to the world a bit prematurely, not fully formed? Certainly we have a ways to go. So yes, I put all questions aside and simply, a bit sublimely—a bit greedily—savored the heralds of this solstice. I wanted to feel like just me, listening to us all. At least, I tried to.

Daily we get a little opportunity to be ourselves in morning minutes after the tide of dreams recedes and takes with it its delights, terrors, and confusions. The welcome new light lifts us, easing the burden of trying to be ourselves with each other, letting us practice briefly being ourselves with just ourselves. And liking our own company. It's not easy. The hardest mind to enter—or to escape from, ironically—is our own. The hardest achievement: just to be always one's self. I watch a mockingbird who seems to be deciding when to begin and what song to play, the way a musician before a performance, testing a new reed and just tooting a few notes, conveys the forecast: a storm is gathering in the tempest of her lungs. Once, I watched a hawk stretching a wing and a leg, showing by the poetry of that extension what those feathers and those feet do for a living, that in the sky there are thunderbolts with intentions. There is something here that is becoming breathtaking. It is how much those birds in the glittering air and in our fluttering chests are packing into so few notes, such economy of motion; it is that through the incomprehensibility of incarnation, a mingling of matter and energy somehow feels itself *yearning*, expresses *desire*. Living beings are bending light and gravity and time; the plasma of the universe is following those notes up into daylight, following the owl into her shaded slumber. Following the hawk to the sky. Following Icarus to the sun.

IT WAS A GLORIOUS MORNING, and I didn't mind being, as always, unable to actually fly. Being rooted has its plus side, too. I quickly located all three owlets—looking great—at the very edge of the woods.

I'd brought my camera on a tripod. Low light and leaf shadows made photography difficult. But Alfie made photography impossible—by landing on my camera. She wanted her food. Now. I wanted more light for photos.

I hated making her wait. But a hunter must be patient. As must a beggar. The circumstances of Alfie's life had made her a bit of both. As am I. Truth was, both of us were giving and getting riches in this relationship. Alfie continually commuted across the blurry threshold of our partly shared, partly distinct life. I've tried for a glimpse of a parallel world, and Alfie has generously provided a little window to peer into, a narrow bridge to cross this span of very special time. For part of each day, she has opened the portal, inviting me to join her. Leading me into the shadows of her own existence, she has allowed me to be, in a very real way, a participant beyond a human-centered world. Through her I've experienced aspects of existence that are rarely humanly available. I did not view these things as earth-shattering; they were small and lovely, surprising and often delightful. But they certainly altered my view of her life and my own. Alfie has been a connector for me, a unifier not only of certain aspects of her world and mine but of my own self with my own world.

I value individuality; mine, Alfie's, and others'. But excessive individualism generates isolation. "Someone once asked me," recalled Native American writer LaDonna Harris, "how I could maintain my individuality as a member of a communal society. I was confused by this question. In fact, I could not even understand it. . . . A strong person strengthens the whole community and a strong community strengthens each person." Such is possible. So it pains me to see individualism hyped in our culture, to see young people raised to be competitors more than contributors. We are taught a kind of "winning" achieved not by helping others flourish but by making others lose. Our system makes this of us, as Rome made gladiators of slaves. With each such win, everyone loses a little. The centurions who stoke the games are devoutly committed to competition not because it is good for us but because our competitions benefit them materially. So we live our gladiatorial existences until the system retires us. Or, if we are lucky, we find a way to live through a different lens.

AT THE MOMENT, A DIFFERENT lens might have gotten me the light I needed and might have prompted Alfie to move off my camera. But she'd put me in a patient mood. And that felt pleasant, because I am often made restless by the pace of our human race.

We tend to spend much of our time in a state of compliance, unable to fully steer our own course, even to fully participate in our lives. "This life of work-or-die is not an improvement" is Tyson Yunkaporta's assessment of industrialized existence versus traditional Indigenous life. Dissociation—even from ourselves—is dualism's contagious ailment, civilization's self-generated epidemic.

Once each of us is sufficiently disengaged from the world and one another, nothing is sufficiently harsh or horrific to unify us. Not mass shootings, nor virus pandemics, certainly not oceans of plastic, nor plummeting populations of birds and bugs, nor intensifying storms and rising floods, nor wildfires that incinerate three billion animals and leave whole towns leveled to smoldering ash. "Those things are *not me*," we are taught. It all works overtime to turn the planet's once splendid living family into a broken home. In this we are stuck for now, because our industrial systems depend on destruction of natural systems. Our way of living, writes Zen master Susan Murphy, "does evil by countless repetitive, cumulative failures of care and conscience." We live in a planetary rape culture, and even those of us who are aghast are enmeshed in its gears. It has become easier to imagine how the world we've known will end—because we're living that trajectory—than how we will end such destructive habits.

ALFIE LINGERED WITH ME IN the still, soft, grief-cleansing air. Dawn's orchestration of light and breath continued. A song sparrow pumped out a declaration. Somehow we are capacitated to discern, from the whole vibrating atmosphere, the different voicings. Somehow, too, the birds' control of forced air tangles our nervous system. Our mind reads the codes sent by our auditory nerves and creates sensations called sounds. Our brain then sends a copy of that analysis down the hall to the emotional department, which labels it *beautiful*. This is the headline of each morning.

A dove tolled. A woodpecker knocked insistently. An early squirrel performed a high-wire act. No traffic yet troubled the road. The air was thick with dewy moisture, brimming with fluted voices and every possibility for the day ahead. It felt nourishing and delicious.

Alfie looked at me intently. Having gotten nothing since landing on my camera, she seemed to be waiting to see whether I was prepared to produce. I positioned her food on the lawn for her viewing pleasure. Promptly yet in no real rush, she plucked it and boomeranged to the trees.

The Hoo converged on her enthusiastically. But, the short night notwithstanding, they'd apparently gotten plenty of food. Again Alfie was more interested in feeding them than they were in getting fed. Quickly stuffed in these days when the livin' is easy, the owlets moved short distances away while Alfie still had plenty left. When one youngster flew about twenty-five feet, Alfie followed with the mouse she'd been holding. An overly solicitous mom, she followed her plump kids from branch to branch, trying to get them to eat even as they moved away from her. She seemed as overindulgent as any mother insisting that her baby finish everything long after hunger has vacated the equation. But let's give the credit and blame where it's deserved: the excess provisions came from me; I was the one providing the help the Hoo didn't need. What Alfie wanted and her babe needed were slightly mismatched in the moment. Yet their fundamental concerns were fully aligned. The interests of giver and receiver created a happy win-win; Alfie's generosity of spirit enlarged her enterprise. This has been the hallmark of good parenting and successful living through the profundity of epochal time.

IS THERE AN ADULT IN the room with us now? Look around you; we are the child with the stick in the lake. We have had fun stirring up a mess. We never thought we would need to undo the extinction crisis, the climate crisis, the toxics crisis—. And in our bulging multitudes, we just stare.

Economists and investment bankers and corporate bosses and the political figurines who serve them cannot allow themselves to understand, because they butter their bread on the coming generations' burnt toast. Growth is their vocabulary. They've been taught to conflate growth with improvement. Making something bigger requires pumping it with more material and energy. But better communities, justice, dignity, and a livable future—none of these require growth. They require stability, which growth disrupts.

We all experienced a period when our bodies' program was growth. When growth stabilized, our focus could become improvement. We could have made a much better deal with the world, one that prioritized the survival of things we touch.

I WOULD HAVE BET THAT Alfie was going to settle in where she was, with the Hoo. But she left that secure, undisclosed location and flew in open daylight to the back-door dogwood and on to the Ivy Tower. There she whinnied her own morning aria. The mind of this owl was not always easy to read.

Nor was the news. From the otherworld portal I'd been transiting with Alfie, I emerged back into human consciousness and confronted the day's headlines. Covid. Political turmoil. Racial frictions. Cultural factions. Lying denials, lying assertions. Shootings. While Alfie and Plus-One had been working to make an honest living in the dark of our night, "troops clashed in disputed areas." Why, over and over, the self-inflicted torments of arbitrary differences? Chimpanzees sometimes kill each other in their territorial clashes; we think them murderous. We routinely kill each other in our wars and call it valorous. The difference: chimpanzees are all they are capable of being. We scarcely aspire toward such success.

Science has gained, and gifted, remarkable understanding of the working story of life. But we have lost the plot thanks to _____. Fill in the blank. Does the blame lie with religious institutions, financial institutions, energy monopolies, tech monopolies, bought-off governments? I'd say, "Not really." It's: *our values.* That's the blank.

Had the founding scientists and economists been freer to choose their faith, they might have led us into a technological revolution and a financial system that acknowledges that the world has value. They might have sought, like the Ionians before Plato, to grasp the forces responsible for creating life on Earth. They might have strived—like other major cultures—to maintain the balances and relationships that hold time together. Reductionists could have zoomed deep into the finest workings of physics and chemistry and cells and zoomed back out with ever-increasing awe for the wondrous world.

We are the beneficiaries *and* victims of millennia of thinking. We mark ourselves by our differences. Can we, like a chimpanzee given the mirror test, recognize ourselves in the reflection and eliminate that mark? Can we keep what is good while rubbing away what is harmful? Because many people *have* done exactly that, we know it is possible. We can make a better deal with the world.

A LOT HAD ALREADY GONE ON. It was nearly six a.m. before the first automobile of the morning passed.

The Hoo had shown themselves capable of flying short distances, twenty feet or so. Yet by day they'd repeatedly bivouacked in the same maples, next to the street, only about a hundred feet from where they'd hatched. These fat little homebodies were more sedentary than I'd expected. I'd expected more wandering and exploring. If "curiosity killed the cat," as they say, the fledgers seemed inclined to remain nonadventurous, near their parents, near each other—and alive.

Speaking of cats: two cats showed up, transiting the area where the youngsters had been spending most of their time for the last few days.

Soon *three* cats were prowling the woods within a hundred feet of where the owls perched. This copious feline presence was made possible through the generosity of my food-for-all neighbor across the street. She's an elderly woman whose admirable kindness to unhomed cats might yet get our owls killed. Alfie sometimes used the bird-bath, or even our chickens' water bowl on the ground, for bathing and drinking. When I set the motion-triggered camera on the birdbath, I captured several images of a cat drinking from it at night, front paws on the bath's lip, hind legs stretched taut. Cats were roaming every-where. So mere bathing or taking a sip of water were mortal hazards for Alfie & Co.

One of the prowling cats now rose with forepaws on a trunk, assessing the climbability of a tree. What had caught the cat's curi-osity, I could not discern. We don't see everything there is to see, even when it's right there. Just yesterday, walking to the studio, I noticed a blue jay landing in the foliage of a maple a mere forty feet from the owls' nest box. There was something suspicious in the blue jay's movements. A furtiveness. I investigated and was amazed to find a hidden nest with an adult jay sitting on eggs—in the tree immediately adjacent to the one the newly fledged owlet had been climbing during that first morning after leaving the nest box. Now it was less surprising that the jays had so furiously knocked the fledger repeatedly to the ground. It was more surprising that these jays had constructed their nest and staked their season—and their lives—just a few wing flaps from nesting owls. The jays had been sitting vulner-ably on their nest all night long for weeks while their mortal enemies crisscrossed the shared airspace, hunting, providing bugs and rodents *and* birds for three growing owlets. But since I'd failed to notice the jays till now, even where I'd spent so much time recently, their teachable moment for me took the form of a question: What else am I missing? Probably plenty.

THERE IS NO GOOD WAY to end the beginning of a perfect morn-ing, or the story of Alfie. We dip into and out of a moving river. That's life. The details mature, perfect themselves, and, in this case, shrink to a small backyard in a new geological formation called suburbia, still filled with songs of the ages on the longest-lit days of the orbital year. Millions of years from the beginning of the story, it gets personal when a man names a dying baby owl Alfie, and one tiny mote of a grand play comes briefly into sharp focus. Whether or not we see the performance, whether or not we read the play, the actors perform this longest-running show. Their intended audiences are their own. It happens beside us or without us. It happens with no regard for us. But it happens.

The air was mild. The Hoo were fed. There was nothing to want at the moment. There was only being here in the net of life. For now.

PART FIVE

Mysterious Messengers

19

Mysterious Messengers

ON SUNDAY MORNING, JUNE 21, I WOKE AT OUR COTTAGE on the bay at four-thirty but lay resting with my eyes closed, listening to the birth of day. I had been dozing when strangely—*very strangely*—I was reawakened by the sound of sharp tapping on glass. I thought perhaps a bird was trying to catch a moth on the skylight. But when I twisted around, I saw a crow rapping at one of the large front windows. Those windows are hinged at the top; they open by tilting outward at the bottom. The bedroom is on the second floor, and there's a jutting window ledge. The tapping crow was on that ledge. The crow now got under the tilted-out glass and began hurling themself at the screen. At that point, between glass and screen, there was no possibility that the crow was reacting to any reflection. And to rule out another possibility: the bird wasn't daintily plucking bugs off the screen. This crow looked absolutely determined to break through and get into the bedroom. I couldn't imagine that anything in the room would be in the crow's interest. With the woods around the house and the beach across the street, why would a crow try so energetically to come into my bedroom with me? I rose. The crow was still trying to enter when I got to the screen door adjacent to the window.

I just said hello. At that, the crow flew to the utility wire in front of the house, joined by two others who'd been nearby. One crouched on the wire, wings slightly spread. Odd. Two flew away, then the third. Their receding caws and croaks rang through the still morning. What were they saying to one another? Were they trying to say anything to me? I didn't feel frightened. I didn't feel that the encounter was either friendly or hostile. The incident felt: spooky.

My journal note at the time: "Well what a strange thing. I guess I'll leave it at that." But then I had a thought, and I added, "—unless somebody has died." A few years ago, a physician told me, matter-of-factly, "Birds appear when someone dies." I had never heard this before. A little research informed me that many cultures view birds as messengers of human deaths. So I started keeping a file. My file is, to me, interesting and perplexing. I don't believe that birds are messengers; I think they are individuals of their species, as we are individuals of our species.

But to imagine a connection between something as soothing as birds and something as unsettling as the death of our beloveds is, well, comforting. A *real* connection between birds and human mortality would upend my entire understanding of reality. Then again, reality could use some improvement. Who would not like to think that existence is an infinite web of eternal being and becoming?

We often put aside critical thinking or logic to enjoy fictional stories that we don't believe, that we *know* are made up. Fiction works when we "suspend our disbelief." Sometimes in moments of need, hitting Pause on disbelief can open us to possibilities that calm and reassure, can help console us when we are grieving a piece of our lifetime.

Perhaps people have made that connection because birds *are* so soothing. Someone died, a bird is here, so the bird must be here because someone has died. It's easy to see our human mind's too-common tendency to fill gaps with imagined cause-and-effect explanations. Hungering for meaning, people routinely make imagined associations when two chance occurrences merely wave at one another from a distance. But when the bird is here doing something very strange, the basic question of science arises: Why? The answer may be: It's a coincidence. The answer may be: The material world is manifesting a spirit world. The problem is, we can't manipulate the situation to prove or disprove either possibility. Even if we don't believe, we can't quite know.

THE CROWS AND THEIR RESONANT caws moved deeper into the pine woods. The crow had rapped on the window so hard it left streaks on the glass. In Native American belief, a spirit can enter a bird for a time and then leave. My mother, age ninety-four, came to mind. I'd spoken with her the previous night. She'd sounded energetic, as always. Maybe, I figured, I'd call her in a couple of hours. That thought, so surprisingly and uncharacteristically superstitious of me, made me feel embarrassed. Superstitions are associations that mean nothing. An irony arises because science is the investigation of associations that might mean nothing—or something. To be truly scientific, one must confront the universe with curiosity about unlikely possibilities. If we simply shut our minds to possibilities that seem unlikely, we can learn nothing further. The universe has responded by being truly bizarre in many proven ways, filled with the strange and the mysterious, with incomprehensible ponderables. We should investigate, but some things are not easily investigated. So we lack information to either confirm or completely dismiss certain weird possibilities. When those weird possibilities soothe us, we might keep them in a special closet of harmless tranquilities. A bird that appears in an odd place at an odd time when something momentous has occurred is a bird we can load with meaning, perhaps lightening our own load in the process.

Jennifer Holland has written beautifully about this in an essay about grief during her mother's final days. She went for a drive to clear her head, and up in a Minnesota sky on February 9, one bald eagle after another appeared, until nine eagles were circling her stretch of road. "After I'd returned home," she wrote, "my mother took her last jagged breath." Holland says that though she's not a particularly spiritual person, she often turns to the natural world to ease stress and quiet her mind. "That night, though, I couldn't help but think that those birds were nature's messenger. . . . I can certainly imagine my mom, a true animal lover, choosing majestic birds, their number matching the date, to prepare me. When I suspended my disbelief," she added, "it made perfect sense." Holland admits to sometimes taking a lingering glance at a chirping bird outside her back door, wondering, "Mom, is that you?" She feels a little silly, yes, but she also feels soothed in the moment. "If that comfort comes in the shape of a fellow creature," Holland writes, "I see that as a wonderful gift. If I were trying to communicate with those I love, I'd certainly do it through something that's beautiful and that breathes, there for a moment, then gone. My mother may have sent those nine eagles; what a lovely thought. But if she didn't, I'm still grateful for the moment of elation and strength those birds brought me at a time when I felt I had nothing left to give."

I GAVE PATRICIA A RING at six a.m., as usual. She'd been up with our dogs and filling the feeders and letting the chickens out. I told her the story of the crazy rap-tapping, body-hurling crow.

"It's J.P.," she said.

This was the first night I'd slept at the cottage on the bay since the passing, ten days earlier, of our beloved across-the-street neighbor J. P. Badkin, who'd built Alfie's nest box—a joyful sprite of a man whom we'd felt lucky to know for about eighteen years. He'd died at ninety-two, after a long and difficult illness.

Patricia reconsidered: "But he would have come back as a gull."

J.P. loved to feed a couple of particular gulls that learned to land on the roof of his Hobbit house–like beach shack and wait for him. One year after not being there all winter and spring, J.P. and his wife, Marilyn, arrived for the summer, and by the time they got to the door with their suitcases, "their" gull was sitting patiently on the roof. There always seemed a little touch of magic around J.P. While I spoke to Patricia, I went to the window to get a direct view of their little house on the dune.

Patricia and I were playing along with each other—*mostly.* Lovely as the idea of messenger birds is, it doesn't pencil out with everything I know. I hold a place for it only because I don't know everything.

I hold that place, too, because I find myself in agreement with Jennifer Holland: there seems little harm in letting the mere notice of something unusual, beautiful, and natural cleanse some of our grief. Why suppress a few soothing moments and the stories that open us to wonder and humility, that remind us that in the vastness of what we do not understand, possibilities remain?

I don't *think* that birds can be spirit messengers. Many things argue against it being true. A crow pecking a window is just a crow. If your beloved neighbor has died, you feel you've lost a rib. But if, after your neighbor has died, a crow pecks your screen, you see a messenger, a guide; you believe in transmigration. And why? Is it because there is more to life and death than you can know? Or simply because there is more to bereavement than you can bear. Everyone knows their answer. The problem is, answers come and answers go. And no one can know with elemental finality whether their answer is correct.

After the crow's visit—or perhaps visitation—the morning's more verifiable realities kept me on my feet. I had a view north across open water, with light wisps of early fog in the first-of-summer air. I had a view east of clouds painted pink by a sun climbing at the year's northernmost point of dawn. The sun would continue trekking across the sky with or without me. I didn't want to be left behind. I dressed and got some tea and sat outside in the breathless stillness to more fully inhabit the day's unfolding. As an ancient poet wrote, "Death plucks my ear and says, 'Live!—I am coming.'" Or as Patricia said on the morning I fell in love with her, "I'm too happy to sleep." House wrens were nesting in a birdhouse a few paces from the door; they were busy delivering insects to their brood. The dewy air was saturated with song. Across the street in J.P. and Marilyn's craggy old cherry tree, a striking yellow-and-black prairie warbler sang. The bay was mirror calm. An osprey hunting along the shoreline swooped upward into a hover, searched for a fish, then swooped low and flew along, until swooping up into another hover. Like that, the osprey worked the shoreline, as if pinning invisible decorations in the sky. My question to myself became, Could I maintain enough presence to make myself worthy of such a morning?

As for Alfie & Co., Patricia had listened hard. She'd detected no owl presence. In the evening, Patricia left a mouse out. In the morning, it remained. That was odd. Of course we hoped they were okay.

Patricia told me that when I'd left for the beach the previous night, Cady had waited for me in the bushes alongside the driveway. "She didn't come in with the other dogs." Cady normally avoids being alone. Last time I went to the beach, Chula was the one waiting up late outside. That the dogs would be waiting for me made me feel as though I'd somehow broken a promise they thought I'd made. I planned to pay extra attention to them when I got home.

And I did.

◆

THE TWENTIETH-CENTURY POLYMATH Bertrand Russell lamented that science was not pursued as a love story between human beings and nature. Russell blamed physics for depriving us of intimacy with our world and the cosmos; he said science gave us "a skeleton of rattling bones, cold and dreadful." But is it because of what's been discovered or because of how we've reacted to the news? Space telescopes' images of galaxies being born grant us views unimagined in the prior sweep of human time. Whether we see them as magnificent and awe-inducing or "cold and dreadful" depends on what bright eye we've brought to the lens. Engineering and tech development still tend too often to be marinated in Bacon's *cri de guerre* of humans against nature. Most economists perpetuate the premise that the world we live in is "external to the market," so pollution is free and future generations are "discounted." Important exceptions to those generalizations exist in designs for low-carbon living, circular no-waste material society, and no-growth economics. But if you consider how engineering and technology continue to push society, it seems apparent that the generalizations still drive. Crises of climate, toxics, plastics, population, and extinction continue to mount rather than be decisively addressed, largely because the ancient architects of Western dualism continue casting long shadows across a bleakly devalued world.

Many scientists, engineers, and economists are taught that reverence for the world is not scientific. In many university laboratories and lecture halls, regarding the world and the cosmos as "value-free" is presented—without a hint of conscious irony—as a core value. That the world has little value is the most consequential—and most religious—Western value, rooted as it is in Plato's influence on Western theology. Despite the millennia during which human thinkers considered how best to live, the global Westernized economy now gallops along behind its three headless horsemen: bigger, faster, more. No plan, no destination, riding a human population that has quadrupled in less than a century. Because pitting ourselves against the world that we rely on remains our main discernible project, we are letting our obsession with control lead to loss of control. By creating problems we refuse to solve, we may be causing problems we will not be able to solve. Of course, an irreverent view of the world is as mythological as any belief—but with this difference: it destroys. It blinds us to what Life is, and what Life needs. And to the better possibilities.

20

⁂

What Goes Around

"*ow. ow. ow.*"

I was always pleased and a little relieved to receive confirmation of their continued existence. I walked outside just before five a.m. on June 23. The cool air was, as usual, textured with birdsong. But of owls I heard nothing further until Alfie showed up softly whinnying in intimate tones, saying, "Hi, I'm right here. Just here."

She was looking at me from the edge of the woods. She didn't come for the food I offered. Her soft greeting constituted acknowledgment of our mutual existence.

Namaste, Alfie. I acknowledge the divine in you.

The divine one looked at me for seven minutes before humoring me by taking the food.

Of young ones I still heard nothing. None of the fledgers' raspy whispers. Had I missed a transition during my day away? Had the young dispersed into the greater woodland? Had they become wild— or had they become food?

I heard no scolding from mockingbirds, cardinals, catbirds, or jays. Nothing. I felt no presence from the fledgers. All was too quiet, too empty-feeling.

I hoped the silence wasn't the end of everything at which these owls had worked so hard. It felt like it might be. I always worried too much about the owls. I feared the great horned owls, the bird hawks, the crows, as well as the cats who roamed so thoroughly not because they needed food but because they'd been fed. I had feared letting Alfie free. But as Aldo Leopold wrote, "too much safety seems to yield only danger in the long run."

IT MIGHT SEEM THAT WE alone among the living can voice our fears. But what if we listen more carefully. Each species, individually, has scant voice to vocalize its tragic opera. But as troubles rise, they sing the blues chorus of living things large and humble, no matter whether they darken skies or rustle grass or attempt to keep their peace among undersea reefs. Everywhere, trouble rumbles. Our problems find them. "Extinction crisis" is a madly mild understatement for the across-the-board tailspins of almost every wild and free-living species on the planet. Any place, any thing that had previously been out of our reach now feels our touch.

Before the early 1800s, extinction was considered a theological impossibility. A species' disappearance would break a window in the cathedral of God's perfect design—something not possible. But extinctions (and species emergences) had been happening, *very rarely*, for millions of years. Between sixty thousand and ten thousand years ago, the dispersal of our species out of Africa and into Australia, Eurasia, and the Americas coincided with extinctions of mammoths, giant sloths, giant kangaroos, and many others. Hunting is a likely cause. But climates, too, were changing. Then, between five thousand and five hundred years ago, waves of extinctions clearly resulted from human arrivals on islands in the Pacific, the Caribbean, and the Indian Ocean. New Zealand's various moa birds became species of the past. Ditto Madagascar's giant lemurs and the enormous elephant bird. On Pacific islands, at least a thousand birds—10 percent of all avian species—went extinct. The Caribbean alone lost about a hundred endemic mammal species. Whether some of the earliest arriving humans into the New World caused a mainland extinction wave remains debated by some. Certainly the New World's European colonizers did. Since 1500, humans have driven at least fourteen hundred animal species out of existence, a rate variously calculated to be between one hundred and one thousand times faster than in prehuman times, and now accelerating. We tend to assume that "endangered species" means animals, but at least sixty-five North American *plant* species are considered to have vanished from the wild since Europeans settled the continent. In 2019, the United Nations estimated that, overall, *a million* species are under threat of extinction worldwide. As I was writing this section, twenty-three species, protected too late, were declared extinct in the United States.

When we speak of extinction, we think that losing the passenger pigeon or the ivory-billed woodpecker was an event confined to each species. Or, more poetically, we speak of threads removed from a great tapestry. A different view is that species *are* relationships. The ivory-billed woodpecker was a manifestation of relationships among certain giant trees and particular insects of southern swamps. When enough trees were cut down, the woodpecker became impossible. A species is a node in a web; its existence is how we can see that relationships are working, that the knots of the net are holding. Whales ate enormous quantities of fish and krill, but when the reckless hunting that Herman Melville called "so remorseless a havoc" caused the near extinction of whales, the fish and krill *declined*. Turns out, whale poop was a major ocean fertilizer; the great whales' collapse severely injured the relationship that had been creating so much krill and fish—and, thus, had been creating those long unfolding generations of whales themselves.

A species is not just a "product" of evolution. When a species declines, it does so because relationships are being unraveled. Extinction is several things. It is a process, an event, a tragedy, a symptom of deeper breakage.

North America has three billion fewer birds than when I was in high school—a 30 percent loss that is very noticeable during migration seasons. Twenty North American birds deemed "common"—species with more than half a million individuals—have declined by more than half in the last forty years. The losses are due mainly to reduction of living space and to climate change. Bobwhite quail—common in every woodlot in my youth—have declined more than 80 percent. In the region we live in, they're gone. Accelerating scarcity among insects is undermining plant pollination and causing some birds to starve. Whip-poor-wills have dropped 70 percent as the larger flying insects they eat have grown scarce. Along our shores, nineteen species of North American shorebirds—Olympians who migrate as much as twelve thousand miles a year—have halved in numbers since the 1970s because of development, hunting, and climate change's disruption of the links between migration timing and food supply. Seabirds including shearwaters, gannets, puffins, auks, and others have declined 70 percent worldwide since 1950, due mainly to food declines caused by overfishing and climate change. Decades of destruction to Brazil's formerly vast Atlantic forest—largely to farm soybeans for feeding cows, pigs, and chickens in North America and Europe—has caused twenty-one bird species to disappear from large areas there, the world's highest density of regional bird extirpations. Of amphibians, 165 species have vanished since 1970, many from their chytrid fungus pandemic. Some 70 percent of America's three hundred species of freshwater mussels are endangered or already extinct. Almost nobody has heard of them, and even their colorful names—heelsplitter, fatmucket, pistolgrip, pigtoe, monkeyface, snuffbox—are fading from memory. A quarter of the world's thousand or so sharks and rays have earned assessments ranging from vulnerable to critically endangered. All ten of the "most charismatic" animals—such as pandas and tigers, the ones we paint on the walls of our nursery rooms—are at risk of extinction in the wild. Elephants are already lost from most of Africa and Asia, their numbers down by around 99 percent from a few centuries ago. Lions have gone extinct in about sixteen African countries and continue declining in their shrinking ranges. Great apes—chimps, bonobos, orangutans, gorillas—are at all-time lows, and their long-term prospects look rickety. In a recent year, the number of "Sophie la Girafe" baby toys sold in France (eight hundred thousand) was more than eight times the number of real giraffes still alive in Africa.

Mainly, we have taken what they all need to live, snipping the webworks of relation that make them possible. We cannot assess the world's tens of millions of species individually. But we have a proxy: habitats. At global scale, all major habitat types except deserts are shrinking or degraded. Forests, despite gains in places such as the eastern United States, are at historic lows globally and continue falling and burning. Plows have claimed most grasslands. Freshwater is at its all-time most degraded and polluted; the oceans and coral reefs are at their most depleted, while also warming, acidifying, plasticizing, and even suffering from a reduced capacity to hold oxygen. The atmosphere today is at its most altered since yesterday. Coral reefs and polar ice systems are fracturing. The World Wildlife Fund's 2022 Living Planet Report estimated that from 1970 to 2020, wild animal numbers declined 69 percent globally. Their decline is linked to forces auguring *our* impending decline; sperm counts among Western men have in the last forty years fallen more than half.

All of this indicates something stark: humankind has made itself incompatible with Life on Earth. If you prefer the tapestry analogy, yes, Life's fabric is becoming threadbare and worn; we are wearing out the world that had welcomed us. We're too much of a good thing. The trajectory should quite reasonably horrify us. As climate disruption leaves towns burned, dries up rivers, and melts the poles; as plastic gets into our food and pollutants of all kinds affect birth and health and even human procreation; as nearly all wild species continue sagging, it is not because we do not know. It is because we are not taught to care.

IN MIDMORNING, A CALICO-COLORED CAT strolled through the woods carrying a limp chipmunk.

At dusk I heard no Alfie, no Plus-One, no fledgers. Absolutely nothing. I walked deeper into the woods. I heard only the robins' vespers.

The owls had moved to somewhere farther and deeper into their world, leaving me stranded in mine. The portal had closed. Alfie had always surprised me. The constancy of Alfie's presence had surprised me most. That set me up to feel surprised by her absence.

Through the example of her mate and the instinctual urgencies of motherhood, she'd acquired the skills and customs of her kind. Her success at becoming wild was bittersweet for me but liberating for us both. It was the completion of a circle that had started with a tiny bedraggled near-death owl chick matted with fly eggs but brought to health, thence to as true a freedom as she had been born to, and it had come to fruition with her own fledglings, forging new young links in the great chain of being.

Mockingbirds and robins, song sparrows and barking dogs notwithstanding, our yard without owls seemed silent.

BUT I WAS GETTING CARRIED away with myself. After all, Alfie had shown up just this morning. She'd been "missing" for only a matter of hours.

Patricia said, "The young ones are moving away, and Alfie is following. I think."

"I think so, too," I said.

At nine p.m. Alfie showed up in the driveway cedars. Alone, as this morning.

"They're exploring, expanding," said Patricia. "But Alfie knows where to come back to."

"Yes, I think so," I said again.

Sometimes what goes around comes around. Over the next few minutes we heard more calling. Soon we could hear the rattles of the fledgers.

Never mind all that stuff about how they're moving into their world and so on. The modern human mind wants to tell a story with a beginning, middle, and end—a linear story, with a timeline. From the owls' perspective—the day, the night, the year, the view—all stories seem circular. They were not verging on an ending. The fledgers' own life stories were barely beginning. And Alfie, early in her prime now, was moving through the cycling phases of a first year in a free-living life. Human stories have endings. Natural stories open possibilities.

Soon the whole Hoo was in the driveway cedars. We could see, silhouetted, Alfie and Plus-One, and the head-waving youngsters.

By ten minutes after nine, they'd all gone silent. Alfie and Plus-One were into the mysterious business of their night. But we'd ascertained that all remained right and tight. They'd made the biggest move since they'd left the nest box. Yet they continued sticking together. They were not "dispersing" as I had imagined it. They were venturing, as a group. I was so pleased. I had grown so fond of their company. Their departures were inevitable. The time was imminent when the youngsters would have to master their world. But if they were in no hurry, neither was I. I wasn't planning to go anywhere. I was content to remain, to feel at home as a visitor in their world while we shared it.

WE'VE HEARD FROM SOME THAT our "destiny" is to colonize other planets. But this has that same old sour smell, an urge to export colonial conquest, this time to space. Their stated reasoning: we are killing this living world. In their logic we can leave Earth for dead and "save ourselves" (a phrase meant to include absolutely none of us) by colonizing—dead worlds. Of course, the idea that salvation must occur off this planet is the old Platonist-Abrahamic impulse, nothing new. For the messianic billionaires stroking their rockets, heaven is Mars. But if they want to try living on a dead planet, it would be more efficient to just stay here and wait for this ailing planetary patient to die. And what ethics could justify seeding other worlds with the only species that has destroyed a world so perfectly suited for Life? Our explorations continue to generate views of galaxies being born in an infinite universe. The perspective is both expansive and humbling. But when will we prove ourselves worthy of a world that we so desperately need to love?

"This disintegration of the world was accompanied by feverish hope in a better future," observed Sylvain Tesson in *The Art of Patience*.

Politicians promised reforms, believers waited for eternal life, the lab rats of Silicon Valley offered us Humankind 2.0. . . . All three instances—revolutionary faith, messianic hope, technological charity—used the idea of salvation to mask complete indifference to the present. . . . Meanwhile, ice sheets melted, plastics proliferated, animals died. There were many of us, in the caves and in the cities, who longed, not for an augmented world, but for a world celebrated in fairness and equality, home only to its splendors.

✦

WE WERE INTO THE HOME quarter of June when one of the chickens began alarm calling from inside the coop at four-thirty a.m. That was unusual. Perhaps she'd seen the same raccoon that had come through the yard a couple of nights back. I dressed and went to check. A few mornings ago, the chickens had been alarmed to see a huge mama snapping turtle that had traveled perhaps a quarter mile from the nearest little stream, looking for a spot that felt right to her for digging her nest and laying her eggs. I'd often thought our humble yard unremarkable. I was coming into a fuller realization that many parallel lives breathed alongside us.

Even before I stepped outside, I heard Alfie calling from the foliage of the back-door dogwood. So we were back to all is well. Of course, all has always been well with her and her family. It's just that for a little while we'd been out of touch.

I admonished myself for worrying. When Alfie first came to us, I was of course immediately concerned about her health. My concern intensified when we gambled on releasing her from the safety of her confinement. I'd been concerned about the wild owl who soon became her mate, then concerned about their three chicks. Why was I so invested in worry? Everything had turned out well, for all of us so far. Alfie had shown us, as do our dogs and chickens, that life is to be lived, not fretted away. Other animals use reasonable caution. Why do we humans create elevated levels of fear? Why insist on being so afraid? Should I have had a little faith? Had we simply been very lucky? Whatever the answer, my worries about the owls had always proved misplaced. Everything I had worried could go wrong—had gone right.

———

THE OWLETS WERE MOVING MORE confidently and assuredly. They remained quite fuzzy, their markings like pastel shadows of their parents' hues, the barring on their breasts finer, altogether a softer beauty. The extravagance of their softness seemed appropriate to their innocence at this stage. Not yet hunters. Not yet responsible for anyone.

Did I say "confidently and assuredly"? One of them stumbled and fell through the cedar boughs before catching themself and righting like a gymnast on a bar.

The ever-surprising Alfie planed directly into the chickens' drinking pan. After flying to a low branch, she let me rub her bill. Owls enjoy bill rubs as dogs do belly rubs. She reciprocated with the gentlest nibbling of my finger, a reciprocal preening. The three fledgers continued carrying on in the cedars while their mother was carrying on here with me. All of this was outside her recent routine. Alfie always acted a bit free-form. She was a jazz improviser. Her unpredictability was one of the most endearing things about her.

Alfie flew to join her young ones. Every few minutes she uttered the strong contact call. Wherever Plus-One was—probably hunting somewhere—he would now know that his family had repositioned to here.

A blue jay landed four feet from an owlet and scolded. The youngster uttered a scratchy threat. I looked down to make a note, and when I looked up, two of the three fledgers had vanished.

In the spring I'd said that the utter silence of owls' wings made keeping track of Alfie and her mate "essentially impossible." To keep track of *five* is quite impossible. You momentarily take your eyes off of one to confirm the position of another, and when you look back two seconds later you see an empty branch. Even if the owl has moved just a few feet, a leaf might obscure the view. I watch. Sometimes I see. But the intricacies and details are theirs to know. I am on the ground picking up crumbs from the ambrosial bakery of their lived experience, trying with a primate brain to understand the vivid lives and minds of these acute birds. Often I merely wait for a sign, hoping the sounds of a catbird or wren, say, will help reveal them. Overall, the experience is quite humbling. Constantly trying to educate myself, I'd come to realize that the true value of an education is not in what you manage to learn but in sensing how little one knows.

Alfie and now Plus-One were suddenly together and giving me a clear view of them in very good light in the cedars. I couldn't understand why they hadn't decided to go to bed for the day. Helping to wish them a good sleep—perhaps a permanent one—several blue jays promptly launched aggressive attacks. After a couple of strikes made contact, Alfie wisely retreated into her ivy citadel. Plus-One, on a bare branch, drew all of the songbirds' ire. He took it, which helped keep their attention off the fledgers. A near-constant parade of onlookers came to pay their disdain. A cardinal. A downy woodpecker. An oriole. None stopped for long. They noted the presence and location of the reviled nemesis, then went to eat. The story continued.

WE HUMANS ARE AUTHORS OF more endings than of well-wrought stories. The end of "plenty of fish in the sea." The end of natural climate, the end of Arctic ice. The end of the epoch during which no turtle had a plastic straw in their nose and no shark was girdled by a discarded packing strap and no whale died from swallowing balloons that read, "Happy Graduation."

A few years ago, United Nations Secretary-General Ban Ki-moon addressed the World Economic Forum, saying, "We mined our way to growth. We burned our way to prosperity. We believed in consumption without consequences. . . . That model . . . is a global suicide pact." (Ban's mother was Buddhist; he himself took a Confucian approach.) "We are part of an earth-eating superorganism and no one is in control of it," wrote the economist and futurist Nate Hagens in an email. And now here we are, "lords of the flies," in William Golding's incisive parable of civilization, adolescents loose on a natural planet with no adult supervision. The late great biologist Edward O. Wilson had written, "The real problem of humanity" is that "we have paleolithic emotions; medieval institutions; and god-like technology."

These problems are enormous and dark, but the path out has been charted. It involves replacing our dualistic indoctrinations with a relational view of existence.

NEAR NINE P.M., AS SUNDOWN deepened, my neighbor John texted that four screech owls were in his yard. He knows this is Alfie's family. They've hopped across our yard, then across our next-door neighbors' yard and into John and Georgia's yard. The owlets delighted them, head bobbing as they assessed their next move. "It's the cutest thing," Georgia said of the swaying young ones, "like they're dancing."

The family was spreading out a little. Plus-One was in the yard between us. Alfie returned to our driveway cedars.

Soon the whole family converged on Alfie.

Soon again the young ones were back in John and Georgia's yard. Every few minutes we heard a strong *"Ow, ow, ow"* from one of the parents. Then all went quiet. Crickets began tuning up their instrumental bodies. Humans retreated into lighted abodes.

IT WOULD NOT DO TO have the family leaving me blind and behind now that they were venturing farther inside the ink of night. So I unwrapped my new pair of light-intensifying night-vision binoculars. These new binocs opened a dark world to view with an eerie, battery-intensified greenness, letting me scan the forest shadows and branchy tangles. I quickly discovered that even from across the night-black backyard, whenever Alfie was looking straight at me, the new binoculars made her eyes seem to glow like headlights. Useful!

Right away the night 'nocs found another owl. Two. Three. Four. In the ghostly green images of the night-vision binocs the owls' reflected eyes turned to embers in space. A constellation of owls. I picked up Plus-One high in John and Georgia's spruce. He crossed air tinted with the last indigo of daylight and the first stars, landing in a maple from which an owlet had just been calling.

He delivered a small, dark mammal with a longish tail, likely a white-footed mouse. The young one took the meal with high-intensity vocals and bill clacking.

Additional intense calling and chattering came from nearby, but I could not see who. And I lost track of the one who had the mouse. The binocs were helpful, but it was still night and they were still owls and I was still having difficulty keeping up with them.

I was hearing a new kind of call. Three or four separate notes, like the strong contact call, but with the first note uttered with the force of an "emphatic declaration." Alfie always varied the intensity and volume of her calls depending on the context. She well understood whether she was in conversation or was broadcasting. Context changes what needs to be communicated; intensity changes the message carried within the call. Researchers usually try to categorize calls. I've been guilty of that with Alfie. When I was in Uganda watching chimpanzees to learn about their communication, researcher Cat Hobaiter explained that other scientists placed their calls into categories such as pant-hoot, food grunt, and so on. She herself had trouble hearing their vocalizations categorically, but she was over it. "I used to just think I was really bad at categorizing," Cat said. "In reality, they all blur." Some researchers discount "partial" or "blended" calls. "But incomplete and blended calls," Cat said, "are a really huge part of their lives." The categories are mostly ours. The calls are entirely theirs.

What I was hearing seemed intermediate between what I'd been calling the "strong contact call" and an "emphatic declaration." It seemed that Alfie was blending notes, for a blended purpose. I always heard nuance in her "whinny." When she broadcast it during her morning song from the Ivy Tower, she was audible two backyards away. If she landed on a limb a few feet away from me, she'd whinny in the softest tones, as confiding as whispered love. Which—speaking for myself—it was.

I PICKED UP THE EYESHINE of two owls sitting next to each other on the same branch. I couldn't tell who, or whether these were two fledgers, a fledger and an adult, or both adults. I could see that one had the mouse but wasn't hungry enough to be eating it, while the other showed no interest in acquiring it.

We think—we *assume*—that survival in the natural world is a constant struggle for existence. Darwin said as much. But there are long stretches of well-being and full bellies and someone to preen you and plenty to go round. And that, too, is normal. It is why Life has persisted these last few billion years, and why it looks like the flagrant success it has been.

Through the night-vision binoculars at a little after nine-thirty, I was again watching an owl, definitely an adult, in possession of a mouse, likely the same one. The owl manipulated the mouse, then began tearing off pieces to feed an owlet. While the parent had plenty left, the owlet hopped away. The dutiful parent flew to the two other kids. Neither was interested.

21

⁂

The Fullness of Youth

CHULA, JUDE, AND CADY—SEADOGS ALL—JOINED PATRI-
cia and me on the boat while we fished for dinner. All three doggies have their accustomed spots and know to lie in secure positions
between the seats while we're underway. They love the ride, and they
watch the fishing activities with a detached and dignified curiosity.
They are good mates and a pleasure to have aboard.

Young birds and parental efforts were visible everywhere. Terns
crossed glittering waters with gleaming fish in their bills, destined for
camouflage-speckled young waiting in nests on isles miles away. We
were living in the season of great nurturing, the hemisphere's annual
bringing forth of new generations who will carry forward the enterprise of being alive in the world. This is also the season of greatest
hazards for the new and naïve. Fuzzy little willets accompanied by
parents treaded the shorelines with their huge feet. (Two got swept off
those feet by the current and were lucky to get retrieved by neighbors
who happened to see them from their boat.) Oystercatcher young followed closely as their parents probed the water's edge, learning what
their bladelike scarlet bills are specialized to accomplish. At the gull
colony, fat chicks stood like cottony softballs, waiting patiently for

parents on long-haul food missions. Also waiting near the gulls round the clock were red-tailed hawks and great horned owls, who took their tolls as needed for their own hungry youngsters.

Meanwhile, back at the cottage, meal-a-minute house wrens were constantly in and out of their nest box on our wooden fence, triggering a small chorus of excitement as they stuffed their little beggars with soft-bodied bugs for the short duration of each rushed visit. J.P.'s daughter Linda greeted me with the news that her tree swallows had just fledged. The young ones had fluttered into the beach grass and were trying to decide what to do next; we watched to be sure their parents were monitoring the situation. On a utility wire, a fledgling blue jay begged a parent for food. Ospreys were commuting across the sea skies and marshes like air traffic, headed to hunt or returning to nests with their talons gripping a struggling bluefish or menhaden or sea robin whose body they firmly and aerodynamically positioned head-forward into the wind. At their nest, the big fish hawks ripped little pieces and—like Alfie—offered them with the utmost gentleness to their young. There is something both informative and innocent about seeing a raptorial bird tearing flesh, then so solicitously and gently proffering it to their hook-billed youngsters. Were velociraptors as gentle and diligent? Did *T. rex* have a soft spot for the kids? Did their impending extinction and the loss of their world feel like anything to them? It does to me.

I HAVE ALWAYS FELT THAT my generation existed in a time spanning the last good years and the beginning of the end of the world. This is, of course, the indulgence that narcissists and religious fanatics have often reserved: the right to pleasure ourselves with this sense of self-importance. A visit with the realities can, it's true, seem like time at the vital bedside of a living world still fighting to stay alive. We can diagnose the problems, so repair must be possible. And already some things have gotten much better. Species that appeared doomed when I was in high school—I'm thinking of ospreys, bald eagles, peregrine falcons, and humpback whales—all got help they crucially needed.

They're again common, making our coast feel younger. Policy people had successfully warded off potentially catastrophic damage to the planet's atmospheric ozone layer. Perhaps we can yet reverse the dangerous changes we're causing to our atmosphere's heat balance. Perhaps this conversation should not be so hard. But does the language we speak limit how we think? Is that part of the difficulty?

Native American writer Robin Wall Kimmerer tells us that European colonization caused "replacement of a language of animacy with one of objectification which renders the beloved land as a lifeless object." This has been profoundly damaging for her people, who use the colonizers' English every day. "Our minds have also been colonized." she writes. "Bulldozers, buttons, berries, and butterflies are all referred to as *it*, as things, whether they are inanimate industrial products or living beings." Kimmerer adds, "I know the world as a living neighborhood, and enjoy my non-human neighbors, [but] the language does not assist me in conveying that." Conversely, many Native languages distinguish between living beings and non-living things. Kimmerer suggests a pronoun that distinguishes what is (or was) alive from the non-living and the human-made. Borrowing from a Potawatomi root referring to land, Kimmerer suggests a new pronoun: "ki," to signify "a being of the living earth." When morning's first bird announces a new day, we can say, "Ki is a robin." Coincidentally, "ki" harks back to *qi* or *ch'i* —the Chinese word for the energy flowing through all things. "Ki" also resonates with the *qui* of Latinate languages, where it means "who." At any rate, it's interesting to think about what our language implies by its inability or unwillingness to distinguish living from non-living. This is no small matter because, as Kimmerer observes, "Naming is the beginning of justice."

Justice means to get what is deserved. For most creatures, what is deserved is the chance to live freely. Injustice begins in misperception, fear, and domination. Justice begins in recognition of relatedness.

So, yes, all the foregoing could have gone differently.

Twenty-five centuries or so ago, Lao-tzu penned an antidote:

There is no calamity like not knowing what is enough
There is no curse greater than the desire for gain.
Therefore, whosoever knows what is enough will always have
   enough.

Would the problems have arisen if we'd known that word:
"enough"? Will the solutions come when we learn it? Will we learn it?

✦

"ACK! ACK! ACK! ACK! ACK!"

Well, *that's* a new one. Alfie? Plus-One? I glanced at the clock:
one fifty-five a.m., June 25. Those five very sharp notes woke me fully,
calling me out into the luxurious summer night.

The air was stock-still. Leafy canopies of maples and the spires
of cedars formed a denser darkness against the star-studded vault of
space. A few fireflies prickled the Milky Way. There appeared to be
two species: one up high, whose flashes seemed to pull the twinkling
stars into the forest canopy, and those shining their shimmers in the
shadows of shrubs. The higher ones signaled two or three blinks in
quick succession; the lower ones semaphored one flash at a time.

The darkness erased all property lines, freeing me like a cat traveling across backyards, searching for owls wherever I might, wherever
I pleased, wherever the heavens led me. I slid between bushes and
glided through shadows as any suburban tabby or possum or raccoon
might. Flickering television light emanated from a neighbor's upstairs
window, shifting every two or three seconds as scenes changed, the
digital blue-light all-night campfire warding off loneliness and the
fear-filled wildernesses of our minds.

At least I knew that my neighbors wouldn't hear my footsteps.
All of them had their windows shut to the summer night, central air
conditioners churning a coolness that pleasantly numbs them to sleep.
The units cycle on and off automatically, their external motors and
fans never all quiet at once, making listening difficult. When the air
conditioner fan next door shut off, I was surprised to feel my entire

body relax; I hadn't realized how tensed up that magic-suppressing sound made me. Previously mentioned: we have no air conditioner. We like to feel the breeze come though, to feel the night air cooling naturally, to savor such delicious sensations and sounds. On nights too hot to sleep, we might turn on a fan for a while, simulating a breeze if necessary. Or even venture out for a bit. But the windows stay open. We want to hear the seasons as spring frogs progress to summer crickets and katydids, to celebrate the sensuous night. And of course, we—at least I—wish to be awakened by any owls inclined to inform us of their whereabouts.

I bade my chilled-down neighbors pleasant dreams while I sleeplessly enjoyed a stroll through the parallel universe. A natural night always seems otherworldly. It is. Whether in the confines of a dark backyard, or in a mountain fastness, or on a black and heaving ocean far from land—anywhere the lights are hiding and stars presiding—barriers and borders external and internal lose their grip on us. Our minds fill the yawning darkness with a bit of dreamscape, putting a gauzy cast on perceptions, quieting voices, for once letting the creative mind edge out the compulsive obsessions of daylight's cramped cages, opening us to what lies somewhere beyond the pale.

"OW! OW! OW! OW!" Sharp, declarative. They are here, somewhere, working the night airs at two twenty-five a.m. This call came from near the street. Possibly even across the street, by Lise and Steve's house. I went to the roadside. With my night binoculars, I scanned. Seeing no owls, I did not want to linger. I didn't want to be caught in the headlights of any police car that might be catting; I didn't want to have to explain my nocturnal owl prowlings with night-vision optics, or have a cop follow me to my front door while I got my ID, setting off all three dog alarms and startling Patricia wide-eyed.

As for wandering around in the dark while avoiding the law—I had little to show; I was learning nothing new about little owls. If I did not own these night binoculars, I'd have drifted happily back to sleep, knowing simply that the owls were populating the night. But because the technology provided added superpowers, I was out here sleepily, a bit delirious, buzzed on summer—knowing simply that: the owls were populating the night. Which, truth be told, I'd known for months now.

At two thirty-three a.m. an owl pinged in with a three-note strong contact call, this time with the first note followed by a momentary delay. It seemed to come from a spruce alongside my neighbor's driveway. I scan, and scan, and—. The light-intensifying binoculars find a bright pair of headlights high up in the tree. The headlights blink. No head bobbing—so that's either Alfie or Plus-One. The owl preens a bit, holding a wing away from the body and going through each flight feather with their bill.

I lower my cheating glasses and the owl becomes unavailable to the mortal human. When I again raise the binoculars, the owl has silently vanished.

I hear a soft whinny to my left. But so what? There's got to be a limit. There will be a piper to pay for this sleep deprivation. I have a workday ahead of me, in just a few hours.

I wander back across my yard. A deer expresses alarm with a snort, surprised to have found a human intruder in a world that is theirs. I hear and can even feel the vibration of hooves striking the ground as the deer bounds away into deep velvet darkness.

It is three a.m. In about an hour and a half it will be getting light. Knowing me, I'll probably want to get up to greet the coming dawn. But I hope not.

Some heavy drops of much-needed rain begin falling, with a rumbling soundtrack. But just as abruptly, the drops cease and the promise fades.

I sneak into my own house.

EACH GENERATION IS GIVEN BOTH the gift of the world and the duty of keeping it safe for those who'll come, observes the writer Jay Griffiths. Technological development would have been possible within the guidance of a great gratitude, pursued as, yes, the love story Bertrand Russell imagined.

I've mentioned that when Indigenous people have acquired

engines, chain saws, and guns, they have often maintained their cultural values of respectful restraint. For instance, an Athapaskan man explained to Richard Nelson that although he'd trapped in a certain area all his life—and his father before him—"it's still good ground." Still lots of beavers, minks, martens, otters, and bears. "I took good care of it . . . don't take too much out of it or you'll get nothing later." Simple enough. After thousands of years of Native use, the area would strike a visitor as essentially untouched. When a society sees a right to take and a need to compete, everyone feels entitled to take all they can. When a society asks, "How much should we leave?," taking means taking care. The coasts and lands that struck European explorers as virgin wilderness had long been home to Indigenous peoples who knew them well—and understood the need to leave enough.

Fabian Jimbijti of the Shuar tribe in Ecuador sometimes forages for several days, gathering wild edible plants, catching fish, and collecting salt. His bounty gets distributed to family members in several villages. "We take enough but not too much," he told a journalist. Taking more than enough "would be a lack of respect for everything and create a total imbalance." In northeast India, Phrang Roy of the Khasi people, author of the United Nations report titled "Indigenous Peoples' Food Systems," said that while the world is "faced with all the crises of climate breakdown, rising inequality, and biodiversity loss . . . Indigenous peoples have a harmony and interconnectedness with nature that is based on balance and collaboration." Such ethics survive; they could realign our thinking.

Nowadays many scientists *do* see an integrated world. Dualism is giving way to a realism that can let us, finally, embrace the love story of the world's deep unity. Ecologists see a big picture of Life having woven itself over eons into fabrics of continuing coadaptation. Geneticists have found all of Life's mind-boggling proliferation growing from one deep root. To finally recognize the overwhelming beauty of the singular living family—it can deliver a jolt.

I SLEPT TILL FIVE-THIRTY—AND FELT ashamed of myself for missing the morning's first wink of light. I was obsessed. The accursed night binoculars enabled an excess that darkness had formerly guard-railed. Too sleepy for real writing, I found myself nodding off while simply trying to answer emails.

So I got up to walk around. Outside, I located no owls. I searched where I'd seen an owl preening around two-thirty a.m. I detected nothing owly. I walked back to my own driveway. Checked the cedars. They were missing.

At six a.m., well past owl hours, I let the dogs out. I went to our little vegetable garden to pick some mint and sage to make tea. Jude, our black dog, the one we call "the poet" for his drifty, dreamy approach to time, waggled over to say hello. You'd never know it, but in his quiet, subtle way he likes to keep an eye on things, without making it obvious that he's checking that everyone's okay.

Soft as a sigh, the faintest of whinnies reached me. Just one. I was being watched by an unseen seer. I heard a fledger growl. And there they were, as if materializing. I found them back in the original biv-ouac area between the raccoon tree and our vegetable garden. Why hadn't I checked *there*?

Two fledgers rested together about twenty-five feet up in a leafy maple close to the street, not far from the stop sign—*as usual*. The third revealed themself by moving on a nearby branch. Around the yard this year, it was always owl time. Whether I knew about it or not, they were always somewhere, doing something, even if they were sometimes doing nothing much.

It is a distinctly human conceit that when they are out of sight we call them "missing." When they are not there *for us*, we feel as though they are "not there." I've mentioned the concept of "object perma-nence" in psychology. It's our understanding that when something we've seen goes out of sight, it continues to exist. This is a capacity humans develop during infancy. Some psychologists have believed that only humans possess object permanence. Any dog who waits for you in the driveway knows what those psychologists don't. The owls call to each other when they need to reconnect, track each other's whereabouts, and rendezvous in known places they return to. What *we* don't quite know—because one's blindness is the hardest thing to see—is how faulty is our own capacity for object permanence. "Out of sight, out of mind." It's why we don't continually bear in mind the existences of owls and every thing that creepeth, though they themselves are always very much there, exerting all efforts to maintain their toehold on our shared bit of galactic dust. The world is always going on. Their lives are always going on.

FROM PLATO TO DESCARTES, the belief was that the thinking mind indicates that the material and immaterial are estranged and at odds. In reality, the mind is perhaps the best evidence that the material and immaterial together create the world we see. Imagine a particular dog, perhaps one you've known. Throw a stick. The happy doggie is chasing that stick. See? Our mind emerges from chemical and electrical impulses along paths of networked nerve cells. Neurobiologists have given the nerves names; they understand the neurotransmitters' chemical pathways. Such understanding represents a triumph for reductionists, but—. Nowhere in the chemical bonds and action potentials is your picture of the dog with the wagging tail traveling along a neuron. When your conscious mind envisions a dog, something pretty wild is going on. The chemical and the cellular facilitate the strangely immaterial experiences we call "sensation," "imagination," and "thought." No one quite knows what goes on or how that happens. Our mind does not fully know itself. We can locate our brain. But thought is an emergent thing. Where are our loves and fears and secrets? Are they in there? Or, like music, do they exist only while they are being played? There is no clear understanding of what, exactly, a thought or a memory actually *is*. But we might say that a thought is the material and the immaterial collaborating in the act of creation. Likewise in loving, and when "the chemistry is right," are we not sharing both bodies and something immaterial? In that sense, the music of life happening—we can call it the spirit if we like—pervades all lived experience. Spirit is a kind of music that living things are always making.

So our physical nervous system somehow creates our emergent mind. Like two personalities in our head, different parts of our prefrontal cortex (often oversimplified as right brain and left brain) may respond to the world a bit differently. After a career studying the human brain, Jill Bolte Taylor experienced her own near-fatal stroke (described in her book *My Stroke of Insight* and her online TED talk). While she was losing her sense of who she was, she was feeling, she says, that "my soul was as big as the universe and frolicked with glee in a boundless sea. . . . I was completely entranced by feelings of tranquility, safety, blessedness, euphoria, and omniscience." She believes that a wise but seldom experienced part of our mind recognizes "this marvelous planet, which sustains our life. It perceives the big picture, how everything is related, and how we all join together to make up the whole." Can we attain such awareness without a near-death experience?

MEANWHILE, THE SLOW-GROWING HOO REMAINED down-jacketed, fluffy, light as the clouds above them. They preened themselves and preened each other. Every few minutes they hopped away from each other. After they'd hopped away, they'd hop back together. Their mutual magnetism maintained their tight-knit residency. They were playing it prudent in a fraught world. Deft little acrobats, they were still getting the hang of their wings and things. I'd still occasionally see one hop toward a limb, miss the grab, fall a few feet, latch onto a clump of leaves, hang upside down for a few moments, right themself, then look around as though hoping nobody noticed. They remained very much children, totally dependent on their parents. On their way to independence, dependence remained the thing they knew best.

Patricia came out. All three doggies wagged round her. She had her good camera. She confronted a difficult photo situation: deep shadows cast by the lush canopy. But she has the technical skill, and she has an exceptional eye. She made some fine images with which she could share the beauty of the owls' steady sanity.

Beauty and sanity seemed increasingly precious in a world unbeautifying itself, fraying and increasingly afraid. The year's painful trifecta—a pandemic, inflamed racial tensions, the international ascent of lying autocrats—made it challenging to stay reasonably well, made it necessary to remain unreasonably sane, made it imperative to step outside of comforts and show up for a better world. Many unfolding events were appalling, much of the news dispiriting. Helping Patricia and me through it, of course, were the non-human aces up our sleeve. Foremost, the impeccably timed salve gifted to us by this owl family, those court jesters daily sprinkling our lives with touches of weightless wizardry. And, of course, the doggies, performing as themselves, were our anchoring smile factory. With their fierce devotion, their proclivity to protect what they loved, their in-the-present joy, and their capacity for forgiveness, they were our exemplars for how to be the kind of humans we wanted to become. And our spring chickens, so companionable in the yard as they grew, reminded us that life remained as capable of renewal as ever. In all, they would have been the best things even in a good year. In this year, they felt crucial. They were our daily instructors, our little gurus, our reasons for getting out of bed early. For the hours daily that they occupied our attentions, they buoyed us sufficiently to distract our minds from the things in the world that were going off the rails. They saved our spirits. Their main lesson: coming into being is the fundamental genius of Life itself.

WHILE OUR LAWN LINGERED IN tree-cast shadows, trees across the street stood in the bright strike of early morning sunshine. From our wires a mockingbird soloed chorus after extended chorus, like an avian John Coltrane.

The Hoo were now so accustomed to our commotions that one of them, dozing, didn't bother to so much as peek when our dogs chased a squirrel, who scrambled up a nearby tree, and the dogs barked and barked and barked, their tails waving gleefully, juiced by the part of their minds that remembered, vaguely, what it means to be a wolf.

Patricia was watering her flower garden indulgently, handling the hose with care in getting around to all her sprouts and plantings. As if pleasure can replicate like some living thing, it gave me great pleasure to see the pleasure she got in nurturing those roots and stems and leaves here in our morning backyard, communing with her buds and blooms.

Me? I was about to discontinue my morning monitoring of the Hoo; I had been standing there a long time and I had my to-dos. But things kept changing. The lower fledger hopped away, to somewhere. I was searching with binoculars for the third owlet, whom I didn't think had gone far, when an adult jumped into my field of view and fairly glared at me. Plus-One. Just past his head, I noticed in the binoculars the talons of the third fledger, gripping a branch. The fledger's entire body was hidden from my view by just two maple leaves; their toes alone were visible. So actually, Dad and all the Hoo were within two feet of one another. And yet so hard for a human—such as I admittedly am—to detect. Now all three young owlets were lined up on the same branch, looking my way. Now they turned a one-eighty, looking at the world from a new angle.

Meanwhile, almost directly under the owls, people jogged past or walked along the street with dogs on leashes. At the stop sign, cars and pickups rolled to a grudging half stop, then growled ahead, their internally combusting grinders clashing with the perfectly meshed light and birds, their heavy-footed occupants scurrying to chilled cubicles or sweaty labors. A swimming pool company's truck followed a landscaper's truck, followed by a car booming something low and loud. The human span of day, the hours of harsh glares, was theirs. The people of the street had various things happening. The thing we alone happened to have was various owls.

Up in the canopy in that sea of leafy shade, it remained a perfect time and place to be a new bird. And what better thing could we and Alfie do than to nurture what is young and growing? If that is the greatest act of faith—as I believe—one might say that Alfie and Patricia and I were practitioners in the same religion.

The owlets were starting to make a very rough version of the whinny, rendering a gravelly *"Owwww, owwwww"* with a guttural texture, like Himalayan throat singers.

I noticed in the front bushes a fledgling mockingbird and what looked like a fledged catbird with a still-stubby tail. All their parents have reason to hate and fear the innocent young wide-eyed owls, whose parents have grown them partly on the corpses of such neighbors.

And yet—our yard remained this full of sound and color. Abundant new life. No discernible diminishment. If predation entails tragedy, it also creates matching beauties. When you step back a bit, you can see the webworks of mutual reliance. All sides are supported. Predator and prey are less enemies than partners in a dance. There's killing, yes, but neither of these unifying opposites destroys the other. A yin and a yang making things whole, maintaining dynamic balances.

Our stories reflect our values. Some stories of our time are money, politics, merchandise, and self-image. What if instead our stories were of community, children, stability, coexistence with the world—? For most cultures, during most of human history, those *were* the stories. Stories of relation. Our world seems worthy of a few more stories of compassion, or simply of love.

How we see determines what we see. Beliefs shape values; values shape cultures; cultures shape history; and history—for better or worse—shapes Life's trajectory. Values flow from a culture's myths and metaphors, from its poetry. Values determine how technology is used. Western values were set centuries prior to plumbing, engines, electricity, petroleum, plastics, and digital devices. The main thing is not the tech, not the financial system, not the political system, not religions; it's this: all human creations *serve the values* of the people who created them. We could have high-tech, stable economies, circular no-waste material flows, government of one sort or another, a financial system, openhearted belief systems, human dignity, a healthy environment, and vital wildness for living beings—if that was what our worldview valued, our pulpits preached, and our institutions pursued. Humans do what they value doing. We are who we keep choosing to be.

BY THE TIME THE OWLETS' varied moves had put them close to one another, the chickens were complaining from their coop. After a night of freedom from danger, the hens preferred the danger of freedom. At a quarter to seven I swung the door open and they came bursting out. The three older hens hustled their bustles along the trail they've made through the cover of yew bushes. But the six young spring chicks turned about and gathered around me. They weren't sure whether I'd be feeding them inside the coop, as I did when they were small, or letting them join the older hens by the back porch, as I've started to do. Turns out, it's the latter. I've already sprinkled their seed off the back porch. So they run down and then spread out among the scattered food like river water fanning into delta shallows.

At three months, the new chickens' internal skeletons were already full-grown. But they remained slim, svelte, leggy birds. Our little flock's breakfast this day was two quarts of barley from our neighbor Travis the brewer, who'd brought us a five-gallon bucket of the stuff left over from his brewing process. I tried it; it tastes good. The chickens love it. They were also getting some wild birdseed mix and some watermelon rinds from which to peck leftovers (we slice the melon generously, with them in mind). The last thing in the world they want are the commercial "complete diet" pellets sold for laying hens. Of this, our chickens have informed us by voting with their beaks. Our hens, we are proud to say, always look gorgeous, even at the peak strain of their egg-laying years. But at the moment, we had a bit of a generation gap. The three older hens hung around together. The six younger ones hung around together. The elders exerted their rank, claiming first dibs. One of our matrons, Stripey, was chasing all the young chicks from all the food. This is how it goes right now, I thought. But the day will come when the young begin to challenge the old order. Zorro ate her fill and then headed up to the coop's egg-laying boxes. The young ones and Smokey trucked into the neighbors' yard where the grass is greener, leaving the entire feeding area to Stripey—who appeared quite pleased to monopolize it.

Chula and Jude know not to bother the chickens' breakfast buffet. But young Cady wants to move in and vacuum up anything that appeals to her. Everything appeals to her. So I distract her by snapping my fingers—her signal to hop up onto the back deck for a treat—and give her a couple of ice cubes. She loves getting what she considers the superior treat, and she crunches away with great satisfaction.

After eating their provided breakfast, the chickens generally drifted off to nip grass tips and scratch for bugs. We were having an unusually severe drought. The leaves on many bushes were wilting. Grass and weeds, often lush at this time of year, were crunching underfoot. Our garden required daily watering to prevent quick desiccation. Droughts can be hard on insects, creating tough times for food chains. Across the continent, severe droughts in California and unusually high temperatures would in coming weeks again help ignite large areas, reducing some human communities to cinders and burning down the homes of two couples I know personally.

I watched as our slender spring chickens hunted for bugs in the leaf litter under bushes, their beaks open, panting in the heat. The high temperatures really stressed them. To cool their coop so they would not have a miserable night, I went to open the big double doors of the shed. Although all the shed's windows were open, I got a blast of heat as I swung the doors apart. Intolerable though much of the nation's news was for me, I was doing what I could to keep things tolerable for them.

WE ARE ONLY HUMAN BEINGS, after all. We come with the inherent privileges and faults thereof. *Humane* being would be a nice step up. But we don't have to reinvent. The human heritage has an abundance of elevated thought from which to choose. Some of the best new thinking—is very old.

As a child in the 1930s and '40s, Elizabeth Marshall Thomas was in love with animals, devouring anything she could read about them. Noticing this love, her school's librarian forbade her from borrowing any more animal books. Henceforth, she would be allowed only books about people. "Her decree was like death," Thomas wrote. The librarian believed that only people mattered.

Thomas later noted that we in our dualistic culture tend to construct two spheres of existence. One is people. The other is everything else: "From amoebas to blue whales, from duckweed to giant sequoias, from the floor of the Mariana Trench to the summit of Everest." In Thomas's unique view, "Every living thing in that second sphere belongs to what I've come to call the Old Way, keeping the old rules that evolution set out for each species, the rules that helped us stay alive and move our genes into the future. The Old Way put us here," she observes, "but we no longer respect that."

Elizabeth Marshall Thomas experienced the Old Way when, as a teenager in the 1950s, she and her family were the first white people to see, live with, and write of the Juwasi people in the Kalahari region of what is now Namibia, in southern Africa. Living their ancient traditional hunter-gatherer existence, the Juwasi got all they needed from that harsh desert in only two or three hours of foraging daily. During droughts, they would move to a region less affected. The people there would welcome them and share what the stark land itself had shared.

Many modern people assume that traditional Indigenous life must have entailed constant drudgery, certainly worse than their own work-for-pay present. In reality, Native people generally enjoyed abundant food and good nutrition. Leisure time was plentiful and often used creatively. Museum collections show that things like fishhooks and spoons were not only useful implements but also ornamented works of art and meaning. No duality separated utility and aesthetics.

Elizabeth Marshall Thomas got a glimpse of people living as they were made to live, in the world that made us. Thomas went on to write many books and traveled to many remnants of a world that was. But, she says, the Juwasi people she came to know remained her lifelong "lodestar," the purest example of the sense of relation and community by which humans are made to thrive. Mind you, these were hunter-gatherers with few and precious material possessions. But also mind you, the Juwasi possessed no word for "theft."

NEAR SUNSET I STARTED LOOKING where I'd left the Hoo. And—they were still there, in a maple twenty feet from the street and the stop sign and our garden, fifty feet from the raccoon tree, about one hundred feet from where they'd hatched. Such stay-at-home little owls! I'd have bet that Plus-One, at least, was also watching me.

Sure enough, he popped into view.

PART SIX

Going, Going

22

⁂

Yarders

AFTER DINNER, I DROVE TO OUR COTTAGE BY THE BAY. Before bed, I phoned Patricia.

"All five owls put on a big show," she told me. Our little roving band of fuzzy homebodies had been flying back and forth from the woods' edge to our huge, old central maple. They'd been begging energetically. So Patricia gave Alfie some food, which she flew to her fluffy kids. Every night was a little different. I was sorry to have missed that performance.

But I was glad, too, to be at the beach, amid its own summer miracles. After several years of alarming declines in the Fowler's toad population, there were so many toads out in the early evening that where the road bends onto our street I had to stop the car. I shooed about twenty toads off the pavement so I could proceed. This recovery would also benefit the last of Long Island's once-plentiful hognose snakes, who hunt mainly toads. They have suffered extirpation across suburbia but are holding on here. In the final hundred yards to our cottage, I had to weave to avoid toads. I'd never seen so many.

I hit the pillow.

I left the house before dawn to head down to the boat for the morning.

BY EVENING ALL THE CHICKS and Plus-One were, yet again, in a young maple near the street, by the stop sign. The fledgers seemed a bit uncomfortable with us tonight. They uttered a growly little threat that sounded like crumpling cellophane. When the dogs walked directly beneath them, they straightened up a little and erected the downy suggestions of their future "ear" tufts.

Two of our older hens, Stripey and Smokey, came around, scratching. Patricia and I were watching the owls, the dogs were watching us, the chickens were watching the dogs, and the owls watched everything. For the first time, I saw the fledgers following the hens' movements. A chicken would be many times too big for a screech owl to tackle. But the owlets watched them with the fascinated curiosity of young future hunters who were feeling stirrings and first urges.

One of the fledgers began to doze. I lifted my camera, and by the time my finger was on the shutter button, they were *all* dozing. Such emotional contagion is a fundamental form of empathy. As with contagious yawning or contagious fear, their minds, like ours, assess and match the moods of those around us. That capacity helps them remain so close together, so sticky.

We left for a couple of hours, returning at a little past eight-thirty p.m.

"*Ow! Ow! Ow!*"

"*Ow! Ow! Ow!*"

Alfie and Plus-One were corresponding. I heard a chick rattle and saw the Hoo flying one by one into the woods near the studio. Their softly stated chitters sounded like they were saying to their parents, "I'm over here. I'm not very hungry. Just letting you know." They were no-drama, like their mama.

Patricia went inside. The three dogs turned their heads to me. How like the owls we were, and how like us the owls were, that the members of our families know each other, know where to find each other, and understand that where we convene is home; home is where we live, together.

Of course, the Hoo will have to strike out on their own separately, will each have to try to make a life of their own somewhere in the world. As all our young ones must. As we all do. And then there will be drama indeed. As there usually is.

It was a Friday night. At the stop sign, a lot of traffic was slowing and going. Tuned as I was to the whispers of owls, internal combustion engines had never seemed so primitive. From the perspective of the owls, Friday in summer meant that the neighboring yards were under human occupation, unavailable for hunting. The neighbors next door had company sitting outside, cackling like poultry. Next door to them, John and Georgia also had noisy company in the backyard—I knew because I'd been one of their noisy guests; we'd just come home from there.

I wondered how the owls themselves, their ears and hearing so finely attuned for the near-silent reveal of a mouse's soft toes, can cope with us. When there's a pause in the street traffic, our neighbor's air conditioner is intrusive even here, at the edge of the woods on the far side of our house. And we live in a relatively quiet neighborhood. But when your ears adjust to softer realities, it's a noisy place in a crowded world that has forgotten how to listen.

Yet under that churn, the magic broadcast continues. If we tune in, we can enter the weave that over long eons kept the fabric of the world together. All these birds and their babies, the seasonal procession of flowerings and seedings, the living and dying of moths and of mice—all of it, enmeshed in this worn tapestry, continues to hold on against and alongside us, even while we unweave the web of life.

◆

WHEN I WALKED OUTSIDE JUST before five a.m. on June 27, I heard the Hoo growling from somewhere high in the big central maple. Against the pale blue of the lightening sky I saw one, then two, then all three owlets fly to the fruit-laden mulberry tree. The move was not approved of by the mockingbird, who chucked at them. Scoldings notwithstanding, the owls dallied. The mulberry tree was busy feeding catbirds and orioles and others, getting its seeds dispersed, paying the movers with fruit. Someone had once advised Patricia and me to cut this tree down, saying, "It makes such a mess." But we love this mess. All the songbirds and even our ground-bound chickens get in on this gig, salvaging fallen berries. Verily the tree turns sunlight into life; the berries turn the tree into growing birds; birds scatter seeds that build more community. I was surprised to see a woodpecker feeding mulberries to a begging fledgling, but woodpeckers know a bargain when they see it. Perhaps this parent woodpecker had been fed from this very tree. Only a human could see a "mess" here, because only a human could be taught blindness to the consecrations and liturgies of birds and chipmunks seeking their sacramental fodders and preaching their ancient faiths to their new young. A recently fledged mockingbird chick appeared. There was much innocence in the yard—much vulnerability. Last summer we found two fledgling blue jays, too young to fly, in our vegetable garden. These fledgling jays could call to their nearby parents, so we left them and wished them well. In the morning we found two small piles of blue feathers. Those unlucky little jays had made an unfortunate choice; they had roosted in the open rather than finding some secluding bit of vegetation. Bad luck was the high cost of inexperience. I wonder now whether Plus-One—who'd been around last summer—had devoured them. For every thing that wants to avoid being eaten, there is another who wants to avoid starving.

Alfie flew swiftly and directly to the ground. She threw her head back and swallowed something soft, a moth or cricket.

The Hoo all flapped heavily to our walnut tree. They were so keyed and cued by each other's movements that it was almost as though each decision was a group decision. They were not just three fledglings begging in their own self-interest. They were Three Musketeers, such a tight little band.

They presented a good opportunity for photographs and today I had my long lens and my tripod. Alfie landed on my camera. Okay, Alfie, no photos of you this morning.

Alfie caught a second moth. Doing well here.

I finally tossed a defrosted mouse onto the lawn. Alfie planed down and grabbed the sacrificial offering, as she had done so many times. Usually she just flies away with it. But this time she grabbed it by the head, biting and pulling as if killing a live mouse. This strongly suggested that she had acquired the rodent-hunting skills of a fully realized owl.

As had long been the case, her owlets were too full to care. My contributions were superfluous. And that's the way I liked it. Plus-One and Alfie were still catching enough food for all five owls in this family.

But I could not deflect the morning's wider metaphor. One wishes to serve the world a mouse that it actually needs, to count for something rather than simply make a motion of good intentions. Then again, perhaps a demonstration of goodwill is enough on some days. Like all beliefs, apathy toward the world is an arrived-at course of action, fueled by the myths we swim in. We blink our eyes open and go schooling in the direction that the whole shoal is swimming, traveling the mythology we were born into. We could instead be like the first fish who came ashore and realized that living in water is only one of the possibilities.

New cloth can be woven from the threads of this unraveling world. The question, as always: How? The thinking and values that got us here will not guide us out. As the physicist Freeman Dyson warned, "The progress of science is destined to bring enormous confusion and misery to mankind unless it is accompanied by progress in ethics." Fortunately, the needed ideas have been around a long time. The values from which to grow new answers have been here for centuries. Much of the world's oldest thinking could scaffold a technological culture in the service of survival, a culture fundamentally different from our current planetary macerator. We could prioritize maintaining the harmonies, as advocated by Confucians. Or attribute to all beings souls of equivalent value, as do many dharmic followers of Buddhist, Hindu, Jain, Sikh, and other beliefs. Or elevate community, place, and all our relations, as do traditional Native American, Australian, African, Hawaiian, Maori, Polynesian, and other Old Way cultures. Their lifeways tend to be based in participation rather than control, inclusion rather than alienation, with knowledge as a source of wisdom rather than a tool of power. These things, perhaps we could relearn.

DAY TO DAY, THE OWLETS did more flying. Compared to a human baby's development, theirs was incredibly fast. But compared to songbirds', their flight competence and the onset of foraging seemed remarkably slow. As for anything like hunting, I'd seen no attempts targeting bugs or even mock attacks on inanimate objects.

Having just considered that thought, however, I next noticed one owlet focusing intently on the ground with what looked like a hunter's attention.

Alfie flew over to feed that owlet. I remained impressed that Alfie was so diligently solicitous in feeding her different youngsters. She was not "reflexively" stuffing food into the "stimulus" of a chick's open mouth. Alfie's approach was further from "stimulus" and "reflex" than a human mother's response to a crying baby. If we watched a human doing what Alfie was doing, we'd describe her as caring and doting. She showed a conscious effort to spread nurturance to each member of her brood. Outwardly, Alfie's parenting inclinations seemed comparable to a human's at mealtime. She knew she had food. She knew she had more than one child. And she was motivated to give each of them a meal.

At last this owlet that Alfie was coaxing took the remainder of the mouse and chugged it down in a big gulp, eyes closed. Of the world, the Hoo knew only that there's plenty of food. They remained ignorant of the effort, the pain, the strain required, the risks. They seemed as oblivious as most of us.

Plus-One whinnied from a sapling. Alfie moved close, into an adjacent tree, calling softly. Plus-One quieted.

Suddenly Alfie piped out, *"Oh! Oh! Oh! Oh! Oh!,"* her voice almost crisp enough to ring.

The black cat came skulking right between the trees in which the adults stood watching. Patricia happened to open the kitchen door and our dogs ran out. The cat turned, sprinting into the woods.

A CHANGE OF DIRECTION REMAINS possible. Ancient values could ease present ills. But we cannot wait for yesterday. Nor need we. Indigenous values could yet help guide a modern rebalancing. Ecological thinking is a modern idea for a livable future. A thing is right when it adds beauty and compassion to the world. Paths exist.

Ubuntu is the Bantu term for the traditional African concept "I am because we are." Its values and practices affirm that a human being is part of a relational world. Desmond Tutu, Nelson Mandela, and the Episcopal Church have all highlighted *ubuntu* as a guiding concept relevant to modern needs. *Ubuntu*, writes philosopher and teacher Mark Nepo, implies "the vow to water the common roots by which we all grow."

Edward O. Wilson advanced the idea that preserving the living world and the future dignity of humankind would require keeping about half of the Earth in a functionally natural state. Indigenous peoples will be crucial in such an enterprise. In Canada, Australia, and Brazil, places inhabited by Native peoples still harbor as much or more living diversity than areas set aside by governments in parks and preserves. In the Amazon, New Guinea, Borneo, Africa, and Canada, Indigenous peoples still struggle to protect their landscapes from the likes of us. They continue defending their lands and waters against our appetites for cheap meat, oil, gas, minerals, metals, and wood. Search online for "Indigenous killed defending"; you'll see that thousands of Indigenous people have been murdered in recent years—an average of one every two days—for protecting their homelands from illegal loggers, ranchers, and miners. Protecting the world requires protecting world-keeping Indigenous cultures themselves, in their ancestral homescapes.

Indigenous answers are already working in the modern world in a very noteworthy way. Haudenosaunee (Iroquois) democracy so attracted American colonists that it was a model for the United States

Constitution. Structured according to the Haudenosaunee Great Law of Peace, the Haudenosaunee Confederacy served their communities and future generations through a two-level democratic legislature that maintained a balance of powers between the confederacy and its constituent tribes. In 1744, an Onondaga man named Canassatego addressed the Provincial Council of Pennsylvania, urging its members to form a nation similar to the Iroquois Confederacy. Colonists also considered government structures from Greek and Roman times, from the Bible, and from Europe. But at the Albany Congress of 1754, representatives of six Native nations and seven colonies heard Benjamin Franklin tell the assembly that if six aboriginal nations were capable of forming a government that "has subsisted for ages and appears indissolvable," a similar union should prove practical for the English colonies.

The United States Constitution did indeed create a republic patterned on Indigenous democracy. There remains much time-tested thinking from which to form an inflection point away from an age of hurting the world to an era of healing.

◆

LATE IN THE AFTERNOON ON June 27, two neighborhood youngsters entering the woods from the street walked right through the bivouac area, unaware that just overhead five owls watched them.

A light rain began, the first since the young owls fledged. It was refreshing to be in cool evening air, listening to much-needed raindrops falling through the trees. After the rain I expected soggy, bedraggled owlets. But under their maple umbrella, their fluffy down slightly matted at the tips into damp little wisps, they looked no wetter than misted pineapples. One preened, pulling the feathers of a wing through their bill. Another sat on the branch like a chicken on an egg.

Speaking of, the spring chicks were now making honklike calls, transitioning between baby squeals and an adult repertoire of clucks and chucks. I closed all the chickens in for the night. Even on what seemed to me a delightfully cool evening and with their coop's windows open, they were all panting, hot past sundown. All things feel; all seek well-being. They sought to create some relief by drooping their wings to get better airflow around their bodies.

IN THIS SLOWLY BAKING, OVERWROUGHT, elbow-to-elbow world, the stakes have become enormous, and so have the needs. But there exists much relational thinking to select from and build on, even in the West's faiths and wisdom traditions. There are the Hellenic ideals, the Judaic Noahic covenant, the Christian call to assist the least of our neighbors, and more to mine in those veins.

New England's Transcendentalists of the 1800s—centered by the writings of former minister and devout abolitionist Ralph Waldo Emerson and of Henry David Thoreau—sought to return the divine to this Earth. "I am part or particle of God," wrote Emerson heretically in his book *Nature.* Emerson viewed all of nature as miraculous. For saying as much at Harvard, he was not invited back for thirty years. When Thoreau wrote, "Heaven is under our feet as well as over our heads," he quite meant it.

Over the last century, the Catholic Church itself has increasingly embraced the physical cosmos and the material Creation. Georges Lemaître, a twentieth-century Catholic priest with a PhD in theoretical physics, was an astronomer, mathematician, and university professor. Around 1930, his calculations formally established the modern notion that the entire universe and all of space and time began from a single point and is still expanding. This Big Bang is perhaps the most fundamental idea in human history. In the 1960s, the Catholic monk Thomas Merton wrote: "I have been shocked at a notice of a new book, by Rachel Carson [*Silent Spring*], on what is happening to birds as a result of the indiscriminate use of poisons. . . . Someone will say: you worry about birds: why not worry about people? I worry about both birds and people. . . . It is all part of the same sickness, and it all hangs together." Not surprisingly, Merton was sharply criticized—but not deterred—for his faith-based concerns about social justice, civil rights, and environmental health. Later, the religious scholar and Catholic priest Thomas Berry wrote extensively on the need to do "the Great Work" of reforming the frameworks of our lives—political, legal, economic, educational, environmental, and religious. Berry believed that "the time has come to lower our voices, to cease imposing our mechanistic patterns on the biological processes of the earth, to resist the impulse to control, to command, to force, to oppress; and to begin quite humbly to follow the guidance of the larger community on which our life depends." He called for a new story of the cosmos and Earth as sacred, ushering us into reverence and care and a new period of ecological renewal he envisioned as the "ecozoic" era. "Our human destiny," Berry understood, "is integral with the destiny of the earth."

In 1995, the Eastern Orthodox Church ecumenical patriarch, Bartholomew I, held a series of conferences for scientists and religious leaders titled "Religion, Science, and the Environment." Bartholomew declared, "For human beings to cause species to become extinct and to destroy the biological diversity of God's creation . . ."—he cited climate change, loss of forests and wetlands and toxic substances—"these are sins." Writing at the beginning of our twenty-first century, the Franciscan Catholic monk and theologian Richard Rohr admonished his Christian audience: "Many Christians have seen the world as sadly inert, non-enchanted, unholy, and even dangerous and evil. . . . just a gratuitous painted backdrop so we could do our Christian thing and be 'saved.'" But seeing God's creation as separate from God, he said, resulted in, "an almost blasphemous waste of time and a shocking disrespect for God's one, beautiful, and multitudinous life." When Cardinal Jorge Mario Bergoglio was elected pope, he took a name no prior pope had chosen, Francis, after the Catholic Church's official patron saint of respect for the natural world and of advocacy for the poor. Pope Francis's 2015 encyclical, *Laudato Si'*, is a unique blend of distilled science and religious imperative. Pope Francis warned of the extremely high costs of environmental deterioration in the present and for the future. The encyclical met a polarized—one might say dualized—reception, embraced and disdained. In 2017, Francis and Bartholomew issued a joint statement acknowledging that "deterioration of the planet weighs upon the most vulnerable of its people."

A small Christian evangelical movement has diversified under the headings "Creation Care" and "ecotheology." Meanwhile, the Yale Forum on Religion and Ecology has provided a portal to some of the world's most compassionate, practical, and needed thinking and writing. Religious recognition in certain quarters is seeking to soften the sharp dualist lines that for centuries have facilitated both human and planetary degradation. It's a start.

"OW! OW! OW!"

Their time had begun. An adult whinnied, and the Hoo made scratchy, screechy versions of the adult call.

The moon rose watercolored by the moist early summer air. Up across dark heaven, a killdeer or two were calling in the flight of night. But why? Who were they? Such creatures see our lights, our houses, roads, and cars. They are more aware of us than we of them. But they live in a world that was ancient before antiquity, a world that swells and subsides to planetary rhythms and immense scales of time. A world of instincts, impulses, discernments, and their own cultures. A world of intricacies and complexities created by no one and maintained by no thing yet proliferating across eons. A proximate but parallel existence. Empirical, resilient, proven, authentic. Theirs is the real world, from which we live in self-imposed exile.

A strong contact call rang across the yard. An adult owl flew close and slipped up into the shadows, vanishing as if through a portal. Chittering and bill clacking indicated a food delivery. Starved for photons, my eyes faded. It occurred to me that the main thing separating our partially overlapping realms of what we call "a day" was the relative abundance or scarcity of that narrow band of electromagnetic wave frequencies that we call "light." What does that even mean? It is "light" only if human eyes can see it? Is any perception of the universe more subjective than that? Truly our eyes deceive us.

A PAUSE HERE TO SHED some light on light. In the former world, light on Earth originated almost solely from the sun, with a meager assist from other stars. Moonlight is sunlight reflected. Wildfires and

volcanoes generated some light, but trivially. Fireflies and phosphorescent mushrooms, yes, but they're hardly a night-light. Phosphorescent
sea plankton, jellies, and the glowing bacteria wielded by a few fish
and squid offer no night guidance to land-bound beings. And none of
that small constellation of glowing beings could have powered pho-
tosynthesis, by which the world uses light to create living matter. The
light for Earth that created life on Earth was solely sun-sourced. That
remains essentially true, despite city nights and fishing fleets visible
from space.

The business of "light" is strange. And "sight," very strange
indeed. "Light" is not a property of those particular wavelengths
within the electromagnetic spectrum. What makes them "light" is
something that happens only within nervous systems equipped with
organs capable of reacting to certain wavelengths by creating coded
nerve impulses, then interpreting the impulses. What we call light
strikes our eyes only; none reaches our brain. In the back of an eye,
the retina consists of several layers of differing cells with differing
functions. When particular wavelengths strike, these cells create
impulses channeled to the optic nerve. The optic nerve carries not the
wavelengths—not the "light"—but only the electrochemical signals.
Next, from the encrypted encoding that the optic nerve delivers, specialized sections of that amalgamated collection of neurons and functions that we call the "brain" construct a three-dimensional facsimile
of the world in space. These illusions, we experience as light and sight.
The images are so convincing, we feel that we are seeing *out*. We use
this grand illusion to navigate at high speed, to catch or strike objects
in motion, to detect someone we might one day love, or even to store
a memory, a retrievable reconstructable imagined image of something
fond or feared. Human optic nerves do not encode impulses from the
infrared or ultraviolet wavelengths adjacent to humanly visible light,
but some other animals see these colors exquisitely well. Human difficulty seeing at night, and the sensation of "darkness" itself, results
from particular limitations of our primate optic system, limits easily
breached by the optic systems of nocturnal beings such as owls.

Plants, lacking nervous systems and visual receptors as we understand them in animals, almost certainly have no ability at all to perceive sensations of light, despite their need of abundant "light," their ability to have their leaves turn to track the sun, and to have their flowers open and shut accordingly. They somehow respond to the density and direction of "photosynthetically active radiation," generally spanning wavelengths between 400 and 700 nanometers—quite similar to what humans use as "light" for eyesight, about 380 to 700 nanometers. (Birds can see ultraviolet radiation starting around 300 nanometers, putting colors inaccessible to us into their world and their plumage.) Plants eat light, and with those meals of pure power, plants create life from water and air. The alchemy of plants makes animals possible. Essentially all food eaten by animals was created by plants, even if it first makes a stop as another animal. Admittedly, the young owls cared little about where their food came from, only about when it came.

COUNTING EACH SUDDEN BOUT OF excited chittering and bill clacking, there'd been three food deliveries in quick succession. It was not yet nine-thirty p.m. The owlets sounded like they were straight overhead, but my light-intensifying night binoculars couldn't see through the leafiness that hid them.

Finally I located two sets of bobbing headlights. They soon flew off in opposite directions. The night binoculars were a slight advantage, but tracking the ungoverned movements of five owls remained humanly impossible. I had their numbers against me, the leafiness against me, darkness against me; an abundance of fallen logs and downed branches made walking in the dark hazardous. I was outnumbered and clearly disadvantaged. But determination counts for a lot. Sometimes for too much. Now that I had night-vision binoculars to "help" me, I scarcely saw any owls, but I *was* stumbling around in the woods in the dark, risking falling hard on a sharp broken branch. The possibility that I *might* find the owls was again depriving me of sleep on these short nights.

An adult blurred past, dissolving into the canopy. Again I heard chitters and clacking, but briefly. That must have been something

small. Six minutes later, my ears—not my binoculars—told me
another snack had arrived. The darkness facilitated my ability to
imagine it. In my mind's mysterious eye, I visualized an adult sweep-
ing in with a billful of moth, whose crumpled wings extended past
the corners of the captor's mouth. I envisioned the anxious owlet I
could hear, and the way the parent leaned forward and the young one
took the gift and chugged it back as the adult dropped off the branch
and planed away through the trees. Who needed light-intensifying
binoculars? Imagination worked better.

It surprised me that after a couple of nights of getting as far
as John and Georgia's yard, the Hoo returned to their accustomed
bivouac between the raccoon tree and the stop sign. Their attitude
seemed to be: Why risk exploring when you've got room service and
a view?

Another hour unwound. The street traffic quelled. The sky
occluded to overcast. In lieu of twinkling stars, fireflies crossed tree-
top openings. A sacred pagan silence seemed to swell up from the
ground and from the trees' thick leafiness, filling the black and humid
air with summer magic. "Hear ye," one cricket chanted. "If you are
my species, I request the honor of your reply. All others simply wit-
ness. No further action on your part is required. That we are together
is sufficient and necessary."

Having heard nothing further of owls in the last little while, I
thought about sleeping out. The neighbor's air conditioner fan went
on. I opened the screen door under our porch light and entered our
house. With the windows open, I could half-listen for owls all night.
If I heard them, I'd perhaps convince myself yet again to stumble
outside. After all, there might never be another summer with such
enchanted connections. Who knew? Not the Hoo. None of us, not
even they who pierced darkness, possessed eyes capable of seeing the
future. We expect only that there will be one, feel confident that
tomorrow will come. But the murky details remain darkened to us all
who constitute merely the now.

Sensing connection to realities larger and more permanent than
ourselves is the basis of religious feeling. All things that scaffold the

life of this world—waters, air, the plants who make the form of oxy-gen that animals breathe—are indeed larger in space and across time. All who have crawled, swum, run, remained rooted, or discovered their wings are our ancestors or relatives. This confronts us with value of such enormity—our entire existence, the sheer possibility of us—that we mostly cannot see it. Retinas and the illusion of sight were not made for perceiving this view of Life. Getting in on that wavelength requires a slightly more engaged attention.

Yet we can say this: one needn't look far. Birds at a feeder, a flower garden, the wolves in our doggies' clothing—they make those con-nections materialize. And, of course: Alfie.

YET ALSO, OF COURSE, ALFIE doesn't always show up right away. Patricia and I sometimes have to wait, talking to the night air—"Where are you?"—as if reciting some sacred incantation in hopes of conjuring her. But if we can have faith in anything and feel certain that our faith is well placed, my faith is in the living. The religion that is followed is not religion. What is prayed is not prayer. Neither is what is spoken to be believed. What lives and how we live: that is reli-gion. To be bound in relation, purest religion. Show me what you are grateful for, and I will know what you believe. All routes to connec-tion converge toward compassion; all arrive at an empowering humil-ity. Migrant birds etching sunset skies, the harbor's humble clams, the long rhythms of whales in the seasons of fishes, these special owls in their leafy abode—. In grand spectacle and subtlest detail, nature is scripture unscripted. The many joined universes above, below, and beside us offer ample fuel for igniting religious experience. Alfie and I live the shared prayer. It's deep, but it's delightful.

23

❧

Countdown, June 28

LUCK WAS WITH MY DREAMS. THE NIGHT REMAINED SUF-ficiently silent for sleep until, at a little after five a.m., I heard loud caterwauling. From cats, to be clear.

My body made a compelling case for staying in bed. But I pushed myself out into dim dawn glimmerings. Light had barely started etching a filigree of sky through the woodland's leaves. Venus floated in the southwest. Robins began logging attendance from all directions, joined by one particularly cranked-up cardinal. I detected nothing owl.

For lack of anything better to do, I simply stood for about ten minutes. The robins' volume occupied almost all the listening capacity; it was hard to hear anyone else. I thought I heard an owl, but—? There. Definitely.

An owl silhouette lands noiselessly on a low branch near me. Hardly more than shadow, but I know her name. I hear the Hoo calling and when I turn, the three fuzzy fledgers are on the gutter edge of our kitchen roof—and Alfie the silent magician has already vanished from the branch and materialized among them. A cult could be founded upon such bewitchery.

Alfie lifted buoyantly into the central maple. One by one, her hard-flapping babes followed, crossing our yard's window of open sky. Their wing feathers were well grown in. But the little pilots still labored for traction in the still air.

They—. Where'd they all just go? I found them back in the walnut tree, having made a little parade procession around the yard.

Alfie dropped to a low branch, scanned the forest floor, and in a few moments she powered into a trajectory that would take her to something she'd spotted on the ground in the woods. Weaving their heads back and forth and in circles, the Hoo peered toward Alfie's disappearance. At the sound of her whinny, they all immediately moved in her direction.

They met their mother in a young locust as one fuzzy head-bobbing mob. Alfie fed one of them something tiny, delivered in a quick meeting of the bills. It vanished in a gulp.

Plus-One arrived, and the family was again in motion. A few minutes later they got something more substantial: part of a small bird. I wondered whether this partial carcass was someone's mate or youngster; those were the only two realistic possibilities. One young owl spent quite a bit of time pulling at this gift that was simultaneously a tragedy and a prize.

Now the Hoo are in the crabapple tree. Now they are in the walnut. Now a maple. Wherever Alfie went, her youngsters followed. Alfie didn't seem hungry enough to pay me much attention, so I did not offer anything.

Again I heard unhappy cats.

One of the youngsters fluttered to the ground and made three quick-hop pounces in the grass—followed by a swallowing motion. Hunting! Their impulse to search, to chase and pounce, was kicking in.

The young hunter hopped to a fallen tree trunk, alongside a sibling. The sib dropped to the ground. Were they copying each other? Some psychology researchers claim that only the most "advanced" animals can copy. But who is to say that owls are not advanced? Anyway, various young birds' learning is enhanced by watching adults. The young terns I studied followed adults miles to sea. There they watched their parents plunge and catch fish. The parents continued feeding them while the young honed their own skills. Likely many birds that are not known to learn by copying—not caring what we know—learn by copying.

The sibling on the ground grabbed at something and then bit it. I couldn't tell if they'd caught a bug or were merely going through the motions, maybe targeting a twig in a bit of play practice. Either way, this was exciting: the first time I'd seen them hunting. Again the breeding process had shifted into a new gear. The Hoo were hurtling toward independence and eventual dispersal into the wider world. Of course, I worried. I worried about them hopping around on the ground. The cats.

At five-thirty a.m., the side door burst open and the doggies came bounding out. Patricia followed them, barefoot and in her nightgown, stretching. "What is going on? Are they all here?" Alfie answered by landing on the lens of my tripod-mounted camera.

By six-twenty, all of the owls had moved to where they were yesterday and the day before and before that: the young maples next to the garden, between the stop sign and the raccoon tree.

A jogger ran past. Earbuds in, he did not hear the scratchy-voiced fledgers who were intently watching him from branches almost directly overhead.

ALFIE AND PLUS-ONE NESTLED TOGETHER on a branch. For the first time since their courtship, I saw them preening one another, grooming each other around the head and bill nibbling. They were going at it so enthusiastically that I could only think of it as "making out." They would soon be empty nesters; perhaps it was a time for rebinding their bond, renewing their owl vows. Eventually, snuggled contentedly up against each other, they settled down.

But not for long. Soon they went at it again. Finally, their ardors spent, they resumed their more usual equanimity. One of the fledgers moved close, sitting up against Mom. Alfie was the center of gravity of her tight-knit little family. Alfie and Plus-One exchanged soft whinnies. The family looked ready to settle in for their daylight rest.

Together, Patricia and I watched them for a few minutes. Then Chula and Cady and Jude came to find us. Alfie was roosting so close to our little veggie garden that when I cut some dandelion and radicchio leaves to sauté for breakfast with our hens' eggs, she started whinnying to me. I felt like I belonged within her family circle. So peaceable a kingdom. That was how the day began.

SCIENTISTS HAVE TESTED MANY IDEAS for evidence. Where evidence warrants, they've pressed deeper into the dynamics of nature. The cosmos of particles that ancient Greek "atomists" conjectured and the unity of interacting parts sensed by Confucian philosophers remain broadly compatible with modern scientific understandings. Conversely, science has no evidence supporting the Platonic-Abrahamic-Cartesian-Baconian conjectures—a soul and body at odds, devaluation of the world—that gave the Industrial and (ironically) Scientific Revolutions their philosophical underpinnings. We know enough to say that from combinations of lesser particles, atoms and then molecules arise, and that gases condense into galaxies whose spontaneously igniting stars whirl like astral fishes in galactic shoals. Buried within at least one galaxy is a sparkling planet that has spawned an explosion of tiny glittering flecks capable of looking out and watching themselves perform. Minds. We are the universe aware of itself. But oh, in our case, how imperfectly so! Perhaps, as we fear, better-perfected beings traffic some distant cosmic intersection. Perhaps they pity us, as we often project; for we seem to know, a bit guiltily, that we are better than we seem, capable of better than we are.

24

◈

Countdown, June 29

A FEW MINUTES AFTER FIVE A.M., THE SLAM OF ANN'S screen door sounded like a breakfast bell to the black-and-white cat who went running through the woods and across the street to her house.

On the ground I noticed a feather from one of the adult owls. Their molt had begun. These perspicacious little owls had busy schedules, scarcely a free moment from establishing territories, cementing their pair bond, then eggs, raising their young and seeing them fledge, and continuing to guard and feed them for weeks as they strengthen and grow and learn what they need to learn. And as those duties and commitments near their end, the adults begin replacing all their feathers. Living is expensive. There is no free lunch. Except—.

I toss Alfie some food. She silently flies it into the tree canopy. She tears a piece and offers it. Her overfed babe shows the mildest interest before moving off. Alfie tugs at the mouse like someone pushing food around her plate; she's not hungry, either. Insisting that a child who has had enough should have more, Alfie repeats the gestures. The youngster flies to a nearby branch. Alfie follows. The owlet accepts a couple of bites and then moves away again. Alfie chases the fledger to another branch. The owlet again moves to put some distance between them. Aren't baby birds supposed to chase their parents around, begging desperately? Survival doesn't always balance on a knife edge. Alfie is still holding most of the food when the youngster grabs some maple leaves and yanks hard on them, more intent on playing at eating than actually eating.

I've been looking forward to full independence for Alfie and the Hoo. Independence is the goal. But I'm really going to miss this crew: the progress, the activity, the sheer delight of getting to know them so well. They yet hold far more mysteries, but the revelations have been beyond all expectations. Our time with them has been what Bertrand Russell wished science could be, a love story between human beings and nature.

IN GRANDILOQUENT TERMS, SCIENCE IS how the universe is beginning to understand itself. We usually assume that science is logical and reasonable. But scientists repeatedly observe some very unreasonable aspects of the universe. The speed of light and its wave/particle nature, gravitational force, the probabilistic behavior of subatomic particles, distantly "entangled" particles interacting by no apparent means, subatomic events altered by merely observing them, and the threshold that opens to the quickened exuberances of the panoply called Life—these are not reasonable things. They just *are*. Scientists are obliged to believe what the evidence indicates. But scientists must also remain curious about new evidence suggesting that things are not quite as they believed, because new tools often reveal that there is more to a story. A healthy humility about one's own ignorance is the beginning of curiosity. Without the curiosity to follow faint whispers and improbable possibilities, there can be no investigation, no improved understanding. Certainty is the end of learning.

Science is supposed to be—and at its best, is—an adventure, fueled by open-mindedness. Simple to say. But science is performed by imperfect beings, so the endeavor is imperfect. For the human ego, open-mindedness requires courage. In Zen, an openness free from preconceptions is called *shoshin*, or "beginner's mind." Beginner's mind opens the book of life not to a fact but to a question. The first question is: How does one ask a question? Every worthwhile answer attained by an open mind spawns multiple questions. To have more questions than answers is not an accident. Right away, you're not even back where you started; you are at a place before your starting point. You can get younger this way.

◆

ALFIE REMAINED COMPLETELY TAME WITH us. Animal behavior specialists might have called her "imprinted." You might say, "She thought she was a person." One might think that if an owl thought people were her people, her chances for a normal owl life would be ruined. Apparently, it's not that simple. Alfie wasn't raised the way she was born to be. But her odd upbringing didn't hurt her ability to pivot and become who she was supposed to be. Alfie showed no difficulty pair-bonding, mating, incubating eggs, or skillfully feeding young. More unexpected was her ability to slide effortlessly between her human culture and her native culture. Self-identity concepts can be fluid. Individuals can be flexible. Alfie ignored our familiar dogs, but strange dogs freaked her out. She knew whom she knew. That's more nuanced than "she thought she was a person." It's more like this: she knew we were family, and she didn't fully trust strangers. Not so different from many of us. We know who we are by knowing whom we're with. Knowing who's in our circle defines our circle. Our circle defines us. As do the questions we pose and the answers we believe.

Among the wonders our human mind can uniquely ponder: Why, in a universe said to be determined toward chaos, do things organize? Why is there anything rather than nothing? Why is the normal so astonishing, the everyday so miraculous? And why is existence simply so strange. That it all is as it is, is mystery. To want to understand it is devotion.

The universe is big, and the more we understand about it, the bigger "infinite" gets. Astronomers at the South African Radio Astronomy Observatory in Cape Town have discovered two new galaxies, each one *more than sixty times* larger than our Milky Way. One can devote a life to exploring the mysteries or one can simply bathe in them a little bit, marveling at our ability to marvel. Unleashing a mind for a walk among the stars is good exercise. A walk through the history of Life helps us stay fit. One gains that most important thing: perspective.

IN THE WOODS, TREE SHADOWS were growing and merging as day's curtain lowered toward night. Overhead, light lingered in a sky still distinctly blue. A mockingbird continued soloing. Inside the woods' edge, several deer snorted notice.

An owlet surprised me by flying strongly about 150 feet into the woods, landing adjacent to the wreck of a huge old multi-trunked maple whose enormous columns lay shattered. The forest floor here remained an obstacle course of fallen trunks, broken and strewn during a violent predawn thunderstorm a few years earlier. Those alarming minutes of darkness and driving downpour had been filled with the crackle of trees being shorn of their canopies and the shuddering thuds of giants falling. Dawn that morning lit extensive damage to the local woodland as well as to homes, autos, and my writing studio. Yet so pinpoint was that bomb of weather that one mile away, not a leaf was disarrayed. Those few minutes of wind left years-long rips in the forest canopy. New saplings wasted no time rising in the ground's newfound light. So through the shadows, I carefully picked my way over and around dark logs and sharp-broken branches, under cadavers of snapped-off boughs still hanging in the embrace of living branches. I had the owlet in sight. What this lone young one sought, I wasn't sure. Was the family together somewhere? Was the fledger traveling toward calls I could not hear?

Then I discerned an adult calling. A slight waver in the call suggested that the caller was in flight. Alfie appeared, flying. She uttered a new rendition of the strong contact call, with long spaces between notes.

Alfie flew back and forth over the fallen-apart trunks. She seemed to be searching. She continued to utter single- or two-note contact calls—while flying. That, too, was something new.

It appeared that she was trying to locate her mate and her kids. She landed, alternating calling and listening. When Alfie moved off a bit farther into the trees, the present fledger followed her. Alfie continued shifting positions, uttering single-note calls.

I detected no sign of Plus-One or the complement of the Hoo. Without their presence, the forest felt a bit emptier. A taste of things to come. For months, Alfie alone could light the whole night for me. The arrival of Plus-One doubled it, and the fledgers quintupled that night-aliveness.

But all high tides must ebb. Shadows swallowed us as day's light drained. Alfie's three-note contact calls shot loudly through the blackening forest. She was indeed searching.

The time for seeing yielded to the time for dreaming. At nine p.m. I heard one emphatic declaration accompanied by a bill clap. Was Alfie getting frustrated in her efforts to locate her family? Plus-One and the others had withdrawn further into their own mystery, their realm and their reality not freely accessible to me. And even for our russet little holder of dual citizenship, Alfie herself, they seemed, for the time, lost.

I STEPPED OUT OF THE WOODS. The sky was framed with familiar silhouettes: our leafy maples, the tall walnut, the generous mulberry, the quiet dogwoods, the lush cherry, the high-spired cedars.

Knowing names helps us distinguish and appreciate what's here. But names also blind us to what is going on, what can get hidden beneath the label.

Forest ecologist Suzanne Simard shows that trees communicate and share food through an underground fungal network she dubbed the "wood-wide web." Robert Macfarlane summarizes some of Simard's findings thus:

The fungal network also allows plants to distribute resources—sugar, nitrogen, and phosphorus—between one another. A dying tree might divest itself of resources to the benefit of the community, for example, or a young seedling in a heavily shaded understory might be supported with extra resources by its stronger neighbors. Even more remarkably, the network also allows plants to send one another warnings. A plant under attack from aphids can indicate to a nearby plant that it should raise its defensive chemical response before the aphids reach it.

The fungal networking penetrates roots, laying a truly vast lacework throughout the forest's velvet underground. Trees sometimes also fuse their roots, and around 40 percent of the carbon in any given root can come from nearby trees, even from other species. In at least some forests, according to Simard, "mother trees" nourish seedlings until they're tall enough to reach sunlight for themselves. Researchers on several continents continue to extend such findings. It is by no means established that plants experience sensations or are capable of intentionality as some of that language might imply. But it always pays to look behind the label. The printmaker and poet William Blake long ago wrote, "The tree which moves some to tears of joy is in the eyes of others only a green thing which stands in the way." A tree is not just "a tree." Alfie is not "an owl." Each of us is not "a person." We embody all precursors. *What* we are is: histories. *Who* we are is: relationships.

SCIENTISTS IN VARIOUS FIELDS ARE working to comprehend the whole-cloth patternings of living diversity, relational webs, and emergent properties. Many—a significant countercurrent—have succeeded in removing the dualist and reductionist blinders of their early training. Ecologists endeavor to understand Life's webworks and how to keep them, astronomers expand the depths of time and space, atmospheric scientists take the temperature, as more engineers work to light a cleaner path ahead.

As constellations of atoms, we are each our own little galaxy. Our components outlast us, as our stardust spirals into the next brief possessor, or into the cosmic storm. We are all works in progress, coping with new possibilities within the immense sweep of time and space. We come and we go, all in our moment on the arrow of changes.

DAY AGAIN YIELDED FULLY TO the time of owls. The moon sailed slowly aloft, hazy with the moisture of late June. Time shifted into "park." I breathed awhile. Eventually I went inside.

25

Countdown, June 30

NIGHT RETAINED PLUSH SHADOWS ON THE FOREST FLOOR, while overhead one star remained in a tinting sky. Another day stretching itself awake. No human-generated sound.

As one soft voice in an empty auditorium can underscore a massive emptiness, the birdsongs of mornings highlight the quiet of the world. Silence is not the absence of sound; it's the absence of noise. Morning among the notes of the first robins is a perfect form of silence. My mind is not yet chattering to itself. Later it will be, when I reenter the peopled day of messages and Zoom calls and things that must be done and errands I must run. For now, before the noise of motors begins pushing our minds into corners, the world remains wide, and dark enough for dreams. Boundaries between myself and the rest of the world remain soft and permeable.

A first automobile broke the silence, barely pausing through the stop sign. Its growl down the road dissipated like a receding wave. Songs of shaded birds rose to erase it.

The owls were not presenting themselves. So I went searching. I stepped into the woodland shadows as if wading. I picked my way carefully toward the wreck of the huge old maple where I'd left Alfie and her owlet last evening.

I heard a rattling peal of scratchy chatter. Two shadows crossed under the canopy about sixty feet up. An adult owl whinnied. All three fledgers descended to low branches just above the forest floor. One adult abruptly issued a strong contact call. I heard a branch break, and turned.

The form of a woman was floating toward me through the morning mist, a diaphanous apparition sparingly clad. Patricia, in nightgown and muck boots. She pointed upward. Brief silhouettes. Callings from leafy shadows. Branches moving. No clear sight. Now they're up there.

Advancing, Patricia pointed: "There's a black cat on a low branch behind the tree over there. Appears to be hunting."

Moments ago, all three fledgers were on low branches, just like this cat we now had our eyes on. The cat might have disrupted their explorations and new hunting urges. Of course, a worse outcome had been possible. And that remained true several times a day and through each night.

"This is very dangerous," I said. These cats can certainly surprise a young owl whose explorations had brought them to touch the ground, whose attention was wholly focused on the new world of the forest floor.

"There's another cat," Patricia said. A calico.

I hurried both cats along in the direction they'd been going, heading toward the street and my neighbor Ann's food bowls after another night of marauding.

"Alfie is right up here," Patricia said. "Hello, Alfie. *Where* are you? *There* you are!"

Alfie began whinnying. She always returned our calls.

She looked away from me, her attention seemingly focused into the realm of owls. My gaze could not take me to where hers took her. The familiar intimacy I'd felt with her for months was becoming eclipsed by mysteries she seemed increasingly to inhabit. Alfie had taken fuller possession of herself. Her world had enlarged as it should.

The bindings felt as though they were loosening—as all parental bonds must.

We didn't know where Plus-One was. The Hoo, who seldom let more than fifteen feet get between them, short-hopped through trees along the fence line, uttering ratchety squeals, ignoring the hectoring robins. They were above a dense tangle of downed wood that looked like good mouse housing, plenty of cover and hiding places.

I put Alfie's food on a log. She looked and looked, taking a sweet while to decide whether a flight of a few yards for a meal was worth her time. She finally planed in and pounced. She turned to me and we locked gazes. I said, "Hello, you."

Alfie flew to the Hoo. Her arrival with takeout in her grasp sparked more chittering and excited bill clacking. They crowded her in a way I hadn't seen before. Looking almost straight up from thirty feet below, I watched through binoculars as she pulled off pieces and fed them. Two owlets crowded close on either side of her as she tore a piece and gave it bill-to-bill to the young one on her left, tore another for the one on her right.

Alfie continued feeding her proximal babes until one got full and hopped away from her. The next got full and hopped away. To the third, who'd been just out of reach, Alfie bestowed the entirety of what was left, fully half a mouse. That owlet pinned the food to the branch with the inner talons of each foot, but pulled halfheartedly.

Lack of hunger notwithstanding, the young whippersnapper suddenly got very interested in a squirrel traversing the contours of the forest floor. Squirrels are much too big for screech owls to tackle, but this inexperienced owlet was clearly fascinated by the flowing rodent motion, watching with the eyes of a future hunter who still had everything to learn.

Plus-One materialized, and all five owls convened. They wanted to be together. All was right with them. That was good enough for me. We'd been gifted another day in each other's company. That thought delivered a simple clarity that made this morning feel particularly fantastic. Patricia and I returned happily through the woods, knowing the owls were well and thriving in their forest, while we took ourselves back toward our house and the human world, where we, too, were still alive and well and so many things in life and living meant so much to us.

SOME SEE A UNIVERSE DEAD and meaningless. Some have faith in divine interventions. Neither appears true to me. One of my friends clings to her faith not because it attracts her but because she is too terrified by an alternative wherein "we are here alone." Therein lies, for me, the middle path. I see no need to choose between believing in a material world and embracing a spiritual world. It seems more a matter of either believing that everything is just a collection of objects or understanding that relationships create meaning. Alone, we could never have become. We are everything *but* alone. Indeed, we are everything. Perhaps the challenge is to realize—by letting ourselves simply feel it—that the world made us.

Have you ever seen a video of cows that have been rescued from some crap-clotted feedlot, brought to a sanctuary, and let out onto lush grass? In the moment when that kiss of sun on the cushioning grass first jolts them, they intuitively understand that they've missed the world they were made for. They experience what their bodies and brains have always longed for but never knew existed. We vibrate at the sight of their spontaneous frolic, and may even be moved to tears, because we know—too well—how those cows felt. And so we await what we were born for to reveal itself, when what we really need is to find the right place to take the necessary step.

26

⫸

Going, Going—

IN THE EVENING I WALKED BEHIND THE STUDIO, IMME-
diately scaring up a black-and-white cat with a black mustache. The
cat trotted straight through the spot where the fledgers had been on
the ground when they'd shown the first glimmers of hunting. Timing
is everything. The cat continued toward the street—where a blond
tabby was waiting. It was as if dear old Ann's food bowls were beget-
ting cats by spontaneous generation.

Robins chatted the sun down like neighbors talking over their
fences. Chula and Cady came around. Cady sat by me. Chula was
smiling at me and wagging her tail, looking me directly in the eyes in
her usual extraordinary way, as no other dog ever has. Jude drifted by,
dreamily taking in everything.

Of owls, I detected nothing. I went into the woods to the wreck
of the big old shattered maple. Nothing there. I walked along my
seldom-seen neighbor's fence. Sounds of a radio and air conditioner
emanated from her yard. Sounds of owls did not. A doe came running
across her lawn, chased by her small brown poodle mix. With an easy
leap, the doe left the poodle behind the chain-link and melted among
the trunks and shadows.

Heavy thunder rolled through the air. Thick raindrops began striking leaves with a dry sound like falling pebbles. But the fat drops fell too briefly to give this place the drink it still thirsted for.

I circled back. The black-and-white cat with the black mustache was reclined about three feet off the ground on a slanting log in the bivouac area, where the owls had convened daily.

I picked up an abandoned rubber ball and threw it to chase the cat from this owl-hallowed spot. The cat hopped down from the log with a friendly attentiveness, as if we were now going to play. In nature, every killer can plausibly plead their innocence.

The shade of night slowly pulled across the vault of heaven. Under a moon already bright, fireflies began threading the lowest altitudes of the deeper darkness rising from the forest floor.

Across the street, someone started a motorcycle with a For Sale sign on it and revved and revved and revved it, adding to the list of ways my neighborhood generates noise. We once had a rooster. Word circulated that one neighbor was going to complain about our rooster's crowing. Another neighbor came preemptively to see me. She was angry that a neighbor would complain about a rooster. "When I think of the mowers," she almost hissed, "the *leaf blowers*. Him over there with his motorcycle, and this guy behind me in his shop every night till eleven p.m. running his circular saw—. And someone's going to complain about your *rooster*? No. I *love* hearing your rooster."

STILL IN THE BACKYARD, I phoned John and Georgia. "Seen the owls?" I asked.

"No," John said.

"They're moving more now. I'm not finding them."

"That's a good thing, right?"

"Right." Of course right.

But as necessary as the owlets' impending dispersal was, I kept thinking about how we would miss their sheer sweetness. And the ability to walk the bridge Alfie had opened between their world and ours.

A flash of lightning lit up the tree trunks. It took many seconds for the thunder to arrive and rumble through. At nightfall, the needed rain finally intensified. This was the first evening with no owl sightings since the Hoo had fledged. They were abroad somewhere, a new part of the wider, freer world.

We humans, too, yearn to be part of something larger than ourselves—and yet we often fear leaving familiar confines. I, too, fear the world's pain, but I've found that one must proceed anyway, or numbness will obliterate joy as well. To snip some of the barbed wire that keeps us in the pens we erect for ourselves, to see ourselves reflected in the eyes of another, then to allow ourselves to feel "something in common" is to donate a piece of our isolation to a wider identity. All the voices of robins and jays, all of Alfie's whinnies and trills, all the world's callings—including our own—seem to have a common yearning: to make contact, to establish connection.

◆

I COULDN'T FIND THEM. Leaves were still dripping and the air still thick from the much-needed rain as I treaded into the coming morning wondering what the young owls might have made of the downpour through the gusting night and their first lightning. I wondered, of course, whether our owls were gone for good or whether I'd reestablish contact. I felt certain I heard one owl, then equally certain that I'd imagined it. I stood at the edge of the woods, more or less waiting. If Alfie was around, she'd be around. If she wasn't, she wouldn't. Whether to come or to release me—that was her choice now. She relied on us less and less. She now needed us perhaps not at all.

We'd kept our promises to her. We merely opened her door, and she took our invitation to explore freedom's risks and splendid realities. Perhaps that is a sufficient rule for good parenting: make promises, keep promises; don't ask for promises.

Screech owl home ranges aren't large, often with a diameter of roughly half a mile to a mile. The Hoo still needed their parents. I felt certain they could not be far. But certainties always exist within mysteries.

I retreated into my ears and stood like a living listening post. In the adjacent backyard, two very small spotted fawns trailed their mother, whose coat was summer russet. The fawns were trying to nurse when their mother noticed me. She stepped forward, looking, looking, waving her head in indecision. She moved toward me, narrowing the distance to about thirty feet. She seemed to want to use the deer path between us. I stepped back. She rushed up the path, into the woods. The fawns hesitated, then scampered to catch up to where she waited for them.

Somewhere this morning, Alfie and Plus-One joined their fledgers, and the fledgers bobbed their heads and growled their scratch-ratchety calls and took their meals, and perhaps hopped around on the dangerous forest floor as they pounced on bugs and continued the beginning of their lives.

Patricia and the doggies came out. Cady barked a demand that I play with her.

"Who's around?" asked Patricia. "No, they're not," I answered. "I haven't heard a Hoo. I haven't seen Alfie. I haven't seen or heard Plus-One. Mama said there'd be days like this."

Patricia made a face, then brought the dogs inside to feed them and to make coffee. I filled the bird feeders. A marble-coated cat walked toward the street.

Nobel-winning physicist Steven Weinberg observed famously and bleakly, "The more the universe seems comprehensible, the more it also seems pointless." But what he added matters more: "There is a point that we can give the universe by the way we live . . . that faced with this unloving, impersonal universe we make a little island of warmth and love and science and art for ourselves."

Regardless of how and why the universe came into being, we love our families and enjoy our days and sometimes we dance. We make the meaning that we decide to make.

Quantum physics astonished its pioneers—notably an initially disbelieving Albert Einstein himself—with the discovery that identical interactions of the universe's tiniest energies and subatomic particles often produce different outcomes. Random encounters, with unpredictable results, affect the cosmos at all scales. They characterize existence and are a major factor in Life.

Cosmic pointlessness, the role of chance in the collisions of matter and energy is, for us little humans over here, existence's great liberating aspect. It means that our lives are not predetermined. There are only probabilities. Consider the role of sheer luck, good and bad, in your own life. The universe has stickiness because everything in the cosmos is in responsive relationship. But because the cosmos is materially uneven, it is unpredictable. Things happen. If you started at the Big Bang and knew all the so-called laws of physics and had limitless computing power, you could *not* predict what has happened, what is happening, and what will occur, in anything more than a vague outline of likely outcomes—of which Life on Earth is perhaps the most unlikely. Our unlikeliness is indicated by the lifeless vastnesses we observe out there. It's a universe so full of non-life that it appeared "pointless" to Steven Weinberg. The point is Life. A singular physics appears to pervade the whole universe. Carbon atoms and water molecules exist throughout. Light maintains its speed everywhere. Gravity holds galaxies together and causes rain to fall. What does *not* pervade is: Life. What if this planet is one in a trillion where conditions are perfect for trees, for owls? What if it's the only one?

On Earth, where things are alive by any definition, we the living burn with a dynamic intensity all our own. Life is fierce, compassionate, merciless, interdependent, durable, fragile. In a universe where chance encounters have major consequences, evolution is living things colliding. Living things take those cosmic probabilities, then bend and sculpt them into extraordinarily improbable outcomes.

A universe that had a point would create complete conformity. If the cosmos had a goal, all things would be like water in a river. No opportunity to run uphill, to do anything but go with the flow. In a universe with a point, there would be no need for reflection, creativity, yearning, no sadnesses or passion, no need of thought. No freedom. If by magic Life did exist in a universe that had a point, it would be one thing, have one idea, would sing one song. Thank goodness the universe is pointless. It allows us to become.

Yet there is another way to see this. Because the universe's probabilities run within certain limited possibilities, the cosmos does in fact have a sort of fuzzy, blurry point. The "point" is: to be free within natural limits. The cosmos acts this way. Life on Earth behaves this way. For most of human history, all people *lived* this way. Only in the last few thousand years, as humans have used hierarchy to impose inequality, has freedom been in need of defense. The desire to "get back to the Garden" is just that: it's our yearning not to achieve something new but to regain the freedom to be our original selves. How are we "supposed" to live? The conditions of the universe and of Life show us: we are supposed to live at liberty in a world of managed hazards. Unoppressed, unsuppressed, but cautious, living up to all our emotional, intellectual, and physical abilities, respectful of greater forces and other beings, while understanding that the source of Life's drama is precisely that nothing is guaranteed.

Fifty years after Michael Collins went to the moon on Apollo 11, he recalled his impression of Earth with the words "It's tiny, it's shiny, it's beautiful, it's home, and it's fragile." For a long time we looked out from our tiny vantage, convinced that the universe revolved around us. Perhaps our only hope of getting it right is to get outside ourselves and look back at our frail shell in the cosmos with awe and curiosity, and to realize how much human fulfillment can result from simply loving living with appreciation and in gratitude.

◆

AT FIRST LIGHT ON JULY 3, I was at sea about eighty miles closer to dawn than was Patricia. In Algonquian terms, I was *abachtuk*, "way out there somewhere on the ocean." Whosoever has not been on the ocean at dawn under a perfect dome of sky, seeing only a round horizon spinning up an incandescent star radiating bright and necessary fire, that person has not yet seen this planet.

"It's 5:06 a.m.," Patricia messaged. "No sign of owls." At six she added, "Still no Alfie show or any owl sounds. I've been in and out, and was back by the trees, calling for a while. I'm sitting outside. But I think I'll go in now."

INDIGENOUS PEOPLE PLANNED for the future. Industrial people created a new future. Some now wonder whether there will *be* a future. Perhaps human beings can evolve toward Humane Being 2.0. What would be required? To win by helping others succeed.

We have one crucial thing, and we lack one crucial thing. We have an unprecedented pool of understanding about the reality of who we are and where we stand. We lack a fundamental sense that the world creates the momentary spark of our lives as it passes through us, connecting us all, connecting us to space and time; that the world exists as something not ours, something we might help maintain but must not harm—something that is sacred. Will we simply decide that the continued survival of living beings is good? Will we understand that we are made for the world that made us, and act to serve our source?

A RAINY NIGHT EMERGED INTO Independence Day in the U.S.A., July Fourth, the day our country celebrates the violent casting off of a minor tyrant. I hope that wasn't just practice. The food I had left out for Alfie the previous night remained untouched—Alfie's own declaration of independence.

Trying a wider search, I crossed the road and headed up a side street to a tiny pond. A flock of grackles chuckled by. Young blue jays begged from their parents. The sound of fighting cats briefly drowned out the morning songbirds.

I returned to our side of the road and walked north along the stone wall between the road and woods, then tucked into the dark shadows of tree trunks still deep in shade under the dense canopy. Amid the dense pileups of storm-felled wood I circled widely, listening, listening. I heard all the birds that had been heralding the first wash of day—except I heard no owls.

WE TOOK THE DOGGIES FOR a run in a nearby meadow and then went to the harbor shore. The island just across the main channel held hundreds of gulls busy with their big, dark fuzzy chicks. Their voices rang across the humid morning air, the water's surface amplifying their cries. Oystercatchers foraged between the high-tide line and the water's edge, their young emulating them. An unusually low tide had exposed mussel beds, oysters, and the clam flats. The place was just reaching the apex of high verdant summer beauty, the banks lined by emerald marsh grass and the thin channels crammed with shoals of small fishes. When we got home I checked the Ivy Tower—just in case.

How might shorebirds and owls and apes survive these billions of us scouring every corner, fathoming every depth, mugging the world for our desperately ravaged "resources"? Bugs and butterflies, jaguars and toucans, fishes, eagles, and whales will continue to exist only if enough people value their survival. Survival hinges on morality. In practical terms, humans deprived of nature cannot live with dignity; humans deprived of dignity cannot maintain the world. Owls and elephants need people; they need people whose goal is justice for all. To answer "Who deserves justice?," ask, "Who does not?"

In his landmark 1972 law journal article "Should Trees Have Standing," Christopher D. Stone observed that the legal world contains various "inanimate right-holders that exist *only* in law": trusts, corporations, joint ventures, municipalities, and so on. Meanwhile, living things are granted few legal rights. To future generations—to the *world*—the law grants none. Thinking of civil emancipations and voting rights, Stone observed, "Throughout legal history, each successive extension of rights to some new entity has been a bit unthinkable." So let us ponder some unthinkables.

Under most countries' laws, "rights" can be extended only to a "legal person." In New Zealand in 2012, indigenous Maori leaders were able to gain protection for their sacred but threatened Whanganui River by getting the river declared a legal "person" with rights to its own well-being. The Maoris' negotiator explained,

"Rather than us being masters of the natural world, we are part of it. We want to live like that as our starting point. And that is not an anti-development, or anti-economic use of the river but to begin with the view that it is a living being, and then consider its future from that central belief." Indigenous values hold untapped potential to guide modernity toward a livable future. The constitutions of Ecuador and majority-Indigenous Bolivia enshrine actionable legal rights of nature and natural processes to exist and flourish. Acting on traditional values of the Andes' Indigenous Quechua peoples, Ecuador amended its constitution to read, "We . . . hereby decide to build a new form of public coexistence, in diversity and in harmony with nature."

In 2013, the government of India decided that dolphins cannot be held captive, because they are "non-human persons" with certain rights. Hungary, Costa Rica, Chile, and Finland have similarly protected the rights of whales and dolphins. In Argentina, a captive orangutan was ruled a "nonhuman person" entitled to life in a sanctuary. Pakistan's high court ordered an elephant named Kaavan and other zoo animals to be sent to sanctuaries on the basis that non-human animals have rights. The Swiss amended their constitution and civil laws to define non-human animals as "beings" instead of "objects." Chilean voters decided against such constitutional changes, but several other countries, including Colombia, Panama, and Bangladesh, have recognized a range of legal rights for natural areas, while a growing international movement seeks legal recognition of crimes against nature. In Wisconsin, the Ho-Chunk Nation amended its tribal constitution, recognizing that "ecosystems, natural communities, and species within the Ho-Chunk Nation territory possess inherent, fundamental, and inalienable rights to naturally exist, flourish, regenerate, and evolve." This helps the tribe protect its homelands from mining, fracking, and extraction of oil and minerals. Tribes have sued on behalf of the rights of fish and plants in Washington and Minnesota. "Maybe now," Robin Wall Kimmerer commented, "we will listen to intelligences other than our own."

Maybe.

Maybe not.

In the United States in 2019, Toledo, Ohio, residents passed the Lake Erie Bill of Rights, giving the lake legal rights so the city or any resident could sue polluters on behalf of the lake. But a judge struck down the law, calling it "invalid in its entirety." After 89 percent of voters in Florida's Orange County granted rights to waterways there, a judge threw the law out. Unthinkable ideas take a while. "In America, the rights of nature sounds like a fringe idea," Harvard law professor Kristin Stilt noted, "but people don't realize how mainstream it is around the world."

AT TEN-THIRTY P.M. ON THE Fourth of July, I thought I somehow heard a soft whinnying, despite the crackles and booms of the neighborhood's backyard fireworks. The racket always terrified Jude. In fact, so thoroughly had Jude hidden himself away from the noise that I could not find him inside our rather small house, despite checking repeatedly under beds and tables and behind the sofa. I finally located him on my third return to the guest bedroom. He was on the bed but had jammed his body so deeply behind the pillows and so flattened himself there and lain so still that I had twice overlooked his fifty-pound black body. He was trembling. I stroked him to calm him a little but let him remain in his chosen spot rather than trying to coax him out to be near us. Clearly he felt better hiding. So I let him hide.

Outside, amid the firecracker noise, the whinnying was real. Alfie, surprisingly, was right there in the back-door dogwood. I gave her just a little fish to reinforce her for finding me. But I didn't want to give her much because I hoped that at dawn she'd reappear—and lead me to her young ones.

INDEED, AT FIVE A.M. WHEN I stepped outside and called, she responded to me instantly, calling from somewhere up in the big central maple. It was still too dark to see; already a slight lengthening of the nights in the two weeks since the solstice was noticeable. I held her food with an outstretched arm, and she fluttered slowly downward at a steep angle, landing on my hand.

Alfie flew into the woods carrying the food, but I lost sight of her. I followed the fence line between the woodland and my seldom-seen neighbor's yard. After a moment's hesitation, I hopped her fence and snuck along the edge of her yard behind some bushes. She was probably still sleeping, but if she was awake, I didn't want the sight of a man crossing her yard to alarm her. So I basically hid and snuck, listening for owls, cupping my ears. I felt a bit foolish, heard nothing, and quickly retraced my steps.

If they were in anyone else's backyard, I'd have little chance of finding them. Or they could be anywhere in the thirty-odd-acre woodland, perhaps at its far edges near the church, the shopping center, or the elementary school. From there they could have moved into any number of private backyards.

I walked deeper into the woods along deer trails, through tangled vines and over fallen logs and between holly trees. The forest mosaic, with sections of native and invasive trees, dense undergrowth or none, reflected patchy histories of human land use and storm damages. The rhythmic tangle of the vegetation and the spicebush-scented air comforted my senses. I was having a pleasant time, letting myself be drawn onward by nothing more than curiosity. Nothing as substantial as the sound of an owl.

In one tiny place in the woods where two large fallen trees let the sun find its way to the ground, an emerald fern glade had sprung up. There I found a chair and a small plastic table. Someone's thinking spot. The place had not been recently visited. I wondered what thoughts and journal jottings might have been prompted forth by the woodland solace. Where had those thoughts gone; what had come of them? What might come of mine here?

I was enjoying my explorations, but in truth it was the owls who kept urging me into discovery—though I had no idea where they were. Their mysteries kept me going, pulling me through my own confines and boundaries like any inspired friendship does.

A little past the fern glen, I entered a thicket, where I found a long-abandoned mattress-sized foam pad. A nice enough spot for making young love. A black cat went slinking away, and a white cat with a black face stared at me from a fallen log.

I had to concentrate on listening. Pleasant though the morning was, my head buzzed with thought fragments and to-dos. A red-bellied woodpecker called. The sound was familiar, so I reflexively filtered it out. Ostensibly I was listening for owls. But tuning in wasn't coming easily. Distraction was. I wasn't accomplishing anything on my lists, and I wasn't accomplishing anything here. Things we allow to accumulate around ourselves are called "trappings" for a reason. A pair of wrens, apparently unaccustomed to seeing a human in their territory here, scolded me with uncommon energies, as though I myself were an owl. The wrens were saying the most important thing they had to say at the moment; their focus was total. But I was having difficulty paying attention to the familiar *and* the unfamiliar. Where did this leave me? The unfamiliar is the path to all that lies undiscovered. The familiar includes the most crucial nodes of our existence. Reminder to self: Pay. Attention. Any little path might be a portal to something deeper. But this morning my things-to-do were winning the tug-of-war.

I emerged from the thicket and circled back to where there was so little understory that I could see a couple hundred yards through the trees. A tiny spotted fawn bounded over to their mother. My binoculars revealed three more spotted fawns. Two sets of twins. But I saw only one doe. I wanted a closer look, but keeping my distance seemed the friendlier thing to do.

HUMANS HAVE ALWAYS CREATED MYTHS and metaphors in a quest for meaning, trying to divine a place and a role for our kind, working through our frailties and our fears, perhaps seeking ultimately to soothe our insecurity and our dread of being alone. People have observed or imagined harmonious webs, necessary balances, benign spirits, punitive gods, good and evil forces, spirit versus flesh, minds without matter, a cosmos as chaos and as clockwork, bodies as machines, brains as computers, man against nature—. The human mind sees pieces of reality and clings to fragments, believes its metaphors, contends absolutes, and winds itself into frenzies. And so each of those mirages has been propounded as reality, sometimes with metaphoric insight, sometimes with blind and radicalized obsession, occasionally with due humility.

Is it possible to be informed by many beliefs yet live without indoctrination? John Coltrane, a kind of spiritual leader of twentieth-century jazz music, said, "I believe in all religions." He sensed harmonies in different chords of thought. Diane Ackerman, the prolific author of many books, including *The Zookeeper's Wife*, writes, "My creed is simple: All life is sacred, life loves life, and we are capable of improving our behavior toward one another. As basic as that is, for me it's also tonic and deeply spiritual, glorifying the smallest life-form and embracing the most distant stars."

Imagine pooling everything human cultures have thought and selecting what's needed for a survivable future. We could call such a transformation "a butterfly event." Butterfly caterpillars don't grow into butterflies. They dissolve into liquid in the chrysalis, and from the DNA in that soup, a newly self-constructed being that we call a butterfly emerges. We could blend the best of connection-oriented, relational thinking. And we could try again.

27

⁂

Departures

AS A FIREBIRD SUN NEARS SETTING, PATRICIA AND I ARE standing on the beach for a small memorial gathering for our beloved neighbor J.P. We have the beautiful view from Lazy Point, and the wide bay. Within easy sight across the street is our cottage and the window where Crazy Crow tried so hard to come into the bedroom. With us are J.P.'s grown kids and their spouses—we're like family—some grandkids, and a couple of friends. A small and intimate and solemn enough group. After we've voiced our remembrances and stories and had our tears and smiles, J.P.'s daughter Nancy pulls a kayak to the shoreline and paddles out a short way. She begins casting rose petals and lilies. They form a floating wreath around her, and into this halo of petals Nancy slowly begins pouring the gray ashes of her father into his beloved waters.

I haven't said much about J.P. This is probably the time and place. J.P. and Marilyn and I were very close. Except for this year and last, when J.P. became ill, they lived across the street each summer in the little gnome house that his parents had built in the 1930s. Many summer mornings I'd visit for coffee with them. If he and Marilyn were having breakfast, they'd each be eating with one hand while holding hands with the other. At every opportunity he'd come help me with a repair—he could fix anything—or with cleaning a catch of fish, and he was delightful company. J.P. was not an ordinary person. He seemed to operate on a plane aside from and beyond the evils of the world, focused on deeper, simpler beauties of being alive. Asked "How are you?," he would usually answer, even at age ninety, with an energetic "I'm *fantastic!*" He possessed an ineffable sparkle. J.P. had stories of a very different United States, such as how in the 1930s, at the ages of fourteen and fifteen, he and his brother, with their parents' permission, hitchhiked across the country and had only wonderful encounters with people, many of whom sheltered and fed them. Or how he'd left his childhood friend Marilyn to go to war (they'd met at age eight on the summer beach right here) and found a very different-looking Marilyn, a head-turner, upon his return. His brother did not return. I never heard J.P. speak of the war itself. He scrupulously avoided the unpleasant; he seemed almost allergic to it. He had lost interest in the dark nonsense of humanity, remaining open only to the beautiful in people and in nature. And for him there was plenty.

While Nancy continued slowly pouring his ashes, a gull landed near the kayak. J.P. loved gulls; two would land on the roof each morning and wait for him to feed them treats. One of the gulls one day brought some soft nesting material and delivered it into J.P.'s hand. But there was nothing remarkable about this gull who was eyeing Nancy; gulls often land near boats that are putting something—usually fish trimmings—overboard. Nancy was still spreading the ashes when an osprey came along, hovered, dived, and caught a fish. People pointed and said this was a sign. Ospreys, however, hunt daily along this shore. The birds helped make the sad scene more pleasant, but neither bird's presence was unusual.

J.P. had long ago—at least two decades, I think—built a birdhouse with multiple apartments for purple martins. Each year, however, house sparrows moved into the apartments just before the migratory martins came back into our region. J.P. never had the heart to evict the sparrows, so his martin house never hosted any nesting martins. A few years ago I'd bought him some new martin houses of a design that house sparrows don't like. Finally, several pairs of martins indeed moved in and raised young. J.P. loved it! But wind had damaged the gourd-shaped houses. Only two remained, not enough to attract the colonially nesting martins, who require the company of others. And with J.P.'s health failing, there'd been no repair. No martins had nested for two years.

A light current began to float the petals slowly away. We were coming back up the sloping shore to where chairs were arranged around a bonfire and tables were set with food when a murmur went through our group. Eight purple martins were fluttering all around the two remaining gourd-nests.

Coincidence? Evidence? Regardless, the birds' abrupt arrival certainly got our attention. They reminded me that we do not know everything. They invited us to ponder possibilities. They affirmed the certainty that existence is wondrously uncertain.

Later in the summer, Crazy Crow would return. Two days after Crazy's reappearance, J.P. and Marilyn's son, Robbie, died after a long illness. The crow banged at our window every morning at dawn for about two more weeks. One morning Chula was on the bed when Crazy Crow started rapping and lunging at the window. Chula hopped off the bed in the direction of the window, and Crazy saw her. Suddenly the crow acted like a regular bird, flew away, and didn't return.

Why would birds, who existed for tens of millions of years on a planet without humans, and who have been so abused by humans, be "messengers" to us? Isn't that just another self-aggrandizing delusion of our own importance? Perhaps it is just the opposite: a sign of humility, a symptom of our fear that we are actually meaningless, an evocation of our desire to connect to something real and beautiful. If it is merely our imagination and our run-amok tendency to make connections, to what, exactly, are we yearning to connect? I see detriment in living according to fears of divine retribution, laws cast in stone, and a universe conniving capriciously to bring or withhold luck. But I don't sense much harm in wondering whether the universe is better than it seems. Meanwhile, we can continue to try to live our best life. If the universe is better than it seems, if there is something more afterward, well, that will be a nice surprise.

Alfie was for me a messenger from the real, authentic, original world, a mentor of sorts. What can we learn from birds? The answer might be "everything we really need to know." During one of the now-frequent California wildfires, a flying owl entered a firefighting helicopter—despite the noise and the rotors—and simply hung out there with the crew for a while. Perhaps the bird, faced with the catastrophic loss of everything needed and known, was catching a breath above the bewildering flames and smoke. Or perhaps the bird was temporarily possessed by a messenger spirit. But no supernatural explanation is needed. The message is clear. The owl and the fire itself bore the same warning about the flight path we are on. It used to be that when we said the world is on fire, we meant it metaphorically.

ARE BIRDS, BUTTERFLIES, STONES, AND clouds all in conversation with each other and with us? Not literally, I don't think. But when you look around at the result, you realize that, yes, they are all corresponding. So they must all have something to tell us. And that makes us—potentially—students of all things. Those many of us who love life cannot avoid sorting through the world's wider ills. It all arrives jumbled together in the net that dumps onto our decks each day's haul of needs and news, the daily catch of the sought and the undesired. We may want to discard the tragedies. But each time we toss a soft broken thing overboard so as to cope and move on, we harden ourselves just a bit. And the harder we become, the more of our own life we cast away. Alfie took on the rigors and dangers of her own life but remained always open to us. I like to think I learned something.

✦

ALFIE DID NOT APPEAR DURING the evening of July 5 but a day later, shortly after dark on July 6. She met us at the back door. I gave her some food and tried hard to watch where she went, in hopes that she might lead us to her family. She flew off in a direction that would take her across two backyards, and we instantly lost sight of her.

Fifteen minutes later, she was back. Had she given the food to a youngster? Eaten it herself? She made three dives to the ground, and caught and ate an insect. She called from different positions in our yard. I thought I heard another adult answer. I thought I faintly heard a distant owlet. I wasn't sure.

AT A CONFERENCE ONCE, WE were asked what we "would be willing to give up" to reverse the destruction of nature. As if risking the world is not already the process of giving up *everything*. Perhaps a reluctance to "sacrifice" is actually a cloaking device for not caring. The most misguided thought is that preventing the world from dying will require sacrifice. It requires love.

High majorities of people across Europe, North America, and Japan say that the natural world has value within itself, and that humans have moral obligations to plants, animals, and nature. The question this raises is how degradation of nature can be accelerating when most people say they want otherwise. Perhaps a sea-change is coming on the next tide; perhaps a groundswell is building. Problems of human making can be solved by human doing. I know we can. And so we must. The ghastly alternative is to sacrifice a livable world.

ON JULY 7, I WENT out at a little after five a.m. and called to Alfie. Again I wanted to try getting her to lead me toward her babes. She spoiled that plan by not appearing.

I fed the dogs and took them to the school grounds for a good run before I got to work. It's always pleasant to be abroad with them, watching them be themselves, seeing them avidly reading signs unseen, and having their warm companionship and the uplift of their antics.

WALT WHITMAN IN HIS LATE years asked a fundamental question about the arc of a human lifetime: "After you have exhausted what there is in business, politics, conviviality, love, and so on—have found that none of these finally satisfy, or permanently wear—what remains?" Whitman had his answer ready for us: "Nature remains . . . the affinities of a man or woman with the open air, the trees, fields, the changes of seasons—the sun by day and the stars of heaven by night." The child of nature draws rejuvenation from the self-renewing world. I've observed that such a person ages without growing old.

FOOD LEFT FOR ALFIE ON the night of July 7 remained untouched the next morning. I felt both pride—her year had exceeded my fondest hope for her success—and pining. Alfie and I were both "empty nesters." Was it too soon for nostalgia? I indulged anyway.

They're gone. That seems clear. I cannot find them. But wherever Alfie and her family are, for them there is only right here now. They are their own possessors. That is freedom as pure as it gets. And yet in their freedoms they remain subject to the fates and the fickleness of the world that enmeshes us all.

So, yes. Alfie, Plus-One, and the Hoo couldn't be too far away. Maybe across the street where the little stream runs through the swamp to the millpond. The human in me is tempted to say, "Who knows?" But I *know* who knows. Alfie knows. Plus-One knows. The Hoo knows. They know.

ALL OF US COME AND go. To keep the living world is a multigenerational relay that can be decisively lost but never decisively won.

Can a world love us? A silly question. On the other hand, what else is this particular world doing—this world that has birthed every breath ever taken? The question becomes whether we remain capable of returning the world's love. If we can't say we love the world, what does that say of us?

BEING "STUCK" AT HOME FREED us to experience real life with deeper consistency. In a "normal" year with a cluttered calendar demanding too much time away, I would not have been able to spend several hours at dawn and dusk watching our little owl find her life. I would have missed the nuances of Alfie and Plus-One's courtship, the fine and delicate shifts from tentative tolerance to nuptial excitement to the business of rearing youngsters. I would have missed the dutifully driven male owl carrying chipmunks at noon. And I would have missed the first fraught and dangerous dawn after fledging, the jays and robins repeatedly knocking the vulnerable young owls from the trees and the fledgers' determination to regain and maintain their new foothold in the world. I'd have missed the weeks when the family's calls convened them and they bivouacked in the same maples day after day. I would have missed seeing a mother owl flying to each youngster in turn, tenderly offering little bites until they wanted no more food. And, of course, all these things and infinitely more are always going on, entirely overlooked, even in our own literal and metaphorical backyards. The real world is seldom on our minds. This year, Patricia and I got lucky.

The owls gave us the opportunity to pay attention. That was their main gift to us: to be present for a while in the always magical here and now.

It was amazing how quiet and empty the air could feel once you subtracted owls. But now I knew they were out there, livening up the nights with or without me. Yes, I felt an empty nester. But I'd been dealt a full house, a winning hand.

Epilogue

ALFIE WAS OUR LITTLE FRIEND. WE SHARED MORE HOURS and more intimacy than I do with most humans I count as friends.

A couple of weeks passed. I was away when Patricia wrote, "5:20 a.m. dogs woke me up howling. Felt like getting up. Came to see if Alfie was around. I started calling her like I do. No response but when scanning the area I see she is right there in the birdbath. Quiet and alone. No babies to be seen or heard. She let me stroke her. She flew up to a low branch, but showed no interest in food."

It was as if, with her family gone, she just wanted to hang out for a few moments with Patricia before going to her day's slumber. After all, we were family.

On the cusp of August, Patricia and I went to the shore for a wide view of the night sky so we might photograph the rare and spectacular comet named Neowise, that summer's celestial celebrity. We returned home around eleven p.m. The yard was absolutely devoid of owls.

Patricia started giving her own signature call: "*Where* are you? . . . *Where* are you?"

I was thinking, wherever she is, she's not here; if she were, she'd be calling.

Patricia said, "I've always gotten the feeling you have to talk to her a bit."

I was in the middle of saying something when I stopped; I thought I'd heard her. Yes, definitely. Now the call was loud. On her silent wings she'd materialized in the back-door dogwood. We gave her some takeout and she vanished into the night—for another two weeks.

I predicted that Alfie would return to her core territory in our yard when the weather cooled toward autumn and insect availability thinned. And that's what happened. She settled back into our presence in the middle of September.

At this writing, Alfie remains our magical russet comet of the nighttime backyard. By day she usually roosts in either the Ivy Tower or the ivy-veiled maple tree she landed in on the first day she was loose, and on some days (as the heckling jays and wrens can attest) she roosts inside her nest box. She has favorite spots, but the choice is always hers. Free within limits—that's the way it is with the universe.

Various friends have asked whether we've seen the Hoo again. I'd expected that they would disperse as young things do, that they'd leave their natal territory to try to stake their own claim in life. And as expected, alas, we never again saw them.

What I did not expect was that I'd never again see Plus-One. On August 4, Hurricane Isaias hit our region hard, with winds up to eighty miles per hour. The gusts snapped or blew down many trees in our yard and in the owls' woods. After a while of not seeing him, I suspected that Plus-One had been killed during that raging night of crackling limbs and trunks.

On a recent gusty night I saw in real time what might have happened. I went out at around eleven to give Alfie some food. Often when I'd call her, she'd show up in a few moments, coming in low and fast, then swoop upward into the back-door dogwood. On this windy night, she swooped upward, but a sudden gust caused her to miss her intended branch and instead strike the trunk; she ended up on the ground about twenty feet away. If, during that August hurricane, Plus-One was sheltering in a tree that snapped, or he was hit by flying branches, or he attempted to fly, it is easy to see how he could have shattered a wing. And it's hard to imagine a better shelter during that storm than Alfie's Ivy Tower, its fifteen-foot-high monumental maple stump invulnerable to the gusts, and the thick cascades of ivy forming an ideal windbreak. If Alfie was sheltering in that ivy as usual, it could well have been the key to her survival. Years ago, after a coastal storm, I found a sanderling in the road. The little shorebird's wing was broken, nearly severed, hanging by some skin and a tendon. It appeared that a gust had driven this unlucky sandpiper into some overhead wires. I finished the amputation with a knife and cauterized it with a soldering gun. That little voyager, that wind bird, got healthy with us and stayed until we arranged her retirement at a public aquarium.

Luck plays a role in life. It can play a roll of the dice in death. We think that death is a mystery. But the mystery is life. And look at us: out of the vast non-living universe, for some brief spark and against all odds, we live. That succession of sparks has been sufficient to let life persist, to proliferate, to sense, to wonder, to love. The most important question is not what will happen after death but what will happen after birth. What—in the poet Mary Oliver's challenging query— will we do with our one wild and precious life? Perhaps the answer can be easy: to care fiercely without apology. If there is a final exam at the end of life and its sole question is "Did you care?," I hope I might at least pass the course. The meaning of life is not given. Relationships are the meaning we make. The Nobelist physicist Frank Wilczek tells us, "Having tasted beauty at the heart of the world, we hunger for more. In this quest there is, I think, no more promising guide than beauty itself." If we attain only what we need to survive, survival has no purpose. Beauty makes life worth the effort it takes. Beauty can save us. So we must be those who save beauty. What is the best we can make of our existence? Connection. That is my answer.

In a year that could make people lose sight of everything known as normal, these are some things that a little owl, whose vision could overcome darkness, helped me see.

P.S.: ON FEBRUARY 17 OF the following year, Alfie and another owl, who was relaxed in my presence, were suddenly side by side in intimate proximity. No preliminaries. From somewhere, Plus-One had returned.

With her doting and devoted first mate, Plus-One, Alfie hatched and fledged three more owlets in her second breeding season. Now, several years later, I am pleased to say that the magic continues.

As I write this, Alfie is coming up on her sixth birthday. (She might live two or even three times as long.) And in her life so far, Alfie has raised a total of ten wild, free-living youngsters. Alfie's life has been much more than just one small tragedy averted. Not only has she survived in a life that was almost denied her, but she has fulfilled her participation into the future. Across time and across the species boundary, Alfie has paid it forward in a big way.

Owls and other birds will remain in or return to their nesting territory for the duration of their lifetime. But in Alfie's third nesting year, Plus-One never showed up. Nor did any prospective new mate. Alfie's internal chemistry responded as usual to the lengthening days. Her fatherless clutch of four eggs was infertile, but she faithfully incubated them well past their due date. It felt to me that Alfie was keeping her promise in a world that had broken its. I knew I was projecting. But there she was, mateless, holding up her end of the covenant. I was almost relieved when she finally abandoned the effort. Almost. A little part of me seemed to wither in those inert eggshells that spring. And Alfie, her body primed by hormones and the long days for another bout of mothering, appeared distinctly at loose ends for a while. It seemed that she sought our company more than usual. It was, certainly for us, a sadder and lonelier springtime.

But Alfie was playing a long game, and she remained in our yard, roosting by day in the Ivy Tower.

Summer, autumn . . . When much of winter passed, Alfie began calling loudly every evening. She was interrogating the night, seeking an answer from the darkness. I thought it would be so sad to see her go through another breeding season with no mate and no brood. Sad for her and—definitely sad for Patricia and me.

When I went outside at 11 p.m. on February 20, Alfie was in the backdoor dogwood. She gave a soft whinny but her attention was not on me. She whinnied again and—I heard a low and unfamiliar trill coming from my left. She snapped to attention looking in that direction and when I looked too, I saw another owl in a cedar along the stone wall, an owl who was wary of my gaze. Alfie had finally attracted a new suitor. We named him Jack.

Whereas Alfie and Plus-One used to meet at dusk each evening, share food he brought, and mate with gusto, Jack proved a secretive, seldom-seen male. He seemed tentative, less than committed, intermittently present, and, frankly, inept. Likely he was young, and this was his first breeding attempt.

Because he seemed awkward and superficial in the couple of mating attempts that I witnessed, I was not confident that Alfie's clutch of five eggs—her largest yet—was fertile. So near when they were due to begin hatching, I waited for Alfie to emerge from her nest and head to the bath. I put up a ladder, climbed, stuck my phone into the nest opening, and took a photo. Stashed in the nest box were the carcasses of three wild white-footed mice, testament that the still elusive Jack was more committed and more competent a provider than he'd revealed to me.

I reached in and pulled out an egg and was about to backlight it with my flashlight to see if anything was going on inside. But that was preempted by the remarkable sound of the egg speaking to me! Was I hallucinating? I was sure I heard it. I made a squeaky noise, and the egg spoke again!

Many birds begin conversations with chicks as soon as the egg is holed. My thumb detected the merest chipping of the shell. That was enough, apparently, to send breath to new lungs. And with those first breaths this just-hatching owlet, not yet into the world, was already adding their newest voice to the age-old planetary conversation, to the symphony of life.

A bird hatching from an egg is something entirely routine, of course. But that little life, yearning to connect beyond all known confines, having faith that on the other side of this dark shell is a mother prepared to nurture, showing that life has firm reason to expect that the world is equipped to welcome it, and those impossible little squeaks, made my eyes misty. I quickly put that egg, that capsule of life with its little time traveler, back in its nest with its wild co-voyagers, back across the fuzzy boundary between my life and theirs.

Four of those five eggs hatched. Eventually all those owlets fledged and dispersed. Another winning year. And Jack? Though he was much more elusive than Plus-One, he proved much more protective—and aggressive. While the owlets were around, Jack frequently came screaming and clacking at me. And the one time he came silently, he came from outside my vision and whacked me in the head. Whoa! When I finally regained my equanimity, I was impressed again at how these little beings possess such individual personalities.

Now as I write, Jack has begun reappearing at the end of a mild winter. But he is still secretive and I seldom see him. Meanwhile Alfie has been visiting her nest box nightly, getting in a broody mood for another nesting season.

Alfie had prompted me to ask whether our disconnection from the natural world is something we are taught. She has brought me out to the classroom, and taught me her answer.

Gratitudes

BLESSED ARE THE COMPASSIONATE, WHO FIND WILD babes rendered helpless by circumstance and feel moved to help. Blessed are the pet sitters: Mayra Marino, Linda Badkin, Sydney Randall, Patrice Domeischel, Abby Costigan, Alex Srp, Jeremy Kimball, Cayla Rosenhagen, and Iris Rosenhagen. Blessed are the hapless mice. Blessed are the dogs who play and chickens who lay, and the birds at our feeders, who give us the gift of accepting our offerings. Blessed is Patricia, who makes us all a family. Praise be to my literary agent, Jennifer Weltz. Praise to the eyes and wise counsel of editor John Glusman. Praise, too, to the extraordinary copyediting of Bonnie Thompson. Praise to the perceptive Paul Greenberg, to Peggy Sloan's insights about my oversights, to the incisive advice of John Grim, and to the far-seeing holy vision of Mary Evelyn Tucker. Praise to all who in so many ways have long supported the journey with their generosity of spirit. Praise to you who have come this far in good faith with Alfie and me.

Alfie's story would never have been possible if the person who found her near death had not called a wildlife rehabilitator. Such people have the expertise to save wild lives. Find out who to call in your community and keep their number handy so there's no time lost if you find a distressed or injured bird.

References

PART ONE: FIRST SUMMERS

CHAPTER 1. DOWN FROM HEAVEN

4 *many Native American languages distinguish*: Kimmerer, R. 2017. "Speaking of Nature." *Orion Magazine*, March–April. Online.

6 *dogs occupy a unique position*: Nelson, *Make Prayers to the Raven*, p. 189.

8 *Algonquian people whose lifeways*: Pritchard, *Native New Yorkers*, p. 33–37.

8 *Algonquian views typify*: Ibid., p. 57.

8 *"We are the land"*: Gunn, P. A. 1981. "Iyani: It Goes This Way." In *The Remembered Earth: An Anthology of Contemporary Native American Literature*, edited by G. Hobson. Albuquerque: University of New Mexico Press. (*Note*: The different capitalizations of Earth are in the original.)

9 *Ken Little Hawk*: Pritchard, *Native New Yorkers*, p. 14.

CHAPTER 2. FLIGHT DELAYED

13 *"Humans and animals share a communality"*: Nelson, *Make Prayers to the Raven*, p. 76.

13 *"An Indigenous person"*: Yunkaporta, *Sand Talk*, p. 36.

13 *Indigenous peoples still constitute perhaps 5 percent*: Taylor, B., Gretel Van Wieren, and Bernard Zahela. 2016. "The Greening of Religion Hypothesis (Part Two): Assessing the Data from Lynn White, Jr, to Pope Francis." *Journal for the Study of Religion, Nature and Culture* 10 (3): 306–78.

14 *When Christopher Columbus*: Letter to King Ferdinand of Spain, 1493, http://xroads.virginia.edu/~Hyper/HNS/Garden/columbus.html.

14 *When James Cook*: Cook, J. 1770. *James Cook's Endeavour Journal*. National Library of Australia. Journal entry of August 23. Online.

14 *"Their souls were those of poets"*: Quoted in Pritchard, E. T. 2015. *Native American Stories of the Sacred*, p. ix.

15 *"an ecological perspective essentially identical"*: Nelson, *Make Prayers to the Raven*, p. 211.

15 *existence is* relational: Marchand et al., *The Medicine Wheel*, p. 158.

15 *always both simultaneously*: Nelson, *Make Prayers to the Raven*, pp. 238–41.

15 *Their spirit-infused natural world*: Ibid., p. xv.

15 *spiritual threads*: Ibid., p. 225. See also: Grim, J., *Indigenous Traditions and Ecology*.

15 *a "watchful and possessive" second society*: Nelson, *Make Prayers to the Raven*, pp. 14–31, 226–29.

CHAPTER 3. TILTING TOWARD SEPTEMBER

17 *Tiny comblike serrations*: Ogden, L. E. 2017. "The Silent Flight of Owls, Explained." *Audubon*, July 28. Online.

18 *two-thirds of young screech owls died*: Belthoff, J. R., and G. Ritchison. 1989. "Natal Dispersal of Eastern Screech-Owls." *Condor* 91:254–65.

20 *the ears have different-sized openings*: Undated. "Owl Hearing." British Trust for Ornithology. Online. See also: Krings, M., et al. 2014. "The Cervical Spine of the American Barn Owl (*Tyto furcata pratincola*): I. Anatomy of the Vertebrae and Regionalization in Their S-Shaped Arrangement." *PLoS ONE* 9. Online. And: de Kok-Mercado, F., et al. 2013. "Adaptations of the Owl's Cervical & Cephalic Arteries in Relation to Extreme Neck Rotation." *Science* 339: 514–15.

22 *Bosch frequently painted owls*: Zuiddam, B. 2014. "The Devil and His Works: The Owl in Hieronymus Bosch (c.1450–1516)." *South African Journal of Art History* 29:1–17. Online.

22 *Messengers of both good* and other powers of prophesy: Nelson, *Make Prayers to the Raven*, p. 105.

22 *The Kiowa see owls*: Swan, H. 2021. "What the Owls Knew." Humans and Nature. org. Online.

22 *Udege people hunted*: "Blakiston's Fish Owls: Conservation Threats." WCS Russia. Online.

22 *the Ainu people of Hokkaido*: Hance, J. 2016. "The Owl Man; Saving the Incredible Bird You've Probably Never Heard Of." *Guardian*. Online.

23 *"Each animal knows way more than you do"*: Nelson, *Make Prayers to the Raven*, p. 225.

23 *Nearly all daily acts*: Ibid., p. 240.

23 *the Maasai lands of Kenya*: Anderson, J. L. 2021. "A Kenyan Ecologist's Crusade to Save Her Country's Wildlife." *New Yorker*, January 25. Online.

23 *Good luck is not random*: Nelson, *Make Prayers to the Raven*, p. 26.

23 *"The interaction here is very intense":*, Ibid., pp. 20, 24, 26.

23 *All members of the offended species*: Ibid., pp. 22–23.

23 *By disrespect, humans create bad luck*: Atleo, E. R. 2004. *Tsawalk: A Nuu-chah-nulth Worldview*, pp. 21, 63–64.

24 *the man froze to death*: Nelson, *Make Prayers to the Raven*, p. 111.

24 *"I was entirely unprepared"*: Ibid., pp. 238–39.

24 *not "religion" in the Western sense*: Pritchard, *Native American Stories of the Sacred*, p. xviii.

24 *Indigenous people generally don't worship*: Lent, *The Patterning Instinct*, p. 86.

24 *"a way of life that nurtures"*: Pritchard, *Native American Stories of the Sacred*, p. xxi.

CHAPTER 4. SHORTENING DAYS

26 *"This is how spirit works"*: Yunkaporta, *Sand Talk*, p. 68.

27 *On Aristotle's authority*: Armstrong, R. 2006. "Ancient Explanations of Bird Migration." Online.

27 *birds annually migrate to*: Simon, M. 2014. "Fantastically Wrong: The Scientist Who Thought That Birds Migrate to the Moon." *Wired*. https://www.wired .com/2014/10/fantastically-wrong-scientist-thought-birds-migrate-moon/.

27 *Thomas Harriot*: Edgerton, S. Y. 2009. *The Mirror, the Window, and the Telescope: How Renaissance Linear Perspective Changed Our Vision of the Universe*. Ithaca: Cornell University Press, pp. 155, 159.

27 *A woodblock print from 1555*: Armstrong, R. 2006. "Ancient Explanations of Bird Migration." Online.

28 *Elliott Coues . . . seemed perplexed*: Allen, J. A. 1909. "Biographical Memoir of Elliott Coues." *National Academy of Sciences*. Online. See also: Coues, E. 1878. *Birds of the Colorado Valley*. Government Printing Office, p 17.

28 *bar-tailed godwit*: Boffey, D. 2020. "Jet-Fighter Godwit Breaks World Record for Non-stop Bird Flight." *Guardian*. Online.

29 *"In these contoured dimensions of existence"*: Ibid., p. 39.

29 *a "way"*: Pritchard, *Native American Stories of the Sacred*, p. xi.

29 *"Our ways, not our things"*: Yunkaporta, *Sand Talk*, pp. 7–8.

29 *"I am always in awe"*: Kimmerer, R. 2017. "Speaking of Nature." *Orion Magazine*, March–April. Online.

29 *Native ways of being and knowing*: Marchand et al., *The Medicine Wheel*, pp. 149–50.

29 *prayers made and plans laid*: Marchand et al., *The Medicine Wheel*, p. 154.

30 *In the long-ago*: Nelson, *Make Prayers to the Raven*, p. 228.

32 *"the extreme profundity of native thought"*: Cireres. 2008. "Christian Motivation for Dialogue with Followers of the African Traditional Religion." *Afrika World*. Online.

32 *The fundamental African understanding*: Beyers, J. 2010. "What Is Religion? An African Understanding." *HTS Theological Studies*. Online.

32 *a person who needs help*: Atleo, *Tsawalk: A Nuu-chah-nulth Worldview*, pp. 12, 47.

32 *"I am here"*: Nepo, M. 2018. "Eight Worldviews and Practices." *Parabola*, October 27. Online.

35 *Artificial units of time such*: Pritchard, E. T. 2001. *No Word for Time*, p. 11.

35 *No word for "work"*: Yunkaporta, *Sand Talk*, p. 141.

36 *Nuu-chah-nulth tradition*: Atleo, *Principles of Tsawalk*, p. 30.

36 *"Science can only ascertain"*: Einstein, A. 1939. Reprinted as "Albert Einstein Solves the Equation." *Lapham's Quarterly*. Online.

PART TWO: OPENINGS
CHAPTER 5. DEPARTURES AND ARRIVALS

44 *The* Tao Te Ching *intuited*: This wording blends two translations, from https:// www.bbc.co.uk/religion/religions/taoism/beliefs/tao.shtml and https://terebess .hu/english/tao/e-m-chen.html.

45 *"When it accumulates there is life"*: Zhou, Y. 2019. "How to Live a Good Life and Afterlife: Conceptions of Post-Mortem Existence and Practices of Self-Cultivation in Early China." Publicly Accessible Penn Dissertations. 3244. https://repository .upenn.edu/edissertations/3244/.

45 *Out of the chaos of energy, Chinese philosophers*: Feuchtwang, S. 2016. "Chinese Religions." In *Religions in the Modern World: Traditions and Transformations*, 3rd ed., edited by L. Woodhead, C. Partridge, and H. Kawanami, 143–72. London: Routledge.

45 *Chinese thinkers generalized*: Tucker, M.E., and J. Berthrong, eds. 1998. *Confucianism and Ecology*. Cambridge, MA: Harvard University Press.

46 *Chinese saw a unity*: "Yin and Yang." Wikipedia. https://en.wikipedia.org/wiki/Yin_and_yang.

46 *Zhang Zai*: As translated and edited by D. A. Mason, http://www.san-shin.org/China-Western-Inscription-ZhangZai.html.

53 *have been known to catch small fish*: Dinets, V. 2011. "Eastern Screech-Owl Catches Fish by Wading." *Wilson Journal of Ornithology* 123 (4): 846–47.

54 *"Detailed study of matter reveals"*: Wilczek, *Fundamentals*, p. xviii.

54 *"The most important thing"*: Suzuki, S. *Zen Mind, Beginner's Mind*, p. 2.

55 *"This patch of earth"*: As quoted in Barash, *Buddhist Biology*, p. 24.

55 *"you are this 'nothing'"*: Nepo, M. 2018. "Eight Worldviews and Practices." *Parabola*, October 27. Online.

56 *David P. Barash says*: Barash, *Buddhist Biology*, p. 23.

56 *"The universe itself is the scripture of Zen"*: Matthiessen, *The Snow Leopard*, p. 31.

CHAPTER 6. ON THE LOOSE

60 *"What people do with their ecology"*: White, L., Jr. 1967. "The Historical Roots of Our Ecological Crisis. *Science* 155:1203–07.

61 *first to invent a sole god* and *Jan Assmann*: Ofengenden, A. 2015. "Monotheism, the Incomplete Revolution: Narrating the Event in Freud's and Assmann's Moses." *Symploke* 23:291–307.

61 *Akhenaten moved spirit*: Lent, *The Patterning Instinct*, pp. 122–24.

61 *boy-pharaoh, Tutankhaten*: Trigger, B., et al. 2001. *Ancient Egypt: A Social History*. Cambridge: Cambridge University Press, pp. 186–87.

61 *Later rulers purged Akhenaten's name*: Manniche, L. 2010. *Akhenaten Colossi of Karnak*. Cairo: American University in Cairo Press, p ix.

61 *"Proto-Indo-Europeans"*: Lent, *The Patterning Instinct*, pp. 136–37.

61 *"brother" is bhrater:* Balter, M. 2015. "Mysterious Indo-European Homeland May Have Been in the Steppes of Ukraine and Russia." *Science*. Online.

62 *Zoroastrianism injected several monumental concepts*: Lent, *The Patterning Instinct*, pp. 139–40. See also: "Zarathustra." Britannica. https://www.britannica.com/biography/Zarathustra. And "Zoroaster." Wikipedia. https://en.wikipedia.org/wiki/Zoroaster.

62 *agrarian civilizations developed straight lines*: Lent, *The Patterning Instinct*, p. 33.

64 *I view the fish as gifts*: See Kimmerer, *Braiding Sweetgrass*, pp. 27–30. See also: Kimmerer, R. 2020. "The Serviceberry: An Economy of Abundance." *Emergence Magazine*. Online.

65 *Historian Colin Wells says*: Wells, C. 2010. "How Did God Get Started?" *Arion* 18 (Fall) Online.

65 *these Ionian thinkers*: "Presocratic Philosophy." *Stanford Encyclopedia of Philosophy.* https://plato.stanford.edu/entries/presocratics/.

65 *Anaximander*: Guthrie, *The Greek Philosophers*, pp. 25–29.

66 *Xenophanes*: "Dinosaur History." http://academic.brooklyn.cuny.edu/geology /chamber/Xenophanes.html. See also: "Xenophanes." *Stanford Encyclopedia of Philosophy.* Online.

66 *Pythagoras*: Guthrie, W. K. C. 2013. *The Greek Philosophers*, p. 33.

66 *Heraclitus*: Graham, D. W. 2021. "Heraclitus." In *Stanford Encyclopedia of Philosophy*, edited by Edward N. Zalta. Online. See also: Guthrie, *The Greek Philosophers*, pp. 40, 81.

66 *"All things were together"*: Quoted in "Presocratic Philosophy." *Stanford Encyclopedia of Philosophy.* https://plato.stanford.edu/entries/presocratics/.

66 "Nous *set in order"*: Burnett, J., trans. "Anaxagoras: Nous." https://www.ellopos .net/elpenor/greek-texts/ancient-greece/anaxagoras-nous.asp.

67 *Democritus*: Williams, M. 2015. "Who Was Democritus?" *Universe Today.* Online. See also: Guthrie, *The Greek Philosophers*, p. 55. And: "Presocratic Philosophy." *Stanford Encyclopedia of Philosophy.* https://plato.stanford.edu/entries/pre socratics/.

67 *Archelaus*: Guthrie, *The Greek Philosophers*, p. 63.

67 *Decree of Diopeithes*: Gagarin, M. 2015. "Diopeithes, Decree of (c. 432 B.C.E.)." *Oxford Classical Dictionary.* Online.

70 *ideal, perfect, eternal "Form"*: Guthrie, *The Greek Philosophers*, p. 47.

71 *guiding souls*: Burkert, *Greek Religion*, p. 317.

71 *in the* Phaedo: "Phaedo," 80b; trans. G. M. A. Grube: http://cscs.res.in/dataarchive /textfiles/textfile.2010-09-15.2713280635/file.

71 *In the dialogues of Plato*: Miroshnikov, I. 2018. "The Gospel of Thomas and Plato," pp. 71–90.

71 *"tainted with human flesh"*: Plato. *Symposium.* Translated by W. Hamilton. Penguin Books, p. 95. https://www.bard.edu/library/arendt/pdfs/Plato-Symposium .pdf.

73 *Plato's star student, Aristotle*: Duignan, B. "Plato and Aristotle: How Do They Differ?" Britannica. https://www.britannica.com/story/plato-and-aristotle-how -do-they-differ.

73 *Lucretius*: "Lucretius." *Stanford Encyclopedia of Philosophy.* Online. See also: Taylor, B. 2016. "The Greening of Religion Hypothesis (Part One): From Lynn White, Jr, and Claims That Religions Can Promote Environmentally Destructive Attitudes and Behaviors to Assertions They Are Becoming Environmentally Friendly." *Journal for the Study of Religion, Nature and Culture* 10 (3): 268–305. Online.

76 *Like fish who don't realize they are in water*: Lent, *The Web of Meaning*, p. 3.

77 *"by any reckoning"*: Kraut, R. 2017. "Plato." *Stanford Encyclopedia of Philosophy.* Online.

CHAPTER 7. CHILLING

83 *"Spinoza is the greatest"*: Viereck, G. S. 1930. *Glimpses of the Great.* New York: Macauley, p. 372–73.

83 *"Those who realize that all life is one"*: Easwaran, E. 1987. *The Upanishads*. Berkeley: Nilgiri Press, p. 149.

84 *"Atman"*: *Katha Upanishad*: http://www.columbia.edu/itc/religion/f2001/docs/laterupanish.pdf.

85 Avatamsaka Sutra: Cleary, T. 1993. *The Flower Ornament Scripture: A Translation of the Avatamsaka Sutra*, pp. 44, 925, as cited at https://en.wikipedia.org/wiki/Avatamsaka_Sutra.

88 *importance of copying parents' behaviors*: Safina, C. 2020. *Becoming Wild*. New York: Henry Holt.

91 *polluting the soul*: Lent, *The Web of Meaning*, p. 45.

91 *things unseen*: Wells, C. 2010. "How Did God Get Started?" *Arion* 18, Fall. Online.

CHAPTER 8. SUSPENDED WINTERLUDE

95 *When the Christian Gospel of Thomas*: Meyer, M., and J. M. Robinson. 2007. *The Nag Hammadi Scriptures: The International Edition*. New York: HarperOne, pp. 2–3.

95 *"makes great sense in light of"*: Miroshnikov, *The Gospel of Thomas and Plato*, p. 71.

96 *Miroshnikov sums up the idea*: Ibid., pp. 71–90.

96 *Tertullian*: Wolterstorff, N. 2010. "Tertullian's Enduring Question." In *Inquiring About God*, edited by T. Cuneo, pp. 283–303. Cambridge: Cambridge University Press.

97 *The Venerable Bede* and *"quite simply, the highest praise"*: Wells, C. 2010. "How Did God Get Started?" *Arion* 18, Fall. Online.

97 *Ludwig Feuerbach advised*: Taylor, B. 2016. "The Greening of Religion Hypothesis (Part One): From Lynn White, Jr, and Claims That Religions Can Promote Environmentally Destructive Attitudes and Behaviors to Assertions They Are Becoming Environmentally Friendly." *Journal for the Study of Religion, Nature and Culture* 10 (3): 268–305. Online.

97 *"I am down here"*: Barash, *Buddhist Biology*, p. 21.

97 *"this useless garment"*: The quotations by Maximus are in Miroshnikov, *The Gospel of Thomas and Plato*, pp. 71–90.

97 *"The whole of that fictitious world"*: Nietzsche, *The Antichrist*, p. 27.

97 *Heather Eaton observed*: Eaton, H. Undated. "Christianity and Ecology." *Yale Forum on Religion and the Environment*. Online.

98 *Here Paul expresses*: Romans 7:14–24.

99 *Augustine of Hippo*: Sheed, F. J., trans. 1943. *The Confessions of St. Augustine*. New York: Sheed & Ward, pp. 236, 242–44.

99 *"is something to be the more ashamed of"*: Augustine. *The City of God* 14:23. Online at: https://erenow.net/common/city-of-god/16.php.

99 *"I am tempted through the eye"*: Augustine. *Confessions*. 1961. Translated by R.S. Pine-Coffin, p. 239. Harmondsworth: Penguin. https://www.sas.upenn.edu/~cavitch/pdf-library/Augustine_ConfessionsX.pdf.

99 *"When I find the singing itself more moving"*: Ibid.

99 *"The Platonists, who approached the truth more nearly"*: Augustine. *The City of God* 14:19. Online at: https://erenow.net/common/city-of-god/16.php.

100 *"is added another form of temptation"*: Augustine. *Confessions* 11:35.

100 *"Augustine's impact on Western Christian thought"*: MacCulloch, D. M. 2010. *A History of Christianity: The First Three Thousand Years*. London: Penguin Books, p. 319.

100 *"developed the intellectual framework"*: Sheed, F. J., trans. 1943. *The Confessions of St. Augustine*. New York: Sheed & Ward, pp. 236, 242–44.

101 *photos of mountain goats*: https://www.theguardian.com/world/gallery/2020/apr /22/animals-roaming-streets-coronavirus-lockdown-photos.

101 *BBC showed us*: https://www.bbc.com/news/world-52459487.

PART THREE: BINDINGS

CHAPTER 9. ISN'T IT ROMANTIC

107 *demoted to demons*: Wells, C. 2010. "How Did God Get Started?" *Arion* 18, Fall. Online.

107 *made it possible to exploit nature"*: White, L., Jr. 1967. "The Historical Roots of Our Ecological Crisis." *Science* 155:1203–07.

107 *"unique in that it 'destroyed belief'"*: Wells, C. 2010. "How Did God Get Started?" *Arion* 18, Fall. Online.

108 *Mather and Onesimus*: Koslov, M. 2021. "Introducing Inoculation, 1721." *Scientist*. Online.

108 *And he wrote famously of his revulsion*: Ryken, L. 1990. *Worldly Saints: The Puritans as They Really Were*. Grand Rapids: Zondervan.

108 *"The worst, the most tiresome"*: Nietzsche, F. Orig. 1886. Preface to *Beyond Good and Evil*. Translated by Helen Zimmern. Online at Gutenberg.org.

109 *"cultural tyranny telling us"*: Popova, M. 2021. "Alain de Botton on the Myth of Normalcy and the Importance of Breakdowns." *Brain Pickings*. Online.

CHAPTER 10. HONEYMOONERS

111 *"From Plato onwards"*: Banville, J. 2018. Review: "The Strange Order of Things by Antonio Damasio." *Guardian*. Online.

111 *"whole essence or nature is to think"*: Descartes as quoted in Dennett, D. 1993. *Consciousness Explained*. London: Penguin, p. 30.

112 *"The rational soul"*: Descartes, R. *Discourse on the Method*. Project Gutenberg. Online.

112 *Pouring Plato through a Catholic filter*: Blum, P. R. 2019. "Substance Dualism in Descartes." In *Introduction to Philosophy: Philosophy of Mind*, edited by H. Salazar, chapter 1. Rebus Community. Online.

114 *"object permanence:"* McLeod, S. 2021. "Object Permanence." *Simply Psychology*. Online.

115 *"This proves not only that the brutes"*: Descartes, R. *Discourse on the Method*. Project Gutenberg. Online.

115 *"If they thought as we do"*: Descartes, R. 1646 letter to the Marquess of Newcastle. Retrieved from http://www.appstate.edu/~steelekm/classes/psy3214/Descartes OnAnimals.htm.

116 *"I do not deny life to animals"*: Kenny, A. 1970. *Descartes: Philosophical Letters*. Oxford: Oxford University Press.

117 *"I had intended to send you"*: Gaukroger, S., ed. 2004. *René Descartes: The World and Other Writings*. Cambridge: Cambridge University Press, p. xxvii. Online.

118 *Newton wrote to a friend*: Berry, R. J. 2011. "John Ray, Physico-Theology and Afterwards." *Archives of Natural History* 38:328–48. Online.

119 *"When I look with a philosopher's eye"*: Descartes, R. *Discourse on the Method*. Project Gutenberg. Online.

119 *"It accords well with reason"*: Descartes, R. 1649. "René Descartes to the Most Erudite and Learned Henry More." *The Cambridge Platonism Sourcebook*. https://www.cambridge-platonism.divinity.cam.ac.uk/view/texts/normalised/Hengstermann1679C.

CHAPTER 11. FULL HOUSE

122 *"It is not less natural for a clock"*: Descartes, R. Orig. 1644. *Principles of Philosophy*. https://www.lancaster.ac.uk/users/philosophy/courses/211/Descartes'%20Principles.htm.

122 *Thomas Hobbes echoed*: Hobbes, T. 1651, 1994. *Leviathan*. Oxford Text Archive. http://hdl.handle.net/20.500.12024/2029.

124 *"turning with united forces against the Nature"*: Peltonen, M. 1992, "Politics and Science: Francis Bacon and the True Greatness of States." *Historical Journal* 35:279–305.

124 *Scholar Heidi D. Studer writes*: Studer, H. D. 2003. "Strange Fire at the Altar of the Lord: Francis Bacon on Human Nature." *Review of Politics* 65:209–35.

125 *Lynn White Jr. wrote*: White, L., Jr. 1967. "The Historical Roots of Our Ecological Crisis. *Science* 155:1203–07.

125 *meatpacking workers*: Funk, J. 2021. "Report: At Least 59,000 Meat Workers Caught COVID; 269 Died." AP News, October 27. Online.

127 *"Modern Western science was cast"*: White, L., Jr. 1967. "The Historical Roots of Our Ecological Crisis. *Science* 155:1203–07.

CHAPTER 12. BLOOMINGS

134 *"Living organisms are chemical machines"*: Jacques Loeb as quoted in Lent, *The Patterning Instinct*, p. 282.

136 *"A feather magnified"*: Beston, H. 1928, 2003. *The Outermost House*. New York: Henry Holt, p. 25.

136 *Schrödinger noted that a chemist*: Schrödinger, *What is Life?*, pp. 5, 78–80.

139 *A computer is merely complicated*: For the distinction between complicated and complex, see Lent, *The Web of Meaning*, pp. 23, 100.

141 *In sleeping male finches, neurons*: 2019. "Do Birds Dream?" All About Birds, Cornell University. Online.

141 *Even cuttlefish dream*: Daley, J. 2019. "Cuttlefish Are Dazzling, but Do They Dream?" *Scientific American*. Online.

143 *Thomas Wentworth Higginson*: Higginson, T. H. 1862. "The Life of Birds." *Atlantic Monthly* 10:368–376, as quoted in Birkhead, T. 2016. *The Most Perfect Thing*. London: Bloomsbury, p. xvi.

144 *For the first billion years*: WNYC Studios. 2008. "Genes on the Move." Radiolab. Online.

144 *For the next billion years*: Pennisi, E. 2018. "The Momentous Transition to Multi-cellular Life Might Not Have Been So Hard After All." *Science.* Online.

PART FOUR: NURSERY DAYS
CHAPTER 13. NURSERY DAYS

153 *"A bat is a machine"*: Dawkins, *The Blind Watchmaker*, p. 37.

153 *Dawkins begins one of his books*: Ibid., p. ix.

154 *Tertullian bellowing*: Wolterstorff, N. 2010. "Tertullian's Enduring Question." In *Inquiring About God*, edited by T. Cuneo, pp. 283–303. Cambridge: Cambridge University Press.

156 *"Life is just bytes"*: Dawkins, *River Out of Eden*, p. 19.

156 *Samuel Butler anticipated the inanity*: Schrage, M. 1995. "Revolutionary Evolutionist." *Wired*, July 1. https://www.wired.com/1995/07/dawkins/.

156 *Ernst Mayr*: Crair, B. 2021. "Where Do Species Come From?" *New Yorker*, September 21.

156 *"do not function independently"*: Collins, F. S., et al. 2003. "A Vision for the Future of Genomics Research." *Nature* 422:835–47.

159 *Eastern chipmunks weigh about four ounces*: The weight of the eastern chipmunk is given as 66–150 g (2.3–5.3 oz) in Wikipedia, https://en.wikipedia.org/wiki/Eastern _chipmunk. The weight of the eastern screech owl: 6 to 7 ounces; https://en .wikipedia.org/wiki/Eastern_screech_owl.

160 *Mice "experience the pain and relief"*: Moutinho, S. 2021. "Mice Feel for Each Other." *Science.* Online.

160 *barn owls could perceive and catch mice*: Payne, R. 1971. "Acoustic Location of Prey by Barn Owls (*Tyto alba*)." *Journal of Experimental Biology* 54:535–73.

160 *"Organisms are algorithms"*: Mukherjee, S. 2017. "Homo Deus." *New York Times*, March 13. Online. See also: Hinchliffe, T. 2018. "How to Hack a Human 101: 'Organisms Are Algorithms,' World Economic Forum Davos." *The Sociable.* Online.

165 *as studies have shown with young barn owls*: Knudsen, E. I., and P. F. Knudsen. 1985. "Vision Guides the Adjustment of Hearing in Barn Owls." *Science* 230:545–48.

CHAPTER 14. ON THE LOOSE

167 *"To wait was to pray"*: Tesson, *The Art of Patience*, p. 140.

167 *"As long as we think of living systems as machines"*: Srinivasan, A. 2018. "What Termites Can Teach Us." *New Yorker*, September 17. Online.

167 *"are resilient patterns in a turbulent flow"* and Woese's quotations on the following pages: Woese, C. 2004. "A New Biology for a New Century." *Microbiology and Molecular Biology Reviews*: 68:173–86.

170 *a physicist and a biologist*: The comparison was suggested in House, P. 2022. *Nineteen Ways of Looking at Consciousness*. New York: St. Martin's, p. 9.

171 *"The ultimate aim"*: Crick, F. H. C. 1966. *Of Molecules and Men*. Seattle: University of Washington Press, p. 10.

171 *The twentieth-century experimental biologist Lancelot Hogben*: Keiper, C. (a.k.a. Nicol, C.) 2007. "Brave New World at 75." *New Atlantis*. Spring. Online.

171 *"Anyone who would hire an ecologist"*: 2009. "An Intellectual Entente." *Harvard Magazine*. Online.

171 *DNA's notably nasty co-discoverer:* Belluz, J. 2019. "DNA Scientist James Watson Has a Remarkably Long History of Sexist, Racist Public Comments." *Vox*. Online.

179 *"We're building stuff."*: NPR Research News. 2008. "Bioengineers Hope to Build Life." Online.

179 *"wonderstruck" by science*: Wilczek, *Fundamentals*, p. xii.

179 *James Somers observed*: Somers, J. 2022. "The Final Frontier." *New Yorker*, March 7.

179 *whether a mammalian fetus lies*: Ryan, B. C., and J. G. Vandenbergh. 2002. "Intra-uterine Position Effects." *Neuroscience and Biobehavioral Reviews* 26:665–78.

180 *Water temperature can affect*: Crozier, L. G., and J. A. Hutchings. 2014. "Plastic and Evolutionary Responses to Climate Change in Fish." *Evolutionary Applications* 7:68–87. Online.

180 *Experiments with certain minnows*: Shama, L. N. S., et al. 2014. "Transgenerational Plasticity in Marine Sticklebacks: Maternal Effects Mediate Impacts of a Warming Ocean." *Functional Ecology* 28:1482–93. Online. See also: Salinas, S., and S. B. Munch. 2012. "Thermal Legacies: Transgenerational Effects of Temperature on Growth in a Vertebrate." *Ecology Letters* 15:159–63.

180 *Studies in more than sixty species*: Salinas, S., et al. 2013. "Non-genetic Inheritance and Changing Environments." *Non-genetic Inheritance*. Online.

180 *wolves infected with a parasite*: Meyer, C. J., et al. 2022. "Parasitic Infection Increases Risk-taking in a Social, Intermediate Host Carnivore." *Communications Biology* 5:1180. Online.

180 *Nigel Goldenfeld*: Cepelewicz, J. 2017. "Seeing Emergent Physics Behind Evolution." *Quanta*. Online.

CHAPTER 15. DOWN TOWN

185 *the regent honeyeater*: Australian National University. 2021. "When Singing the Wrong Song Spells Trouble." *SciTechDaily*. Online.

185 *"I should have loved biology"*: Somers, J. Undated. "I Should Have Loved Biology." Online.

185 *"Half of our first-year students"*: Robbins, J. 2021. "Why Local Legends About Birds Matter." BBC.com. Online.

189 *the Oxford Junior Dictionary began dropping words* and *Author Robert Macfarlane*: Flood, A. 2015. "Oxford Junior Dictionary's Replacement of 'Natural' Words with 21st-Century Terms Sparks Outcry." *Guardian*. Online.

191 *"without any imperative to know"* and *"What kind of creature are we?"*: Challenger, *On Extinction*, pp. xiii, xvi.

CHAPTER 16. OUT AND ABOUT

197 *"waiting for and hastening"*: 2 Peter 3:12.

198 *Calvin Beisner*: Weaver, A. 2014. "The EPA and Evangelical (Anti)Environmentalism." *Religion Dispatches*. Online. See also: Taylor, B., Gretel Van Wieren, and Bernard Zahela. 2016. "The Greening of Religion Hypothesis (Part Two): Assess-

ing the Data from Lynn White, Jr, to Pope Francis." *Journal for the Study of Religion, Nature and Culture* 10 (3): 306–78. Online.

199 *"a good candidate for the originating idea"*: Sartwell, C. 2021. "Humans Are Animals; Let's Get Over It." *New York Times*, February 23. Online.

200 *Willie Jennings*: Undated. "Eco-Theology and Zoning Meetings: An Interview with Willie Jennings." *Reflections*. Online.

200 *"a metaphor based on deception"*: Yunkaporta, *Sand Talk*, p. 49.

203 *"Animals, whom we have made our slaves"*: Darwin, C. 1837–38. *Notebook B: Transmutation of Species*. Darwin-online.org.uk.

CHAPTER 17. ALL TOGETHER NOW

208 *Tu Weiming*: Weiming, Tu. 1998. "Beyond the Enlightenment Mentality." In *Confucianism and Ecology*, edited by M. E. Tucker and J. Berthrong, pp 3–21. Cambridge, MA: Harvard University Press.

211 *"animals are not self-conscious"*: Infield, L. 1963. *Lectures on Ethics*. New York: Harper and Row, pp. 239–41.

211 *"the animal in this case"*: Kant, I. 1900. *On Education (Ueber Pädagogik)*. Translated by Annette Churton. 1:5. Online.

211 *people annually kill roughly 50 billion chickens*: Thornton, A. 2019. "This Is How Many Animals We Eat Each Year." World Economic Forum. Online. See also: Our World in Data: https://ourworldindata.org/meat-production#number-of -animals-slaughtered.

211 *humans, cows, pigs*: Bar-On, Y. M., R. Phillips, and R. Milo. 2018. "The Biomass Distribution on Earth." *Proceedings of the National Academy of Sciences* 115:6506–11.

212 *"justice consists in the superior ruling over and having more than the inferior"*: Plato, *Gorgias*. Translated by Benjamin Jowett. Part 2, p. 12. Online.

212 *"In the case of those whose business it is"*: Aristotle. *Politics*. Translated in 1885 by Benjamin Jowett. Book I, Part V. Online.

212 *"a common power to keep them all in awe"*: Hobbes, T. *Leviathan*, chapters 13–14. Online at Gutenberg.org.

213 *paycheck to paycheck*: LendingClub Corporation. 2022. "The Number of Consumers Living Paycheck to Paycheck Has Increased Year-over-Year Across All Income Levels." Online.

213 *half of Americans don't have enough savings*: Velasquez, F. 2021. "Over Half of Americans Have Less Than 3 Months Worth of Emergency Savings." CNBC. Online.

213 *"morally independent of animality"*: Sartwell, C. 2021. "Humans Are Animals; Let's Get Over It." *New York Times*, February 23. Online.

213 *"Western technology and the people"*: Notes, *Basic Call to Consciousness*, pp. 89–90.

213 *"What we're seeing now"*: Sengupta, S., C. Einhorn, and M. Andreoni. 2021. "There's a Global Plan to Conserve Nature: Indigenous People Could Lead the Way. *New York Times*, 11 March. Online.

CHAPTER 18. INTO A NEW DAY

218 *As Wade Davis observes*: Davis, W. 2020. "The Unraveling of America." *Rolling Stone*. Online.

220 *"Someone once asked me"*: Harris, L., and J. Wasilewski. 2004. "Indigeneity, an Alternative Worldview." *Systems Research and Behavioral Science* 21:489–503.

221 *"This life of work-or-die"*: Yunkaporta, *Sand Talk*, pp. 139–40.

221 *incinerate three billion animals*: 2020. "Australia's Fires 'Killed or Harmed Three Billion Animals.'" BBC. Online.

221 *our industrial systems depend on destruction*: Yunkaporta, *Sand Talk*, p. 67.

221 *Zen master Susan Murphy*: Murphy, S. 2014. *Minding the Earth, Mending the World*. Berkeley: Counterpoint, p. 4.

PART FIVE: MYSTERIOUS MESSENGERS
CHAPTER 19. MYSTERIOUS MESSENGERS

231 *a spirit can enter a bird for a time*: Pritchard, E. T. 2013. *Bird Medicine*. Rochester, VT: Bear & Co., p. 22.

231 *Jennifer Holland*: Holland, J. S. 2014. "Wild Messengers." *New York Times*, November 1. Online.

234 *a love story between human beings and nature* and Bertrand Russell: Keiper, C. (a.k.a. Nicol, C.) 2007. "Brave New World at 75." *New Atlantis*. Spring. Online. See also: Russell, B. 1931. *The Scientific Outlook*. London: George Allen & Unwin.

CHAPTER 20. WHAT GOES AROUND

237 *as Aldo Leopold wrote*: Leopold, A. (1949) 1989. *A Sand County Almanac*. New York: Oxford University Press, p. 133.

237 *extinction was considered a theological impossibility*: Freeberg, E. 2021. "The Long History of Those Who Fought to Save the Animals." *New York Times*. April 14. Online.

237 *waves of extinctions clearly resulted from human arrivals* and *Since 1500*: Johnson, C. N. Undated. "Past and Future Decline and Extinction of Species." Royal Society. Online.

238 *a rate variously calculated*: Ceballos, G., et al. 2015. "Accelerated Modern Human-Induced Species Losses: Entering the Sixth Mass Extinction." *Science Advances*. See also: De Vos, J. M., et al. 2014. "Estimating the Normal Background Rate of Species Extinction." *Conservation Biology*.

238 *sixty-five North American plant species*: Renault, M. 2020. "How Many Plants Have We Wiped Out? Here Are Five Extinction Stories." *New York Times*, October 16. Online.

238 *the United Nations estimated*: 2019. "World Is 'on Notice' as Major UN Report Shows One Million Species Face Extinction." *UN News*. Online.

238 *twenty-three species*: Einhorn, C. 2021. "Protected Too Late: U.S. Officials Report More Than 20 Extinctions." *New York Times*, 4 October. Online.

238 *whale poop was a major ocean fertilizer*: Yong, E. 2021. "The Enormous Hole That Whaling Left Behind." *Atlantic,* Online.

238 *three billion fewer birds*: Rosenberg, K. V., et al. 2019. "Decline of the North American Avifauna." *Science* 366:120–24.

238 *Twenty North American birds*: 2014. "Common Birds Are Declining in North

America." Bird Life International. http://datazone.birdlife.org/sowb/casestudy
/common-birds-are-declining-in-north-america.

239 *Bobwhite quail*: "Northern Bobwhite." IUCN Red List. http://www.iucnredlist
.org/details/22728956/0.

239 *Accelerating scarcity among insects*: Jarvis, B. 2018. "The Insect Apocalypse Is
Here." *New York Times Magazine*. Online. See also: Hance, J. 2019. "The Great
Insect Dying." *Mongabay*. Online.

239 *Whip-poor-wills have dropped*: 2009. "Are Whip-poor-will Populations Declining?" All About Birds. Cornell University. Online.

239 *nineteen species of North American shorebirds*: Fitzpatrick, J., and N. Senner. 2018.
"Shorebirds, the World's Greatest Travelers, Face Extinction." *New York Times*. Online.

239 *Seabirds including shearwaters*: Paleczny, M., et al. 2015. "Population Trend of the
World's Monitored Seabirds, 1950–2010." *Proceedings of the National Academy of
Sciences*. Online.

239 *Brazil's formerly vast Atlantic forest*: BirdLife International. 2004. "In the Neo-
tropics, Many Species Have Been Driven Extinct Across Large Parts of Their
Range." BirdLife International. Online.

239 *chytrid fungus*: http://www.amphibianark.org/the-crisis/chytrid-fungus/.

239 *freshwater mussels*: "Chytrid Fungus." Amphibian Ark. https://www.fws.gov/mid
west/endangered/clams/mussels.html.

239 *sharks and rays*: IUCN. 2014. "A Quarter of Sharks and Rays Threatened with
Extinction." IUCN. Online.

239 *All ten of the "most charismatic" animals*: Courchamp, F., et al. 2018. "The Paradox-
ical Extinction of the Most Charismatic Animals." *PLoS Biology*. Online.

240 *sperm counts among Western men*: Davis, N. 2017. "Sperm Counts Among Western
Men Have Halved in Last 40 Years—Study." *Guardian*. Online.

242 *"This disintegration of the world"*: Tesson, *The Art of Patience*, pp. 123–25.

245 *"We mined our way"*: United Nations. 2011. "Warning of 'Global Suicide,' Ban
Calls for Revolution to Ensure Sustainable Development." https://news.un.org/en
/story/2011/01/365432.

245 *took a Confucian approach*: Walsh, B. 2006. "Can This Guy Run the U.N.?"
Time. https://web.archive.org/web/20061104180556/http://www.time.com/time
/magazine/article/0%2C9171%2C1543932%2C00.html.

245 *"We are part of an earth-eating superorganism"*: email to the author.

245 *"The real problem of humanity"*: Edward O. Wilson quoted in Hagens, N. J. 2019.
"Economics for the Future—Beyond the Superorganism." *Ecological Economics* 169.

CHAPTER 21. THE FULLNESS OF YOUTH

251 *damage to the planet's atmospheric ozone layer*: UNEP. 2021. "Making Peace with
Nature." Online.

251 *Native American writer Robin Wall Kimmerer*: Kimmerer, R. 2017. "Speaking of
Nature." *Orion Magazine*, March–April.

252 *"There is no calamity . . ."*: This is a composite translation from: Lao Tsu, *Tao Te
Ching*, trans. G. Feng and J. English (New York: Vintage, 1972), chapters 44, 46;
Lao Tzu, *Tao Te Ching*, trans. Ellen M. Chen (St. Paul, MN: Paragon House,

1989); and Lao Tzu, *Tao Teh Ching*, trans. John C. H. Wu (Boston: Shambhala, 2005). See also: Lent, *The Web of Meaning*, p. 220.

254 *Jay Griffiths*: Quoted in Challenger, *On Extinction*, p. xvii.

255 *"it's still good ground"*: Nelson, *Make Prayers to the Raven*, p. 200.

255 *Fabian Jimbijti and Phrang Roy*: Lewis, N. 2021. "Nature Is Not a Commodity." CNN. Online.

258 *Jill Bolte Taylor*: Taylor, J. B. 2006. *My Stroke of Insight*. New York: Penguin Books. See also her TED talk online.

263 *Elizabeth Marshall Thomas*: Thomas, *Dreaming of Lions*, pp. 24, 64.

PART SIX: GOING, GOING
CHAPTER 22. YARDERS

271 *"The progress of science is destined to bring"*: Dyson, F. 1997. *Imagined Worlds*. Cambridge, MA: Harvard University Press, p. 99.

273 *Ubuntu*: Mugumbate, J. R., and A. Chereni. 2020. "Editorial: Now, the Theory of Ubuntu Has Its Space in Social Work." *African Journal of Social Work*, April 23.

273 *Desmond Tutu, Nelson Mandela*: LoGiurato, B. 2013. "Obama's Tribute to Nelson Mandela at Memorial Service." *Business Insider*, December 10. About the Episcopal Church, see also: Episcopal Church in Mississippi, 76th General Convention, July 8–17, 2009, https://www.dioms.org/Archives/general convention2009page2.html.

273 *"the vow to water the common roots"*: Nepo, M. 2018. Eight Worldviews and Practices. *Parabola*, October 27. Online.

273 *Indigenous peoples will be crucial*: Sengupta, S., C. Einhorn, and M. Andreoni. 2021. "There's a Global Plan to Conserve Nature: Indigenous People Could Lead the Way." *New York Times*, 11 March. Online.

273 *thousands of Indigenous people have been murdered*: Lawlor, M. 2022. "One Person Is Killed Every Two Days Defending the Environment." *Euronews.green*. Online. See also: Watts, J. 2021. "Murders of Environment and Land Defenders Hit Record High Last Year." *Guardian*. Online.

273 *Haudenosaunee (Iroquois) democracy so attracted*: 1987. "Iroquois Constitution: A Forerunner to Colonists' Democratic Principles." *New York Times*, 28 June. Online. See also: Hansen, T. "How the Iroquois Great Law of Peace Shaped U.S. Democracy." *Native Voices*. PBS. Last updated December 17, 2018. https://www.pbs.org/native-america/blogs/native-voices/how-the-iroquois-great-law-of-peace-shaped-us-democracy/.

275 *Ralph Waldo Emerson*: Wineapple, B. 2022. "New England Ecstasies." *New York Review*. Online.

275 *Thomas Merton*: Kramer, V. A., ed. 1996. *Turning Toward the World: The Pivotal Years. The Journals of Thomas Merton*, vol. 4, *1960–1963*. San Francisco: HarperSanFrancisco, p. 274.

275 *Thomas Berry*: Berry, T. 1988. *Dream of the Earth*.

276 *"For human beings to cause species"*: A video of Bartholomew's pronouncement is online at YouTube; search for "Harming the Environment Is a Sin." See also:

Stammer, L. B. 1997. "Harming the Environment Is a Sin, Prelate Says." *Los Angeles Times*. Online.

276 *Richard Rohr*: Rohr, R. "Creation as the Body of God," in Vaughan-Lee, *Spiritual Ecology*, pp. 236–41.

276 *Francis and Bartholomew issued a joint statement*: "Joint Message of Pope Francis and the Ecumenical Patriarch Bartholomew for the World Day of Prayer for Creation, 01.09.2017." Vatican Press Office. Online.

279 *"photosynthetically active radiation"*: Liu, J., and M. W. van Iersel 2021. "Photosynthetic Physiology of Blue, Green, and Red Light." *Frontiers in Plant Science*, March 5. https://www.frontiersin.org/articles/10.3389/fpls.2021.619987/full.

279 *what humans use as "light" for eyesight*: "Visible Light." NASA Science. https://science.nasa.gov/ems/09_visiblelight.

279 *Birds can see ultraviolet radiation*: Withgott, J. 2000. "Taking a Bird's-Eye View . . . in the UV." *BioScience* 50 (10): 854–59. https://academic.oup.com/bioscience/article/50/10/854/233996.

CHAPTER 24. COUNTDOWN, JUNE 29

288 *have discovered two new galaxies*: 2021. "Two New Giant Radio Galaxies Discovered." *Sci.News*. Online.

290 *Robert Macfarlane summarizes some of Simard's findings*: Macfarlane, R., 2016. "The Secrets of the Wood Wide Web." *New Yorker*, August 7.

291 *around 40 percent of the carbon*: Owens, B. 2016. "Trees Share Vital Goodies Through a Secret Underground Network." *New Scientist*, April 14. Online. See also: Jabr, F. 2020. "The Social Life of Forests." *New York Times Magazine*, December 2. Online.

291 *according to Simard*: Hooper, R. 2021. "Suzanne Simard Interview: How I Uncovered the Hidden Language of Trees." *New Scientist*. Online.

CHAPTER 25. COUNTDOWN, JUNE 30

296 *Have you ever seen a video of cows*: See, for example, the short film *73 Cows*: https://vimeo.com/293352305.

CHAPTER 26. GOING, GOING—

299 *or numbness will obliterate joy*: Macy, J. "The Greening of the Self." In Vaughan-Lee, *Spiritual Ecology*, p. 154.

299 *Screech owl home ranges*: Smith, D. G., and R. Gilbert. 1984. "Eastern Screech-Owl Home Range and Use of Suburban Habitats in Southern Connecticut." *Journal of Field Ornithology* 55 (3): 322–29.

300 *Steven Weinberg observed*: Weinberg, S. 1993. *The First Three Minutes*. New York: Basic Books, p. 154.

300 *"There is a point that we can give the universe"*: Steven Weinberg, *Faith and Reason*, PBS; interview transcript: https://www.pbs.org/faithandreason/transcript/margaret-frame.html.

302 *"It's tiny, it's shiny, it's beautiful"*: Chang, K. 2019. "For Apollo 11 He Wasn't on the Moon. But His Coffee Was Warm." *New York Times*, 16 July.

302 *abachtuk*: Pritchard, *Native American Stories of the Sacred*, p. lxiii.

304 *landmark 1972 law journal article*: Stone, C. D. 1972. "Should Trees Have Standing? Towards Legal Rights for Natural Objects." *Southern California Law Review* 45:450–501.

304 *The Maoris' negotiator explained*: Cheater, D. 2018. "I Am the River, and the River Is Me: Legal Personhood and Emerging Rights of Nature." *West Coast Environmental Law Alert Blog*, March 22. www.wcel.org/blog/i-am-river-and-river -melegal-personhood-and-emerging-rights-nature.

305 *Ecuador and majority-Indigenous Bolivia*: Balch, O. 2013. "Buen Vivir: The Social Philosophy Inspiring Movements in South America." *Guardian*. Online.

305 *government of India* and *Hungary, Costa Rica, Chile, Finland, and Argentina* and *Pakistan's high court*: Wright, L. 2022. "The Elephant in the Courtroom." *New Yorker*, March 7. Online.

305 *The Swiss amended*: Michel, M., and E. S. Kayasseh. 2011. "The Legal Situation of Animals in Switzerland: Two Steps Forward, One Step Back—Many Steps to Go." *Journal of Animal Law* 7: 1–42. https://www.afgoetschel.com/de/downloads /legal-situation-of-animals-in-switzerland.pdf.

305 *Chilean voters decided against*: Surma, K. 2022. "Chilean Voters Reject a New Constitution That Would Have Provided Groundbreaking Protections for the Rights of Nature." *Inside Climate News*. Online.

305 *several other countries . . . have recognized*: Surma, K. 2022. "Indian Court Rules That Nature Has Legal Status on Par with Humans—and That Humans Are Required to Protect It." *Inside Climate News*. Online. See also: Surma, K. 2021. "As the Climate Crisis Grows, a Movement Gathers to Make 'Ecocide' an International Crime Against the Environment." *Inside Climate News*. Online.

305 *"ecosystems, natural communities, and species within the Ho-Chunk Nation"*: CELDF. September 17, 2018. "Press Release: Ho-Chunk Nation General Council Approves Rights of Nature Constitutional Amendment." Online.

305 *Tribes have sued*: Surma, K. 2022. "In the Latest Rights of Nature Case, a Tribe Is Suing Seattle on Behalf of Salmon in the Skagit River." *Inside Climate News*. Online.

305 *"Maybe now"*: Kimmerer, R. 2017. "Speaking of Nature." *Orion Magazine*, March–April. Online.

306 *Lake Erie Bill of Rights*: Gillett, M. T. 2020. "Federal Judge Rules Lake Erie Bill of Rights Unconstitutional." *Jurist*. Online.

306 *After 89 percent of voters*: Surma, K. 2022. "Two Lakes, Two Streams and a Marsh Filed a Lawsuit in Florida to Stop a Developer from Filling in Wetlands. A Judge Just Threw It Out of Court." *Inside Climate News*. Online.

306 *"In America, the rights of nature"*: Surma, K. 2022. "Ecuador's High Court Rules That Wild Animals Have Legal Rights. *Inside Climate News*. Online.

309 *"I believe in all religions"*: Shatz, A. 2021. "Coltrane's New 'Love Supreme.'" *New York Review*. Online.

309 *Diane Ackerman*: Ackerman, D. 2005. *An Alchemy of Mind: The Marvel and Mystery of the Brain*. New York: Scribner, p. 60.

CHAPTER 27. DEPARTURES

313 *an owl flew into a firefighting helicopter*: 2020. "Owl Flies into Helicopter Mak-

ing Water Drops over Creek Fire." https://abc30.com/creek-fire-owl-updates-in
-helicopter-firefighter/7029352/.

314 *High majorities*: Taylor, B., Gretel Van Wieren, and Bernard Zahela. 2016. "The
Greening of Religion Hypothesis (Part Two): Assessing the Data from Lynn
White, Jr, to Pope Francis." *Journal for the Study of Religion, Nature and Culture*
10 (3): 306–78. Online.

314 *"After you have exhausted"*: Whitman, W. 1876. "103: New Themes Entered Upon."
Specimen Days. Online at bartleby.com/229/.

EPILOGUE

319 *Frank Wilczek tells us*: See On Being. 2016. "Why Is the World So Beautiful?" onbe-
ing.org, July 25. http://m.dailygood.org/story/1343/why-is-the-world-so-beautiful
-on-being].

Selected Bibliography

Ackerman, D. 2005. *An Alchemy of Mind: The Marvel and Mystery of the Brain.* New York: Scribner.

Atleo, E. R. 2004. *Tsawalk: A Nuu-chah-nulth Worldview.* Vancouver: UBC Press.

———. 2011. *Principles of Tsawalk.* Vancouver: UBC Press.

Barash, D. P. 2014. *Buddhist Biology.* Oxford: Oxford University Press.

Berry, T. 1988. *Dream of the Earth.* San Francisco: Sierra Club Books.

Burkert, Walter. 1985. *Greek Religion.* Cambridge, MA: Harvard University Press.

Challenger, M. 2013. *On Extinction.* Berkeley: Counterpoint Press.

Dawkins, R. 1986. *The Blind Watchmaker.* New York: W. W. Norton.

———. 1996. *River Out of Eden.* New York: Basic Books.

Grim, J., ed. 2001. *Indigenous Traditions and Ecology.* Cambridge, MA: Harvard University Press.

Guthrie, W. K. C. 2013. *The Greek Philosophers.* London: Routledge.

Kimmerer, R. 2013. *Braiding Sweetgrass.* Minneapolis: Milkweed Editions.

Lent, J. 2017. *The Patterning Instinct.* Amherst, NY: Prometheus Books.

———. 2021. *The Web of Meaning.* Gabriola Island, BC: New Society Publishers.

Leopold, A. (1949) 1989. *A Sand County Almanac.* New York: Oxford University Press.

Marchand, M. E., et al. 2020. *The Medicine Wheel.* East Lansing: Michigan State University Press.

Matthiessen, P. 1978. *The Snow Leopard.* New York: Viking Press.

Miroshnikov, I. 2018. *The Gospel of Thomas and Plato.* Leiden, Netherlands: Brill. Accessed online: https://brill.com/view/book/9789004367296/BP000003.xml.

Nelson, R. K. 1983. *Make Prayers to the Raven.* Chicago: University of Chicago Press.

Nietzsche, F. (1895) 2010. *The Antichrist.* New York: SoHo Books.

Notes, A., ed. 2005. *Basic Call to Consciousness.* Summertown, TN: Native Voices.

Pritchard, E. T. 2001. *No Word for Time.* Bentonville, AR: Pointer Oak (Millichap) Books.

———. 2007. *Native New Yorkers.* Chicago: Council Oak Books.

———. 2015. *Native American Stories of the Sacred.* Woodstock, VT: Skylight Paths.

Schrödinger, E. (1944) 2019. *What Is Life?* Cambridge: Cambridge University Press.

Suzuki, S. 1970. *Zen Mind, Beginner's Mind: Informal Talks on Zen Meditation and Practice*. New York: Weatherhill.

Tesson, S. 2021. *The Art of Patience*. London: Oneworld Publications.

Thomas, E. M. 2016. *Dreaming of Lions*. White River Junction, VT: Chelsea Green.

Tucker, M. E., and J. Berthrong, eds. 1998. *Confucianism and Ecology*. Cambridge: Harvard University Press.

Vaughan-Lee, L., ed. 2014. *Spiritual Ecology: The Cry of the Earth*. Point Reyes: Golden Sufi Center.

Wilczek, F. 2021. *Fundamentals*. London: Penguin.

Yunkaporta, T. 2020. *Sand Talk*. New York. HarperOne.

Index